Teaching Values and Citizenship Across the Curriculum

Educating children for the world

Edited by RICHARD BAILEY

KOGAN
PAGE

First published 2000

Kogan Page Limited
120 Pentonville Road
London N1 9JN
UK

Stylus Publishing Inc
22883 Quicksilver Drive
Sterling VA 20166-2012
USA

British Library Cataloguing in Publication Data

A CIP record for this book is available from the British Library.

ISBN 0 7494 3209 8

Typeset by Saxon Graphics Ltd, Derby
Printed and bound in Great Britain

Contents

Contributors

Richard Bailey is a Reader in Childhood Studies, at Leeds Metropolitan University. He was previously Subject Leader for Physical Education in the School of Education, University of Reading. Dr Bailey has worked in Primary and Secondary schools as well as in teacher training. He is the author of *Education in the Open Society* (Ashgate, forthcoming), co-author of *Schools and Community* (Falmer, 1999) and Editor of *Teaching Physical Education 5–11* (Continuum, 2000). His current research focuses upon child development and evolutionary life history theory.

Eve Bearne has taught English, Drama and Education in schools and colleges for over 30 years. She was a Project Officer for the National Writing Project and Editor of a number of their publications. She is Co-editor of a series of books about children's literature (for Cassell) and has written and edited several books about language and literacy (for Routledge). She is currently Assistant Director of Research at Homerton College, Cambridge, dividing her time between teaching, running in-service courses, researching and writing.

Michael Bottery is Reader in Education, and Director of the Centre for Educational Studies at the University of Hull. He has published widely on questions of professional and educational values, and has lectured in the UK, mainland Europe, North America and the Far East. His book *Education, Policy and Ethics* will be published later this year by Continuum.

Lynne Broadbent is Director of the British and Foreign Schools Society's National Religious Education at Brunel University. She is course tutor for PGCE secondary and primary courses in Religious Education, an RE Consultant to two LEAs and has written on the contribution of RE to pupils' spiritual, moral, social and cultural development. Her main research interest is the relationship between subject knowledge and pedagogy.

Karen Evans is Professor of Post-compulsory Education at the University of Surrey, and Director of the Postgraduate Centre for Professional and Adult Education, a centre providing postgraduate education and training from Certificate to Doctoral level for 400 practitioners from Further, Higher, Professional and Continuing Education. She has directed numerous research studies of learning in the transition to adult and working life. Her recent books include *Becoming Adults in England and Germany* (Anglo-German Foundation 1994), *Shaping Futures: Learning for Competence and Citizenship* (Ashgate 1998) and *Learning and Work in the Risk Society*

(Macmillan 2000). She is a school governor and member of the Further Education Funding Council S.E. Regional Committee.

John Gardner is Professor and Head of the Graduate School of Education, Queen's University Belfast. He entered the teaching profession as a chemistry teacher at a Belfast grammar school in 1978. In 1982, he took up a seconded research officer post with Queen's University to provide training for teachers in computer-based learning. He was subsequently appointed to a lectureship in education (1984), readership in education (1990) and a personal chair in education (1995). Over the years, he has developed a national reputation for his research in the use of computers in education and in the evaluation of education policy and its implementation. Professor Gardner has acted frequently on advisory bodies for government departments and associated education agencies. He is presently (1993–2001) Head of the University's Graduate School of Education.

David Malvern is a Professor of Education working in both Mathematics and Science Education. He is Dean of the Faculty of Education and Professional Studies in the University of Reading, and Convenor of the Mathematics Education Division of the School of Education. Professor Malvern has directed a number of research projects, and has published numerous books, academic articles and governmental reports, including being a Co-author of a series of 10 mathematics textbooks and the *Macmillan Guide to Assessment: Mathematics*.

Ann McCollum is a Sarah Fielden Research fellow in the Faculty of Education at the University of Manchester. Her current research interests include the development of critical theory and practice in citizenship education and the relationship between different forms of socially critical education.

Gill Nicholls is Professor at the School of Educational Studies, University of Surrey. She is the convenor for the Centre of Professional Development and Education. Her research areas are Science Education and Professional Development. She has significant publications in the area of Science Education, and is the author of *Pupils in transition: practices and principles* (Routledge, 1998). At present, Professor Nicholls is the Project Director of the Millennium Satellite project, which brings satellite technology to the classroom.

George Skinner is Lecturer in Education in the Centre for Ethnic Studies in Education, Faculty of Education, University of Manchester. Originally a secondary school teacher of Religious Education, for the past 15 years he has been researching and teaching in the areas of Ethnicity, Religion and Equality of Opportunity.

Fraser Smith is Senior Lecturer in Art and Design in Education at the University of Reading. Before joining the university he taught in a primary school, several secondary schools, an art school and a polytechnic. A prize-winning exhibitor with the London Potters group, he has also exhibited drawings and paintings and contributed prints to the limited edition artists' journal, *Real Art*. He has published a number of articles and reviews and his research interests in Art and Design focus on aspects of artist/teachers' teaching and learning to teach and on values, beliefs and attitudes in relation to Art as a discipline in educational contexts including galleries and museums.

William Stow is a Senior Lecturer in Primary Education at Canterbury Christ Church University College, specialising in history. Research undertaken into the development of primary children's sense of chronology has informed a chapter to be published in a forthcoming book on Issues in Teaching History. He is currently engaged in research into Citizenship and Democracy in primary education, which involves comparative work in Sweden and the UK, and will result in joint publication of a book in 2000.

Roger Straughan is Reader in Education at the University of Reading. He is the author of many books and articles on moral education, philosophy of education and bioethics. His books include *Can We Teach Children to be Good?* (Open University Press, 1988), *Beliefs, Behaviour and Education* (Cassell, 1989) and *Freedom and Indoctrination in Education: International Perspectives* (Cassell, 1991).

Helen Walkington is a Geography Education Lecturer at the University of Reading. Prior to this she taught Geography in a rural secondary school in Zimbabwe with the organization Voluntary Service Overseas (VSO). Dr Walkington's current research interests concern the teaching strategies, which contribute to participatory, collaborative learning. This interest has been focused most recently upon Geography Education and Global Citizenship Education practice in primary schools and collaborative fieldwork in higher education.

Patrick Walsh entered the teaching profession as an English teacher in 1976 and over the next 20 years taught at a number of secondary schools in the Belfast area. Dr Walsh became Head of English in St Malachy's College, Belfast in 1992 and took up a lectureship in Education at the Graduate School of Education, Queen's University, Belfast in 1998. His research interests include issues as diverse as Anglo-Irish Literature, Culture and Community, and the application of IT in the Humanities.

Chris Wilkins is a lecturer in Education at the University of Reading, and a former primary school teacher. He has been closely involved in research into citizenship education issues for a number of years, and is also actively engaged in research and writing in the social context of education and educational policy making.

Series Editor's Foreword

The issue of citizenship and values has been a major discussion point for schools following the Crick Report. With a formal emphasis on educating young people about values and their roles and responsibilities as citizens, teachers across the compulsory phases of education are now faced with delivering a curriculum related to citizenship and values. This book aims to help teachers in this role by giving authoritative guidance and practical tasks, backed up by extensive theoretical perspectives for engaging with ideas and concepts of citizenship and values across the curriculum.

Teaching Values and Citizenship Across the Curriculum has been included in the Kogan Page Teaching Series because of the importance and significance of the subject to the delivery of the national curriculum.

Richard Bailey has assembled a rich resource that reveals an awareness of the broad social, political and cultural contexts in which the challenges of teaching and learning about values and citizenship are addressed. The chapters draw widely from leading experts in the field and reflect both pragmatic and theoretical issues that are of relevance to the delivery of the curriculum. All of the chapters have a commitment to providing a high-quality learning experience. They reflect not only on the teaching of the subject area itself, but also on the learning outcomes from engaging with the concepts of citizenship and values across the curriculum.

The key element of this book is its combination of generic and specific teaching ideas, theoretical perspectives and vision for future developments. These significant elements are presented to help experienced and newly qualified teachers alike. By addressing issues across phases, this book will be uniquely helpful for all teaching professionals.

Professor Gill Nicholls
University of Surrey
April 2000

Preface

Teaching values and citizenship education across the curriculum

Few topics in education generate greater debate than those of values education and citizenship education. Few are as topical. The last few years have witnessed the publication of a series of widely discussed documents, such as reports for the National Forum for Values and the National Advisory Group on Personal, Social and Health Education, as well as the Crick Report on Citizenship. Each has emphasized something that is self-evident for most teachers: formal education, and each of its constituent elements, should contribute systematically to all aspects of pupils' development, not least of which to their social and moral development.

Research suggests that while this is acknowledged, many teachers feel uncertain regarding just how to carry out this aspect of their work. This is hardly surprising. Questions of values will always be hotly contested, and it is right that teachers question the simplistic views sometimes presented to them. At the same time, however, there is a need for guidance that is useful and accessible to those required to deliver values and citizenship education day to day. The recent publication of Programmes of Study for Citizenship at Key Stages 3 and 4, and the announcement that OFSTED inspectors will be seeking evidence of appropriate provision in this area in *all* age groups, has only heightened the need for support and information.

The content and structure of the book

Teaching Values and Citizenship Across the Curriculum has been prepared during this period of change and challenge. My aim in organizing this book was to attempt to address these two needs. On the one hand, teachers ought to be aware of the background and contemporary issues underpinning the debates in values and citizenship education. On the other hand, they also need guidance on how to meet the requirements currently being presented to them.

Each chapter is written by an author who has wide experience and understanding in his or her particular field, and who is well-able to offer constructive advice to those feeling perplexed or simply daunted by the new demands being made of them.

The book is structured around three parts. Part 1 includes chapters on the central themes of values and citizenship. These chapters trace the historical background and the contemporary manifestation of the debates in these areas. They also suggest relationships and possible tensions between values education and citizenship education.

Part 2 takes up the challenge, made for example in the Crick Report and the Key Stage 3 and 4 National Curriculum for Citizenship documentation, of subject-based work in this area. Each chapter in this section draws out the distinctive contribution that the subject can make to values and citizenship education, and suggests ways in which this might be done at all phases of schooling. Also, each chapter contains a series of focus boxes, that offer the reader the opportunity to reflect upon a specific piece of research or upon some aspect of Values and Citizenship Education that relates to classroom practice.

Finally, Part 3 contains three chapters exploring other aspects of the debate that, perhaps, have not been adequately addressed in current discussions and legislation. Issues of spirituality, intercultural education and post-compulsory education are indicative of a need to continue to question guidance and policy.

Each chapter presents the authors' own viewpoint and interpretation of the current debate. As such, each can be read as a discrete contribution to that debate. Together though, the different chapters aim to make a coherent and comprehensive text that is both challenging (in the best sense of that word) and accessible to the practitioner.

Acknowledgements

I would like to acknowledge the cooperation and effort of the contributing authors. For those working in education, there are never any quiet times to write, and the time-scale of this book coincided with an unusually busy period for many of the contributors. Thanks, therefore, is a very slight gesture. Nevertheless, it is earnestly meant. I would also like to offer my great appreciation for those who agreed to comment upon draft chapters: Patrick Carmichael, Tony Macfadyen, Russell Jago and Andrew Lambirth. Finally, many thanks to Gill Nicholls, the Series Editor, and Jonathan Simpson, from Kogan Page, for their support and advice.

Richard Bailey
Reading, February 2000

Part 1

1   Values education

Michael Bottery

Introduction

Many teachers, as well as members of the general public, would probably agree that increased attention has been paid by governments to the topic of values education over the last few years. Yet whilst, in the UK at least, governments increasingly believe that they can and should intervene in the workings and values of the school, values education is not a new governmental interest. Historically, many have seen it as important to equip members of their societies with the kinds of dispositions, attitudes and values needed for the future, and which would facilitate the kinds of projects upon which they intended to legislate. As Green argues (1997: 35), one kind of values education was central to the inception of many educational systems. As he says, schools were designed: '... to spread the dominant cultures and inculcate popular ideologies of nationhood, to forge the political and cultural unity of the burgeoning nation states, and to cement the ideological hegemony of their dominant classes'.

Nevertheless, there is nowadays a feeling of an increased pace of change in the world, and of an urgency, through some form of values education curriculum, to deal with the problems thrown up by this speed, which may well be unique. Not only that, but particularly in the UK, this is now an aspect of schooling which is subject to official inspection. To that extent then, values education today has an enhanced profile which makes it imperative that it is taken seriously and that a clear understanding is gained of what it means for school practice. This chapter addresses the issue by utilising an historical perspective to highlight continuities and discontinuities of practice, to show that whilst many things necessarily must change, other issues remain constants in the debate within this area.

A brief history of values education

An initial authoritarianism

There is always great danger of over-simplification by suggesting that the history of thought upon a complex issue falls into particular eras, as there are always dissident voices and nonconformist groups against a dominant value code. Nevertheless, there has been a general movement over the last 200 centuries in most western societies from fairly authoritarian value systems to more liberal ones, followed by a recent swing back. In the US, whilst there was a separation of the religious and the secular in the public school system, there was still considerable concern over the melding of a nation, and the creation of individuals with the right character which had quite profound authoritarian overtones:

> The danger to civilisation is not from without, but from within. The heterogeneous masses must be made homogeneous. Those who inherit the traditions of other and hostile nations; those who were bred under diverse influences and hold foreign ideas; those who are supported by national inspirations not American, must be assimilated and Americanized . . .
>
> (Hersh, Miller and Fielding, 1980: 57)

In other western countries, there existed a value code which was seen as essential for preserving the existing class divisions, which provided different schools for different classes, and which inculcated into the working class the 'right attitudes' to factory work. In 1867, Robert Lowe described specific ideas about the education of different classes in Britain:

> The lower classes ought to be educated to discharge the duties cast upon them. They ought also to be educated that they may appreciate and defer to a higher cultivation when they meet it, and the higher classes ought to be educated in a very different manner in order that they exhibit to the lower classes that higher education to which, if it were shown to them, they would bow down and defer.
>
> (*Times Education Supplement*, 1985:4)

In terms of its epistemological foundations, it was unremittingly objectivist. As an editor of *The School Board Chronicle* wrote (9 November 1872), 'its members. . . have to instil into the minds of children knowledge. . . not to undertake the Quixotic task of indoctrinating the rising generation of the working and labouring classes with the dogma of equality. . . but with. . . knowledge of their place in society.' Finally, it was backed by a particular hierarchical form of Christian ethics, as illustrated by a – now expurgated – verse from the hymn 'All Things Bright and Beautiful':

> The rich man in his castle
> The poor man at his gate
> God made them high or lowly
> *And order'd their estate.*
>
> (*Hymns Ancient and Modern*, 1924: emphasis added)

The reasons for the decline in this value code are varied: both industrialism and capitalism led to the breakdown of rigid class divisions; the need for a more educated workforce led to the production of one that was necessarily less compliant; the experience of two world wars led to a greater recognition of inadequacies in social and educational provision for those lower down the social scale; the greater influx of immigrants led to a comparison of cultural and value perceptions; and religious objectivism declined to a point where a Church of

England bishop could write that: '. . . we are reaching the point at which the whole conception of a God "out there". . . is becoming more of a hindrance than a help' (Robinson, 1963: 15–16).

This different 'inductivist' approach to religious belief seemed more necessary but also much more dangerous, for within it: 'The ends are not prescribed, the answers are not settled beforehand. But this is only to say that a real *decision* is involved in any responsible moral choice'(Robinson, 1964: 41).

More liberal times

The values code which emerged in the 1960s was predicated largely upon the notion of moral choice. Until that time, 'values education' had very largely consisted of a set of objectivist values defined by a religious, educational or political authority, and values education had largely consisted of teaching the difference between them. Now it seemed permissible to consider not only a personal approach to values, but even that there might be a plurality of approaches, and an incommensurable plurality at that.

This in its own way had profound difficulties. If value objectivism has epistemological and ethical problems, so does a more liberal code. At its most extreme, it can lead to a relativism of choice, a supermarket of values, such that no single code is more acceptable, or rejectable, than any another. For example, a Nazi value code would have to be as acceptable as any other. As an illustration of this, take the *Values Clarification* approach, used mostly in the US during the politically liberal 1960s and 1970s. It argued that the dominant value concern for schools should be that of individual rights, and of helping students to clarify their values through using a seven-step process in order to arrive at their own self-chosen stance. Raths, Harmin and Simon, the most famous advocates of this position, argue that, 'It is not impossible to conceive of someone going through the seven values criteria and deciding that he values intolerance and thievery. What is to be done? Our position is that we respect his right to decide upon that value' (1966: 227).

This kind of relativist position is one possible consequence of rejecting objectivism. Other 'liberal' approaches attempted through a variety of strategies to avoid this position, but it is doubtful if they fully resolved the problem. In the UK, for instance, McPhail (1982) adopted a content and value approach based upon what pupils regarded as the important issues in society. In so doing, he avoided the charge of authoritarianism, but also failed to answer adequately what he would have done if his respondents had come up with categories like 'burning Jews' or 'stealing from others'. Would he have accepted such views simply because students vocalized them; and if he had rejected them, on what basis would he have done so?

In the US, Kohlberg (1981) suggested that there are universal, invariant stages of moral development which could be scientifically assessed and then, by the use of appropriate moral dilemmas, children could be helped to progress more quickly through them. In so doing, Kohlberg claimed that an objective development in values thinking was possible. This approach, at first enthusiastically adopted, was increasingly subjected to a barrage of different criticisms, as commentators came to doubt whether these stages existed in the form that Kohlberg claimed, whether they were underpinned by a philosophically adequate moral theory, and whether their pedagogical effects were significant.

An increasing number of commentators argued that the teaching of these approaches provided students with little moral foundation. Kilpatrick was not alone in arguing that all they did was to encourage students '. . .to develop their own values and value systems. . . The ground rule for discussion is that there are no right or wrong answers. Each student must decide for himself/herself what is right or wrong. . .' (1992: 93).

Economic and social concerns

Lumping these approaches together may well be unfair (particularly as cognitive developmentalists have been amongst those who have accused values clarificationists of value relativism!), but it is important to recognize that undergirding any direct criticisms of such approaches was the change in the political climate in western societies. This began in the early 1970s with widespread economic problems, dramatically increased oil prices, an apparent failure of Keynesian economic policies, and an inability to finance welfare state policies. In such circumstances, the political right enjoyed a resurgence, which led on both sides of the Atlantic to a curious mixture of ultra-liberal market economics and moral authoritarianism. Feeding into any values agenda, then, was a strong economic argument that national economic competitiveness could only be maintained by the education of a suitably qualified workforce, with the 'right' kinds of work attitudes. Indeed, by the late 1990s the policies of the notionally more liberal Clinton-Blair governments had superseded the Thatcher–Reagan nexus, and there have been attempts to exert more policy control. Thus, Clarke and Newman (1996) argue that whilst governments increasingly believe that they must reduce the amount of policy 'rowing' that they do, they also feel the need to increase their involvement in policy 'steering', particularly with respect to the economy. This concentration upon the prioritisation of economic concerns is seen strikingly by the British Secretary of State for Education in the introduction to his Green Paper *The Learning Age*. It begins with the statement that:

> Learning is the key to prosperity – for each of us as individuals, as well as for the nation as a whole. Investment in human capital will be the foundation of success in the knowledge-based global economy of the twenty-first century. This is why the Government has put learning at the heart of its ambition.
> (Blunkett, 1998: 1)

If there are new economic problems, new social ones have appeared as well. The heady days of free love and 'flower power' have long since receded, and have been replaced by very different concerns. Commentators such as Lickona suggest that: '. . . everyone is concerned about the breakdown of the family; everyone is concerned about the negative impact of television on children; everyone is concerned about the growing self-centredness, materialism and delinquency they see among the young' (1991: 19).

Through the 1980s and 1990s, therefore, more conservative counsels have taken dominant policy positions on both sides of the Atlantic, and part of the blame for this perceived societal breakdown has been laid at the feet of liberal approaches. As Kilpatrick argues: 'If anger is called for in the schools, it should not be misdirected at forms of political oppression visible only to the eagle eyes of the politically radicalized; rather it should be directed at the culture of self-gratification, sexual permissiveness, and irresponsibility visible elsewhere' (1992: 163).

In place, of concerns about individuals and their rights, this approach has been underpinned at the philosophical level by modern versions of Aritistotelian virtue ethics (MacIntyre, 1982), leading to a very different set of assumptions:

- that the 'good' should take priority over the 'right', and be defined by what the community takes to be its core values;
- that these goods and duties should be prioritized over individually chosen goods and duties;
- that the state should take an active role in implementing such prioritisation.

Writers like Etzioni have been influential in the thinking of both the Clinton and Blair governments on social issues, through calling for '. . . a moratorium on the minting of most, if not all, rights' (1993: 4). Emphasis has also moved steadily from the belief that values agendas are to be taught through providing students with the reasoning skills by which they might arrive at their own preferred position, to one in which values, and their teaching, are to be embedded within a set of accepted core values. This forms the basis of the development of movements like *Character Education*, in which policy makers and educators attempt to specify what kinds of characters their students will need to leave school with, and so what virtues should be transmitted.

Of course, the picture on the ground is not as simple as this description suggests. Within any society, there is a plurality of interests and opinions, and within democratic ones, diversity and criticism may be seen as positive virtues. Furthermore, there are genuine attempts at building bridges between differing views (see, for instance, the volume by Nucci (1989), on bringing cognitive developmentalists and character educators together). Indeed, a reading of recent documents like the Qualifications and Curriculum Authority (QCA) and Department for Education and Employment (DFEE) document on Citizenship (1998) argues a quite different course for society, and it is a matter of speculation as to how – or whether – different policy and value directions can be harmonized. Nevertheless, there is good evidence that economic and social concerns are having considerable influence, and as they place new demands upon teachers and schools in the delivery of a values education framework, it is advisable to be aware of them.

Indeed, this modern example only serves to highlight the continuities and discontinuities of practice which the historical perspective of past practice, as well as the brief overview of present pressures, also provide. They help to indicate that whilst some things necessarily must change, others remain a constant in discussion upon this area. The remainder of this chapter now utilizes these descriptions in order to discuss five of the major issues to be considered in the implementation of any values education curriculum.

Implementing values education

1. Characteristics and controversy

Defining 'values' and 'values education' continue to be sources of concern for policy makers and teachers alike (see Halstead, 1996). Whilst there are debates about other curriculum areas, they do not change their names or their curriculum content nearly as much as this imprecisely defined yet vital area of school life. However, what may seem criticisms of values education – its imprecision and changeability – may actually be necessary character-istics, because it should reflect current concerns and problems within society. Thus, descriptions under this term have included:

- values education;
- values clarification;
- religious and moral education;
- moral education;
- personal and social education;
- personal, social and moral education;
- personal, social and health education;
- justice reasoning;
- citizenship education;
- character education.

The sheer number of these is a reflection of the fact that the content and description of values education curricula have changed, at least in part, because what are seen as the most pressing issues to which schools should attend have also changed. Clearly, this is an area that is ripe for educational controversy and debate, as value areas and issues are rearranged and redefined. A recent example from the UK is in the separate location of Citizenship Education outside a value framework in *Preparing Young People for Adult Life*, which instead gave in its terms of reference the principal areas of focus as being those of parenthood education, sex and relationships education, drugs education, and personal finance (DfEE, 1999a: 24).

Good reasons can be made for making this separation, and Chris Wilkins, in this volume, follows Crick's (QCA/DfEE, 1998) argument in suggesting that the overlap between these areas is progressively reduced as a more sophisticated understanding of the area is required in the later years of schooling. Similarly, the exclusion of Religious Education from this list is noteworthy, particularly in the light of the arguments made in this volume by Lynne Broadbent, and for spirituality made by Roger Straughan. The purpose here is not to enter a debate but to point out that no single list is likely to be definitive. An openness to different analyses and an awareness of potential areas of concern do, however, seem to be essential in this area. Furthermore, different approaches indicate not only that there are a variety of problems to be addressed, but also that there a variety of means of doing so.

This is, then, a second characteristic of this area for it must not only reflect current concerns, it must also provide strategies for remediating such concerns. This may seem much less controversial, yet it is hardly less so, for the strategies advocated may reflect the particular value stance taken. Thus, as described above, whilst some codes advocate rational, critical, and individualistic approaches, others are characterized more by communal, virtue-inculcating approaches to form desired character. So even when one talks of matters of implementation, there is considerable room for controversy. What is being argued is that the title given to this area, its content, and even its implementation, to some extent reflect the prevailing concerns of a particular period in time. Educationalists, therefore, need to be critically reflective about whether present specifications reflect current concerns. However, they also need to be critically aware that there may be disagreement on the nature of these pressing concerns. Values education, therefore, probably more than any other curriculum area, can be hijacked by extra-educational pressures. This then indicates a third characteristic of any definition. Not only should part of its content be determined by present concerns, and its methods go some way to ameliorating such concerns, but it should also be recognized that there is an inherent controversiality to both of these. This then helps to explain why teachers may feel nervous about this area, for it demands of them that they deal with issues, about which they might feel unprepared, unqualified or uncomfortable to teach. It also asks of them that they be politically aware, and perhaps even politically critical, and this is a position about which many understandably feel very nervous.

2. Questions of epistemology

This leads directly into a second area for discussion. It will be clear that the different value codes described above adopt very different stances as regards certainty about facts and values. Authoritarian codes adopt, for political, religious and epistemological reasons, an essentially objectivist stance to facts and values. There are few problems (at least for its proponents) in terms of deciding what to teach: the problems are largely problems of implementation. Yet this kind of stance is unacceptable in a democracy, where a degree of uncertainty about both facts and values needs to be reflected both in terms of their selection and their teaching. A more liberal code, on the other hand, is faced with a very different set of problems. It may lead to a relativist stance where a mass murderer's code cannot be adjudged as less desirable than that of Mother Theresa's. Yet whilst not adopting an absolutist stance, there are good reasons for believing that we can hold some facts and values with more certainty than others (Bottery, 1988).

However, such a provisionalist approach to epistemology is also strewn with difficulties, as absolutists ask for more certainty, and relativists for less. It is no surprise then that, yet again, in this area of inherent controversiality, teachers should feel a distinct degree of discomfort, which ultimately may never be totally resoluble. Nevertheless, there are ways forward in this area, and ways of dealing with controversy. As the Crick report argues:

> When dealing with controversial issues, teachers should adopt strategies that teach pupils how to recognize bias, how to evaluate evidence put before them and how to look for alternative interpretations, viewpoints and sources of evidence; above all to give good reasons for everything they say and do, and to expect good reasons to be given by others.
>
> (QCA/DfEE, 1998: 56)

Ultimately, these questions are epistemological ones, asking what can we know, of what can we be certain. They may not be fully answerable, but that does not prevent the attempt, nor the ability to pass on to students the skills with which to make this attempt.

3. Specifying content

Concerns about content specification are closely related to issues of epistemology. In an area of such potential controversy, a specification of content that is too precise may well leave teachers feeling open to charges of absolutism and indoctrination, or of feeling that they are being asked to implement an absolutist curriculum, and may increase their reluctance to deal with this area in the classroom. Yet a failure to specify content may be one of the main reasons why implementation has lacked coherence, and in an age when there is a clear need for students to be aware of and to be able to deal with controversial issues, such reluctance is problematic. In the UK, the School Curriculum and Assessment Authority (SCAA), now the Qualifications and Curriculum Authority (QCA), has attempted to provide partial resolution to this problem by the setting up of a National Forum for Values in Education and the Community in order to develop a statement of values. This has resulted in the description of four possible areas of value concern and principle (DfEE, 1999a: 8):

- The self: we value ourselves as unique human beings capable of spiritual, moral, intellectual, and physical growth and development.
- Relationships: we value others for themselves, not only for what they have or what they can do for us. We value relationships as fundamental to the development and fulfilment of ourselves and others, and to the good of the community.
- Society: we value truth, justice, human rights, the rule of law and collective effort for the common good. In particular, we value families as sources of love and support for all their members, and as the basis of a society in which people care for others.
- The environment: we value the environment, both natural and shaped by humanity, as the basis of life and a source of wonder and enthusiasm.

These, it might be argued, are a good basis from which a school may begin to think about this area, as they have all been major stimuli for the derivation of the major moral codes, though there are arguments (Bottery, 1990) for suggesting a fifth, a Religious/Mystical, as many individuals have claimed access through contemplation of these four– temporally earlier – areas. This approach, because it goes no further than specifying areas, helps in avoiding charges of indoctrination, and thus might be seen as providing a sufficient but not overly prescriptive framework for development.

4. Processes in values education

Rote learning and didacticism have formed the core of approaches in authoritarian codes, and were effective in leading to internalisation and acceptance. Yet their centrality in this code suggests that these approaches need to be supplemented, perhaps even replaced. In a democratic society these techniques may fail to provide individuals with the tools needed to participate fully in society. Central to values education for a democracy, then, would seem to be four other major processes, examined below.

The promotion of rationality

Rationality is needed for at least three reasons. First, it is needed in complex areas of judgement where one must balance the effects of actions in the short-term against long-term consequences, or where an ability to comprehend and deal with issues of clashing principle is required. Second, rationality is needed in a sophisticated understanding of the distress of others, as feelings for the distress of others may be felt just as keenly by those with limited rationality, but the execution of appropriate help depends upon the ability to master cognitively complex situations (Israely, 1985). Finally, and as Popper (1945) argued, the adoption of rationality is in actuality a moral decision by society, for its rejection – the surrender to irrationality or blind obedience to others' decisions – invites all the brutalities of totalitarian regimes. Peters (1966) expanded this by arguing that the adoption of reason involves the making of various second-order moral commitments, such as impartiality, a willingness to listen to others' points of view, and fairness. In any approach to values education, therefore, the promotion of rationality is a core process.

The development of empathy

Whilst empathy needs reason to be fully effective, reason needs empathy. The Native American saying that one should never judge another person until one has had the chance to walk in his or her moccasins is a graphic way of saying that cognitively understanding an action is never sufficient if one wishes to fully comprehend why it is performed. The development of empathy, then, is a vital ingredient in values education which not only provides for reflective understanding and tolerance, but also acts as the mainspring to action. It is only by providing students with such opportunities that qualities like tolerance and the appreciation of others' difficulties, sufferings and viewpoints can be gained. As the Buddha said: 'See yourself in others. Then whom can you hurt? What harm can you do?'

The fostering of empowerment and self-esteem

Rationality and empathy encourage understanding in both cognitive and emotional ways, and provide a motivation for doing something about it. Yet there may still be some distance from action, for even with a strong comprehension of an issue, and empathy for others, individuals may still not feel able to reach out. A crucial part of movement to action lies in a person's self-esteem – how individuals see and treat themselves. Those who have low self-esteem, who feel insecure and unloved, are usually the last to help others. Self-esteem and empowerment are, then, closely linked processes. An essential prerequisite process for values education is, therefore, that students should feel sufficiently secure and trusted that they then feel able to reach out and help others.

Furthering cooperation

Under previous authoritarian codes, much teaching was didactic, individualistic and highly competitive, and implied that the only valid source of opinion was the teacher. Such structures and processes helped to maintain an authoritarian and hierarchical value code. In the highly competitive, exam-oriented world of today, there exist similar dangers. Thus, students may well come to view themselves as pursuing independent, individualistic routes through their educational careers, ones in which others are seen as, at best, irrelevant, at worst as competitors. Education then fails to be an activity contributing to some common good, in which other students are viewed as those with whom they might collaborate, and who might contribute to and improve their own learning opportunities. Cooperation, therefore, is valuable in helping to improve basic teaching processes, it helps students to like and trust each other as part of the actual activity of learning, and it might well be seen as a crucial means of educating students to a less authoritarian way of learning and living in society.

5. Questions of implementation

If this analysis of the historical development of values education has so far looked at questions of what (in terms of its definition and content), at questions of why (in terms of education, politics, and epistemology), and at questions of how (in terms of processes), it finally needs to look at questions of where (in terms of its location within school activities). The historical overview of this area strongly suggests that values impact at more than one level. Indeed, recent official publications give increasing prominence to the role of cross-curricular provision and to the 'ethos' of the school, and this suggests a need to build a picture of likely sites of impact. It may also help to explain disputes between those who would prefer to talk of 'Values in Education' as opposed to 'Value Education' (Barr and McGhie, 1995).

One way of conceptualising this is to suggest that values education may have different layers to it, like those of an onion. Its outer layer would then consist of external influences, such as cultural norms, government policies, the nature of the catchment area of the school, and the values of parents and other 'stakeholders'. A second layer would be in terms of the management and ethos of the school – things like its stated mission and aims (and its real values if these are different), its view of what 'management' means, and its stance on the mediation of external suggestions and directives. A third layer would consist of cross-curricular influences – both in terms of the selection of values material which are incorporated into different curriculum areas, and the manner in which these curriculum areas are taught. A final layer would consist of the taught lessons in values, again in terms of what and how they are taught.

This kind of approach does two things. Firstly, it allows the teacher to conceptualize the variety of ways in which values education can be taught. But secondly, it suggests that some values may be taught in all these layers in a manner which, deliberately or accidentally, bypasses the critical faculties of students, and sometimes teachers as well. This is the hidden curriculum of values education, and it is important to note that it can have effects in at least four different ways:

- A school curriculum and activities may be used to bend the attitudes and dispositions of the unwary. An example of this manipulative hidden curriculum would be aspects of previous authoritarian codes, which used seating rows, bells, and didacticism to inculcate school children into the kinds of values and behaviour which would be of use to their future employers in the factory.
- Such manipulative practices may be frowned upon within a democratic society, but when the reasons for such practices are forgotten, these then become a second form of hidden curriculum which may be no less dramatic in its effects.
- Some activities may seem so obviously worthy that no justification is felt to be needed, and these, therefore, become part of an assumed hidden curriculum. However, all too often, one person's or era's assumed hidden curriculum is another's manipulation.

- Activities may take place designed for one thing which achieve entirely different, positive or negative, results. These then become part of an accidental hidden curriculum.

Conclusion

This conceptualisation of a layered curriculum 'onion', as well as the differentiation of kinds of hidden curriculum, brings home not only the variety of means by which values education may be taught, but also that teachers need to be constantly vigilant that the practice of schools is both overt and benign, and not, with so many possible sites of impact, covert and malign. This chapter has shown ways in which values education occurs. It has also attempted to raise other critical issues with which teachers must come to grips if students are to be provided with the values and social skills they need as they enter a changing and challenging world. Values education, therefore, must be manageable, but it cannot afford to be neat and simple, for as someone once said, to every complex problem there exists a solution which is neat and simple – but invariably wrong.

2 Citizenship education

Chris Wilkins

Introduction

Citizenship education has long occupied the margins of the UK curriculum. At times, elements of Citizenship, such as Political Education or Civics, have appeared, then fallen out of favour. When the National Curriculum was first introduced, it appeared as a non-statutory cross-curricular theme (NCC, 1990), only to be effectively sidelined by the Dearing Review of 1993. Finally, however, the subject has become the subject of statutory entitlement at Key Stages 3 and 4, and whilst remaining non-statutory at Key Stages 1 and 2, the expectation of rigorous inspection will probably ensure a more significant impact than ever before is made across the entire span of compulsory schooling. This chapter examines the development of the notion of citizenship education as envisaged by the Crick Report, the model adopted as part of the Curriculum 2000 Review, and explores the possible impact of both classroom practice and school management and organisation.

The development of citizenship

Before we consider how best we can educate people to be citizens, we need to define citizenship. The notion of citizenship dates back to the era of the Greek city states, and has evolved continually since that time, both deepening (by increasing the scope of 'democratic involvement') and broadening (by ever widening the franchise beyond the male property-owning elite class). Citizenship is normally taken to mean the membership of, and participation in the activities of a community or group of communities. It implies an abstract sense of loyalty, a sense of bonding to the concept of the state, or the civic order, rather than to an individual monarch or chief. The notion of *belonging*, the emphasis on commonalities is central. Citizens are members of a club that imbues these common attitudes and practices with positive virtues, such that they become the criteria for membership. Citizens are rewarded for their conformity by certain privileges, or rights.

Naturally, different communities hold different views as to what constitutes citizenship; the rights bestowed upon citizens and the duties performed in order to 'earn' them differ. However, although all political cultures produce different conceptions of the citizen, since citizenship is rooted largely in Western political philosophy there are certain common features. The traditional model of citizenship identifies key spheres of allegiance (the nuclear family, the nation-state) and a political and economic context (liberal democratic capitalism). Some commentators have come to take the view that this state of affairs actually represents more than a stage in the cycle of history, but a 'final victory for liberalism and the market'; the 'End of History' (Fukuyama, 1992).

However, at a time of radical social and political change world-wide with the globalization of capital, the rise of nationalism and the perceived crisis of declining respect for 'civic virtues' in liberal democracies, this may be premature judgement. A contrasting view of recent historical developments sees the break up of 'the Old Order' as the beginning of a new, fluid, dynamic period, history 'accelerating, even overheating' (Habermas, 1994: 20). In this unsettling world, the nature of citizenship must be fundamentally reassessed to take account of the apparent decline in the status of the nation state as 'a given natural order', and the parallel growth of global capitalism, rapidly outstripping nationally located institutions of democracy.

The concept of citizenship has historically lain at the centre of western political discourse. Much western political philosophy has concerned itself with the nature of the rights and responsibilities of the citizen. Individual rights and freedoms have always been at the heart of liberal democratic theory; the right of an individual to not only possess certain resources, but also the liberty to utilize them in order to live out their lives in accordance with their own beliefs (Kymlicka, 1991: 12–13). This emphasis on individualism and rights as a commodity locates citizenship in the social contract theory of classical liberal political philosophy (Frazer and Gordon, 1994: 95). It is this interpretation of citizenship that led Marx to argue that liberal democratic citizenship depoliticizes class, and allows class-based inequalities to go unchallenged within the political arena (Marx, 1975: 219).

As the citizenship net has widened, the reality of inequalities of social power and status present a greater challenge, for where socio-economic power differentials are entrenched, a distinction arises between *formal* and *actual* realisable equality (Barbalet, 1988: 18). Perhaps the most significant extension of citizenship theory this century is T.H. Marshall's essay 'Citizenship and Social Class' (1952). The distinctive feature of Marshall's analysis is his separation of citizenship into three identifiable strands: civil, political and social. Whilst stressing that this is a division based more on historical convenience than on any rigid demarcation between the three, he broadly assigns the development of the three elements to successive centuries. Civil citizenship, the product of the 18th century, comprises the rights of individual liberties: freedom of speech and thought, religious freedom and the right to equality before the law. Political citizenship was developed in the 19th century and it brought the rights of *participation*, the right to play a role in the exercising of political power. Finally, in the present century, we can see the growth of social citizenship, the rights to a minimum level of economic and material security:

> . . . a universal common floor *not* proportionate to the claimant's 'market value' together with the rights of participation in the broad range of social spheres which are commonly accepted as comprising the 'social heritage' of a people; possessing the consciousness and skills to fully participate with both self respect and the respect of one's peers.
>
> (Marshall, 1952: 11)

Marshall, writing whilst the welfare state was under construction, saw this as the point in history when 'true citizenship', with the civil, political and social strands united, finally emerged, as the universal welfare state enabled all citizens to escape the debilitating drudgery of mere survival (1952: 13). Social citizenship insulates the status of citizens against market forces, turning citizenship into a non-economic concept (Dahrendorf, 1994: 13). However, whereas Marshall saw the extension of global social citizenship as an inevitable historical evolution, the experience of the 1980s, certainly in the USA and the UK, saw the growth of welfarism thrown into reverse.

Recent political history has exposed a range of tensions other than those of social class and power. Perhaps the most exacting of these is the crucial concept of 'community'. Traditional models of citizenship tend to treat this concept as uncontested, viewing communities in simplistic, one-dimensional and static terms, perhaps arising from the emphasis on the nation-state as the primary locus of community identification. Political history shows us that this is a relatively recent development, and the late 20th century has witnessed a globalization of capital, the break-up of the Soviet Union, the rise of devolutionary movements in the UK, the growth of federalism across much of continental Europe, and a resurgence of religion as a political force. These diverse phenomena clearly indicate that the nation-state is not a 'natural order', and present a considerable challenge to a model of citizenship.

The second half of the 20th century has seen a burgeoning of 'multiple community' identities. The civil rights movement challenged the exclusion of black people from full citizenship status and feminism engaged in the same struggle for women. Thus, ethnicity and gender have become recognized both as instruments of structural inequality and as sites of 'communal belonging', where lived experience of social power leads to social, cultural and political identification. Individuals are no longer seen as members of a single community as class, gender and 'race' are augmented by a host of 'allegiances of scale', ranging from the small unit of people who share daily life, the local community and regional and national communities. The rapid growth of interest in the politics of environmentalism and animal rights has added a further dimension to the concept of 'community', effectively claiming citizenship rights for future generations, non-human species and the earth itself. Many of these 'new social movements' are in essence 'virtual communities', with individuals communicating via the Internet, such as the J18 'anti-capitalist movement'. These communities provide the most significant challenge today to the conventional liberal democratic notion of citizenship.

Whilst some theorists and commentators call for a radical restructuring of citizenship to take into account new concepts of community, others, such as the US communitarian Etzioni (1993), respond by reasserting the traditional homogeneous model. This view of citizenship and community is a critique of the 'undue extension of welfare provision. . . in the corrupted liberal orders where the politics of dutiless rights prevails' (Selbourne, 1994: 63). This attempt to recapture citizenship for conservatism is a significant one, since it has had a clear impact on the current citizenship agenda, and therefore on the model of citizenship education introduced into our schools (Arthur and Bailey, 1999).

Educating citizens

The history of state education in the UK illustrates the tension between conflicting methods of schooling, between the 'progressive', enquiry-based learning model, and the 'traditional', knowledge-transmission approach. John Dewey, perhaps the most influential educationalist of the 20th century, was acutely aware that for citizenship education, the teaching approach was as important as the content. His heuristic approach was driven by the need to educate the 'democratic citizen', arguing that problem-solving is the best way of developing a critical outlook, the key to producing actively engaged citizens (Dewey, 1961).This progressive model of schooling has dominated educational theory throughout this century, and yet it has remained contentious at a political level. All liberal/social democracies require critically aware citizens in order to operate effectively, and this need for a sophisticated, politically literate citizenry, is complemented by the skills and outlook encouraged by an educational system whereby students are taught to question rather than obey, experiment rather than learn by rote (Heater, 1990: 104). However, the critical citizen also creates a potential threat for a political establishment driven by a desire to maintain stability and a grip on power.

The history of state education in the UK clearly illustrates the importance attached to schooling as a means of fostering 'appropriate' values and practices amongst citizens. Long before the growth of state schooling, the public school system had acknowledged the importance of schooling in preparing students for their social role. These students were being groomed for leadership, in the qualities and skills considered necessary for playing their role in the governance of Britain and its empire, and inspired by the Athenian model, were taught the classics, history and government and rhetorical skills. In contrast, the children of the poor were not to be educated for leadership, for exercising democratic power, but to be instilled with a modicum of skills necessary for the workplace and a sense of duty and obedience. They were, in essence, second class citizens, forced into conformism and passivity by a combination of nationalistic patriotism, religion and an authoritarian code of discipline, in order that they should 'properly understand their own position in society' (Batho, 1990: 91).

This political dimension has ensured that citizenship education has always been steeped in political controversy. Educating people to be 'good citizens' has frequently been equated with indoctrination and propaganda from both the left and the right of the political spectrum. The left use theories of cultural reproduction to explain the role of schooling as an agent of capitalism (Bowles & Gintis, 1988), and the right see 'liberal educators' as relativists attempting to impose egalitarianism through attacks on 'standards' and 'excellence' (Hillgate Group, 1986). As a result of the tone of these public discussions of the role of education, citizenship education has understandably been viewed with a fair degree of scepticism and caution. If citizenship education is to finally become a genuine feature of the curriculum for *all* schools, this caution must be taken into account.

The development of citizenship education in Britain

Although social theorists and educationalists representing a wide spectrum of views have come to accept the strong relationship between the nature of schooling and society, attempting to apply this principle to the development in citizenship education in Britain is no easy task. The piecemeal progress from education purely for the elite to education for all, and eventually on to a unified curriculum within the last decade, presents a confused picture. Elsewhere, greater coherence in the development of educational systems with central control of the curriculum makes it easier to trace the relationship. In the US, courses in citizenship were established in the curriculum of most states from the early part of the 19th century. These courses were designed with the clear aims of fostering a sense of national identity, a patriotism and loyalty to the American Constitution amongst a country of immigrants from a wide range of backgrounds (Heater, 1990:83–84). By the turn of the century, the influence of John Dewey was being felt, and education for citizenship was seen more as a form of democratic training. Despite this 'progressive' philosophy, however, the social studies curriculum model remained relatively static until the social upheavals of the 1960s led to an imperative for change (Heater, 1990:108).

In Britain, although local control of the curriculum gave schools a high degree of autonomy, successive Board of Education reports dating back to the end of the 19th century strongly recommended that schools should pay attention to the interests of the wider community in devising school curricula (Batho, 1990:93). By the beginning of the 20th century, the philosophies of John Dewey had crossed the Atlantic, and the social and cultural upheaval of the First World War reinforced the need for a civic and international perspective to the curriculum, and various pressure groups emerged to lobby for an increased profile for citizenship education in some form or other, periodically supported by government reports which offered guidance to schools, reminding them of their social obligations. However, this guidance was always tempered with caution that schools should stay clear of contentious areas, leading to a generally conservative approach to citizenship education.

From the hierarchical English school system, two differing models of citizenship education evolved. In independent and grammar schools, citizenship tended to be delivered through the regular curriculum, through history, economics or sociology, in addition to studies such as British Constitution. In Secondary Modern or Technical schools, separate subjects called Civics or Citizenship were more likely to be found (Edwards and Fogelman, 1991:17–18). The socialising purpose of these subjects was often transparent; in the 1960s, secondary modern students were taught how to cope with the intricacies of the social security system, under the label of Social Arithmetic (Batho, 1990: 96).

Citizenship education in the National Curriculum

The 1988 Education Reform Act (ERA/The Act), the culmination of an intensely politically volatile period in education, recognized the central role schooling plays in shaping social values, making it a statutory requirement of schools to promote 'the spiritual, moral, cultural, mental and physical development of pupils and of society' (ERA, 1988). This emphasis on society as well as the individual placed citizenship education, the 'making of good citizens', in a key role. The Act makes it clear that the core and foundation subjects were not the *whole* curriculum (NCC, 1990a). Citizenship education was identified as a key theme within the whole curriculum, and *Curriculum Guidance 8: Education for Citizenship* (NCC, 1990b), was intended to determine the direction in which citizenship education was to be developed through the National Curriculum. However, when the Dearing Report of

1994 recommended a 'slimmed down' curriculum, the cross-curricular themes rated scarcely a mention, leaving schools unsure of their status (Lawton, 1995: 8). The effect was an even greater variety in provision than before, as schools already providing for citizenship education took advantage of the increased space in the curriculum to cover more cross-curricular ground. Conversely, those schools who had previously been using the non-statutory nature of the subject as an excuse to avoid confronting the subject, took the curriculum review as justification of this (Kerr, 1996).

Right from the start, those involved were fully aware of the acute political significance of citizenship education, with Duncan Graham, head of the National Curriculum Council at the time, recalling 'ministerial panic and interference' (Arnot, 1997: 276). The concept of citizenship portrayed by the National Curriculum Council is clearly the product of the conventional notion of the active citizen, stressing the participative nature of civil society and the importance of citizens exercising their responsibilities.

The notion of the 'active citizen' might seem self-evident, since citizenship clearly depends on active participation. However, it is a problematic concept, since the individual is essentially reactive, and, in the neo-liberal model of the 1980s, the *citizen's* rights are reduced to mere *consumer* rights. The ill-fated Citizen's Charter, launched by the Major administration in the 1990s, demonstrates this restricted view, with the focus on the defence of contractual rights; the embodiment of the 'possessive individualism' which lies at the heart of democratic capitalism (Beck, 1996: 24). Research has shown that the 'citizen as consumer' model impacts on public perception of citizenship. Particularly for a younger (18–35) generation, the role of the 'good citizen' is restricted to minimal public duties (obeying the law, paying taxes) and the defence of private property (the growth of the culture of Neighbourhood Watch) (Wilkins, 1999: 225).

All curriculum initiatives need to be seen in their political context, and this is particularly true of citizenship education. Both the *structure* (the philosophical and ideological framework of citizenship) and *content* (the application of this framework to classroom resources and subsequent practice are rooted in the ideologically contradictory post-1979 era. The 1980s and 1990s have seen a drive towards economic neo-liberalism alongside social and moral authoritarianism, creating a simultaneous 'rolling back and rolling forward' of the state, by turns interventionist and privatising, libertarian and authoritarian, populist and elitist (Gamble, 1988: 28–29). Despite the current administration's fondness for all things 'new', for all its presentation of bold new projects and 'new visions' for community, Tony Blair's language is deeply conservative, invoking images of an old order, a *recreation* of 'family life, civic virtues and mutual obligations' (Giddens, 1994). This ideology of citizenship will underpin citizenship education into the next century.

Education for citizenship: The Crick Report model

The renewed interest in citizenship education engendered by the result of the 1997 General Election can be readily understood. The 'regeneration of community' was a key element of the 'Blair Project', and the fact that the new Secretary of State for Education, David Blunkett, was a long-term enthusiast for citizenship education was also significant. Just two months after taking office, the new administration's White Paper *Excellence in Schools* announced the need to enhance the place of citizenship and political education within the National Curriculum. The Secretary of State appointed his old university mentor, Professor Bernard

Crick, to chair the Advisory Group on Citizenship and the Teaching of Democracy in Schools, with the remit to 'provide advice on effective education for citizenship in schools' (QCA/DfEE, 1998).

The Advisory Group produced its final report in September 1998, and this set out detailed proposals for revision of the National Curriculum from September 2000. The Qualifications and Curriculum Authority (QCA), the body responsible for National Curriculum review, has largely taken on board these proposals, with the one significant shift being the decision to make only the Key Stages 3 and 4 learning outcomes statutory (DfEE/QCA, 1999a).

The Crick Report identifies three key dimensions: participation in democracy, the responsibilities and rights of citizens, and the value of community activity (QCA/DfEE, 1998: 4). The Report first sets out to define 'needs and aims', attempting to clarify what citizenship education is, and why it is important. The second section details a set of 'essential recommendations', how the curriculum should be refined to accommodate citizenship goals, including statutory entitlements. The third section, 'spelling it out' does just this; detailing underlying principles, learning outcomes at each Key Stage, and the essential elements of citizenship to be covered. This section encompasses key concepts, values and dispositions, skills and aptitudes and knowledge and understanding, and sets out the general shape of citizenship education in the post-2000 National Curriculum. The implications of the Report for schools are significant, and we therefore need to examine carefully the model of citizenship education it recommends.

The Crick Report draws heavily upon Marshall's three strands of citizenship: the civil, the political and the social. However, Marshall emphasized the citizen's rights as the essential element of the civil and political domains, and the role of the state in providing the conditions for social citizenship, reflecting the era in which he was writing. The Crick Report is similarly of its time, accurately representing the Blairite model of citizenship. It stresses the need for a much greater reciprocity between rights and duties, reflecting the post-1979 agenda set by Margaret Thatcher and enthusiastically taken up by Tony Blair. This model echoes the communitarian analysis that the importance to citizenship of civic duties has been neglected in the pursuit of rights. The Crick Report also recognizes the communitarian view, supported by Tony Blair, of the welfare state as a 'safety net not a blanket', seeing a much more prominent role for voluntary groups and organisations. However, perhaps the most significant departure in terms of definition comes in the political domain. Crick criticizes the Speaker's Commission of 1990, which drafted the curriculum guidance on citizenship education at the inception of the National Curriculum for downplaying the importance of the political domain. Crick argues that although 'civic spirit' and 'voluntary community activity' are important, citizens must 'shape the terms of such engagements by political understanding and action' (QCA/DfEE, 1998: 10).

For Crick, effective education for citizenship is therefore a deep and complex process. Cutting across Marshall's three domains, the Report outlines 'three heads on the one body'; three related mutually dependent dimensions, *social and moral responsibility, community involvement* and *political literacy*, which nevertheless each require a different space and treatment in the curriculum (QCA/DfEE, 1998: 11). These dimensions, or 'three heads on one body', underpin the Crick model of citizenship education.

Social and moral responsibility

Clearly there is considerable overlap between citizenship and values education in this dimension, and fostering the growth of desirable personal, social and moral values and behaviour. From the earliest phase of schooling, this learning clearly has a major role to play in the curriculum, and both Personal, Social and Health Education (PSHE) and whole-school Spiritual, Moral, Social and Cultural Development (SMSC) contribute to this learning. For Crick, however, this guidance on moral values and personal development is not citizenship by another name, rather that it promotes the 'essential preconditions of citizenship' (QCA/DfEE, 1998: 11). Without socially and morally responsible values, children cannot effectively become citizens; however, merely possessing such values is not enough. Citizenship education involves supporting children's learning of concepts of fairness, attitudes to laws, rules, decision-making, and the social context (locally, nationally and globally) in which these develop. Learning is, therefore, attached to 'institutional knowledge', and 'limits of tolerance' need to be discussed in terms of public order and political doctrines' (QCA/DfEE, 1998: 63). The Crick Report sees responsibility as a political as well as a moral virtue, as it implies premeditation and calculation of the effect actions are likely to have on others. This requires a skills and knowledge dimension as well as an attitudes and values one.

Community involvement

Educating for citizenship cannot be confined to the school community, and 'active citizenship' is clearly a desirable goal. Involvement in community groups requires both a sense of civic responsibility and political skills. Both of these can be promoted from the beginning of schooling, and therefore the remit of PSHE, SMSC and citizenship education also overlap here. There is clearly much common ground, particularly in the primary phase. However, Crick argues that in Key Stages 3 and 4, a different emphasis is desirable. Community involvement cannot be divorced from the social and political reality of the community, and teachers need to address not only 'what is the case?', but 'what ought to be the case?' and 'can it be done better?' (QCA/DfEE, 1998: 63–64). Arguably, Crick could have gone further, as there seems no reason to avoid this critically reflective approach in Key Stages 1 and 2.

Political literacy

The political literacy dimension is the one that most explicitly distinguishes citizenship education from PSHE, SMSC and values education. Put simply, political literacy involves children 'learning about and how to make themselves effective in public life' (QCA/DfEE, 1998: 13). Even in the primary years, Crick argues that it is well within children's abilities to have a simple awareness of the broad nature of democracy, the key institutions of government and the role of community organisations. This is the '. . .essential base on which to build towards the aim of a politically literate citizenry' (QCA/DfEE, 1998: 64), and establishes a clear need to draw a distinction between citizenship and values education.

The Crick Report's notion of citizenship education is, in essence, that it should be education *for*, not *about* citizenship; not just thinking like a good citizen, but acting like one too. This implies that schools have a responsibility to develop both knowledge of citizenship and civic society, and to develop values, skills and understanding. In order to do this, citizenship education must work alongside PSHE, SMSC and values education, sharing common aims and teaching approaches, but also demanding separate provision.

Main recommendations

The Crick Report sets out 13 key recommendations for citizenship education, and many of these have direct implications for schools. Most importantly, it recommends that it should be a statutory entitlement in the curriculum, with specific learning outcomes set out for each key stage, defined tightly enough for the provision of these to be assessable by schools and inspected by OFSTED. To support this, primary and secondary working groups developed a framework for citizenship education, and used these to develop learning outcomes (see the Box below). The QCA, responsible for incorporating citizenship into the National Curriculum review, have broadly accepted the framework, although two key modifications emerged from the consultation period. Firstly, the entitlements remain non-statutory at Key Stages 1 and 2, with 'learning outcomes' becoming 'guidelines', and these form a joint framework with PSHE. Secondly, at Key Stages 3 and 4, the 'outcomes model' envisaged by Crick is modified to Programmes of Study. The Crick Report argued that an outcomes model would allow schools the flexibility to take account of local contexts, and utilize a cross-curricular approach where appropriate. It also arguably gives the subject a degree of objectivity, distancing it from the potential direct influence of government dictat over content. Furthermore, the tight definition of learning outcomes give the subject 'rigour and bite', and allows for assessment of progression, and a measurable sense of the collective school approach to citizenship (QCA/DfEE, 1998: 28–29). Potentially, the shift in emphasis towards broad attainment targets could create the potential for less rigorous provision, although the model is still a tightly defined one, and the current culture of rigorous external assessment may ensure schools address the subject seriously. The same may still apply to the non-statutory guidelines, although the fate of the cross-curricular guidance issued in the early 1990s does not inspire confidence for citizenship education in primary schools, as teachers wrestle with the pressures of delivering ever more challenging literacy and numeracy objectives. Much is likely to depend on the attention given to citizenship and PSHE by OFSTED.

Delivering citizenship education

The challenge to schools is a significant one. With the subject intended to occupy no more than 5 per cent of curriculum time across each key stage, schools must consider carefully how this might be balanced. At different key stages, and for different elements of citizenship, different approaches might be necessary; schools may want to use blocks or

Framework for Citizenship Education: (QCA/DfEE, 1998: 35–46)

Guiding principles:
- breadth and balance;
- coherence;
- continuity and progression;
- relevance;
- quality;
- access and inclusion.

Factors affecting the learning process:
- whole-school approaches;
- teaching approaches and learning opportunities;
- special educational needs.

Teacher assessment of learning components:
- aims and purpose;
- strands;
- social and moral responsibility;
- community involvement;
- political literacy;
- essential elements;
- concepts;
- values and dispositions;
- skills and aptitudes;
- knowledge and understanding;
- social;
- moral;
- political;
- economic;
- environmental.

modules, use weekly slots now allocated for 'general studies or tutorial time', or they may rely more heavily on a cross-curricular approach. Subsequent chapters will address in detail the possible ways in which citizenship education might be addressed through curriculum subjects, though this overview points to some general issues schools will be considering. Clearly some curriculum subjects provide greater opportunities for addressing citizenship issues than others. Some will focus more on the *skills* and *knowledge* dimension, others provide a useful space to deal with the *values*-related dimension of citizenship. Helen Walkington's chapter on Geography highlights some of the productive ways in which values and citizenship education cross-fertilize. However, a glance at just an example of the QCA's specific recommendations suggests that there are elements within knowledge and understanding that can only be met through discrete provision:

Citizenship education outcomes (QCA 2000)

In Key Stage 1, pupils should be taught:
- to take part in discussions with one other person and the whole class;
- to take part in a simple debate about some topical issues;
- to recognize choices they can make, and recognize the difference between right and wrong;
- to agree to follow rules for their group and classroom, and understand that rules help them;
- to see that people and other living things have needs, and that they have responsibilities to meet them;
- to see that they belong to various groups and communities, such as family and school;
- to recognize what improves and harms their local, natural and built environment and about some of the different ways people look after them;
- to make a contribution to the life of the class and school;
- to realise that money comes from different sources and can be used for different purposes.

In Key Stage 4, pupils should be taught:
- the legal and human rights and responsibilities underpinning society and how they relate to citizens, including the role and operation of the criminal and civil justice system;
- the origins and implications of the diverse national, regional, religious and ethnic identities within the UK and the need for mutual respect and understanding;
- the work of parliament, the Government, and the courts in making and shaping the law;
- the importance of playing an active part in democratic and electoral processes;
- how the economy functions, including the role of business and financial services;
- the opportunities for individuals and voluntary groups to effect social change locally, nationally, in Europe and internationally;
- the importance of a free press and role and influence of the media in society, including the Internet, in providing information and affecting opinion;
- the rights and responsibilities of consumers, employers and employees;
- the UK's relations within Europe, including the European Union, and relations with the Commonwealth and the United Nations;
- the wider issues and challenges of global interdependence and responsibility, including sustainable development and Local Agenda 21.

Apart from its profound impact throughout the curriculum, citizenship education reaches beyond the taught to 'the whole curriculum'. Schools have long recognized the importance of school ethos and organisation in contributing to values *and* citizenship education, not to mention the role of wider community involvement. School ethos impacts upon every aspect of school life, and in particular, in the relationships within the school which have such a bearing on citizenship values. As stated elsewhere, pupils need to be prepared *for* as well as taught *about* citizenship, and so schools must consider the values implicit in the way individuals relate to one another within the school community. Education for citizenship is about *empowerment* and *access*, and just as citizens in wider society need opportunities to act as citizens as well as an understanding of democratic institutions, so pupils must have opportunities to play a part in the school community (Vlaeminke and Burkimsher, 1991: 51). A commitment to democratic schooling lies at the heart of effective education for citizenship, and this commitment, if it is to be sustainable, must permeate every aspect of the institution, from school management structures, to codes of conduct and the way in which a school positions itself in the community.

Wider implications of citizenship education

The curriculum review relating to citizenship education which is underway has profound implications for schools, cutting across National Curriculum subject teaching, cross-curricular issues and school organisation and ethos. However, the QCA recommendations carry implications not simply for schools, but the inspection services and by providers of initial and in-service teacher education and training. Knowledge requirements at Key Stage 4 are demanding (see citizenship education outcomes above), and even assuming both an enthusiasm for delivering citizenship education and a sophisticated level of personal citizenship knowledge and understanding amongst teachers, the challenge may be overwhelming. In any case, research evidence suggests that this enthusiasm and personal confidence, particularly with a newer, younger generation of teachers, may not be universal. One study of student teachers has revealed that generally positive attitudes towards teaching citizenship may be offset by the students' own lack of 'civic awareness', which in turn affects their confidence in teaching about citizenship (Wilkins, 1999). Wider studies amongst young people during the 1980s and 1990s consistently report a decline in both enthusiasm for, and knowledge about, political and social engagement (Crewe et al, 1998; Jowell et al,1996; Wilkinson and Mulgan, 1995).

The history of citizenship education in the UK reflects a long-standing scepticism amongst educators about the explicit teaching of political citizenship, with the general view being that citizenship was 'caught, not taught' (Hahn, 1999: 239–40). This view, set alongside the declining public confidence and interest in democratic processes and institutions, clearly sets up a potential conflict with the model of citizenship education proposed by the Crick Report and endorsed by the QCA. The experience of the Cross-Curricular Guidance for citizenship education in the early days of the National Curriculum suggests that schools' attitudes towards non-statutory citizenship goals may be varied, largely determined by individual school's and teacher's personal motivation. This, the political message clearly states, is no longer acceptable, and there is likely to be a call for specific advice and resources to support schools throughout all four key stages. The threat of OFSTED may 'concentrate minds', but it will not win hearts. Citizenship education reluctantly delivered, by teachers lacking personal knowledge, skills, confidence and positive enthusiasm for the subject, will undoubtedly fail, as many other attempts to introduce these vital issues into the curriculum have done before.

The Teacher Training Agency (TTA) must take account of the National Curriculum 2000 review, and consider the implications of the demand to educate pupils to take their place in a sophisticated, politically and socially literate society. Research shows that young people entering teaching, whilst positive about the socially beneficial role of education in general, and citizenship education in particular, often lack the necessary knowledge and skills for fully engaged citizenship themselves (Wilkins, 1999: 227). The educational ideology propounded by the Blair government creates a tension here. Whilst the current attention given to citizenship appears to suggest an acknowledgement of the need for a more critically reflective curriculum in schools, the National Curriculum for Initial Teacher Training (NCITT) heads in an opposite direction, down a road of highly prescriptive 'teaching standards'. The demands of NCITT inevitably means that trainee teachers have less opportunity to develop a sense of the wider social agenda of schooling, whilst curriculum review now demands this very quality in serving teachers. Perhaps the major implication of the QCA's proposals is that it gives weight to the view that teacher *training* is not enough; that teacher *education* is still of central importance, producing critically reflective teachers willing and able to educate tomorrow's critically reflective citizens.

Conclusion: a vision of citizenship education

In considering the potential role of citizenship education in schools, we can simplify the position by identifying three broad approaches. It can be *conforming*, following the traditionalist model of teaching right from wrong and respect for the institutions in a society, with its sole aim the preservation of an established order. The second approach is a *reforming* one, and is more analytical; not content with teaching uncritical respect, but recognizes conflict and ambiguity in society (Lynch, 1992: 103–106). The overall aim of this approach is to reform society by individual understanding, knowledge and prejudice reduction and broadly corresponds with the Crick Report's model of citizenship education outlined in this chapter.

A third approach, one not evident in the QCA recommendations, is *transforming*, where the aim is not simply to develop understanding, but to empower individuals to change their material circumstances (Clay, Cole and Hill, 1990). It makes explicit the political context of schooling which remains at the implicit level in the reforming model; the teacher is a critical pedagogue committed to a 'counter-hegemonic' project (Hill, 1989: 7).

For Henry Giroux, citizenship education has, at its core, issues which are normative and political, the fundamental question it asks is *should* society be changed, and if so, *how*. This model, that I would call education for *critical citizenship*, therefore questions the aims of education itself, and to do this, it must incorporate three essential elements: historical critique, critical reflection and *social action*. (Giroux, 1983: 193). This requires that teaching is a process conducted within '. . . a metanarrative of emancipation and egalitarian social justice' (Hill, 1989: 33).

All educators possess a vision that infuses their educational goals and practices, this is nothing new. The most exciting consequence of the work of the Crick Committee may be that it brings 'the vision thing' into the open. Schools can no longer afford to focus narrowly on the National Curriculum, and in addressing education for citizenship, they must first articulate their own vision of citizenship. The very action of introducing the subject into the curriculum is the beginning of the reflective act. Through teaching about citizenship, teachers must inevitably enrich their own concept of citizenship.

Part 2

3 The contribution of the Arts to values education and citizenship

Fraser Smith

Introduction

There is a story of a young woman taking her boyfriend, an Art student, home to meet her parents for the first time. 'Well,' said her father, 'and what do you do?' After several anxious attempts at what he thought might be an acceptable answer and suddenly remembering something he had once read about Picasso, the young man suggested that, as an artist, he brought order to chaos. 'Oh, terrific,' replied the girl's father, 'you can make a start on the garage.'

It is possible that this is not a true story, but what is most certainly the case is that the Arts in general and in education in particular are thought to confer certain skills, abilities and values on those who appreciate, practise or study them. Furthermore, these attributes, although very often recognized simply in terms of what utility they might bring to bear, are generally, if rather vaguely, thought to be beneficial, worthwhile and in some senses distinctive. The hostess's instruction, 'Look, you're arty – be a darling and do something with these flowers while I get dressed', is somehow informed by perhaps quite complex assumptive evidence. It is also clear that these sets of assumptions about the potentially beneficial outcomes of Arts education are widely accepted, largely unquestioned and, due perhaps to the nature or inadequacy of language, most often tacitly formed and held. No one is surprised if the Art teacher is asked to design and make posters for the school play nor if the drama teacher is assumed to have a significant role in improving pupils' pronunciation.

Understanding and recognising the educative outcomes of the Arts at anything other than this lowly instrumental level is as demanding for many as it is irksome for teachers of the Arts to be given such roles. At the same time, Arts teachers sometimes find it difficult to convey the form, nature and benefits of the higher order values, practices, skills and outcomes implicit within the best Arts educational encounters.

It would be mistaken, however, for Arts educators wholly to disown or unduly diminish what they tend to see as the more peripheral or extrinsic benefits of study in and of the Arts. More so if, in pursuit of the less tangible but higher stakes of core, intrinsic elements and values, this results in appearing to reject support from influential friends and informed sources. For example, the recent publication of the final report of a National Advisory Committee, *All Our Futures: Creativity, Culture and Education* (DfEE, 1999), is to be welcomed as much for its support of the Arts in schools as for its endorsement of creativity across the curriculum. In this respect, the report may be seen further to amplify and extend aspects of a series of prior reviews and reports such as *The Gulbenkian Report: Arts in Schools* (Calouste Gulbenkian Foundation, 1982); *Whither the Arts* (SHA, 1995); *Guaranteeing an Entitlement to the Arts in Schools* (Rogers, 1995); and *Secondary School Pupils and the Arts* (O'Brien, 1996).

As these sources clearly suggest, part of the case for the Arts in education does lie in communicating the nature of these ancillary benefits effectively, more so as they appear to connect with and support some of the aims and strategies of Citizenship education. It is difficult to see, for example, how well organized experience of good practice in Drama can fail to contribute to pupils' effectiveness as communicators, not only within the studios but also in the wider community. The sense of personal identity, confidence and achievement resulting from rising successfully to the challenge of conceiving, choreographing and performing a dance piece for younger pupils will be further enhanced by performances in a community arts festival.

The most recent National Curriculum documents for Art and Music contain non-statutory but most useful statements outlining aspects of their respectively unique importance within the curriculum as ways of knowing, understanding and behaving (DfEE/QCA, 1999b and c):

The importance of music

Music is a powerful, unique form of communication that can change the way pupils feel, think and act. It brings together intellect and feeling and enables personal expression, reflection and emotional development. As an integral part of culture, past and present, it helps pupils understand themselves and relate to others, forging important links between the home, school and the wider world. The teaching of music develops pupils' ability to listen and appreciate a wide variety of music and to make judgements about musical quality. It encourages active involvement in different forms of amateur music making, both individual and communal, developing a sense of group identity and togetherness. It also increases self-discipline and creativity, aesthetic sensitivity and fulfilment.

The importance of Art and Design

Art and Design stimulates creativity and imagination. It provides visual, tactile and sensory experiences and a unique way of understanding and responding to the world. Pupils use colour, form, texture, pattern and different materials and processes to communicate what they see, feel and think. Through Art and Design activities, they learn to make informed value judgements and aesthetic and practical decisions, becoming actively involved in shaping environments. They explore ideas and meanings in the work of artists, craftspeople and designers. They learn about the diverse roles and functions of art, craft and design in contemporary life and in different times and cultures. Understanding, appreciation and enjoyment of the visual arts have the power to enrich our personal and public lives.

Although regrettably we no longer find Drama as a specific area of study and expression in the National Curriculum, Drama and Dance both have dedicated sections in English and PE respectively. In both cases, creating, performing and presenting are statutory requirements and their importance is reflected in non-statutory information. From this it can clearly be seen what both Dance and Drama share with Art and Music in offering challenges to pupils and young people who, in responding creatively to these, both contribute to and gain from values and attributes of the Arts as a whole.

The purpose of this chapter, however, is not simply to repeat and endorse existing statements of the values and benefits of the Arts in education, whether these are expressed in the form of considered and supportive national documentation or as friendly and well-meaning expressions of popular belief. Rather, it is an attempt to explore beneath the surface of the Arts in schools and to draw out and exemplify some of the ways in which these may contribute to, connect with and support significant approaches and features of citizenship in education. As many of these connections and contributions are associated with, and essentially contained within, sound Arts methodology and good teaching practices, it will be useful to note some features of the increased professionalism of teachers of the Arts. Following that, some elements of good practice will be examined further for the support they may offer to citizenship education.

There is no argument here for the Arts as a special case, except in the sense that all subjects have unique contributions to make in a balanced, entitlement curriculum. Other curriculum disciplines may make a more easily recognized, but hopefully not over-valued, contribution. An excellent case is made in Geography, for example, (Walkington, in this volume and 1999) and no doubt other colleagues will contribute to the common good. Indeed, the nature and quality of our citizenship might be assessed in terms of how thoughtfully and conscientiously balance is achieved in and endorsed by the National Curriculum for schools.

The professional development of teachers of the Arts

Some years ago now, in the context of writing on values and evaluation in education, I developed a typology of Art teachers based on their expressed beliefs, teaching strategies and practices (Smith, 1980). Suffice it to say that my endorsed type of that time, the 'Pedagogue', has emerged in increasing numbers over the intervening period to exemplify enhanced professionalism and good practice in the teaching of Art. There is no reason to suppose that teachers of the other Arts have not risen to the same challenges in equally thoughtful ways. For example, since 1980, when it was not too difficult to find some Arts teachers reluctant or even refusing to engage in meaningful analysis and assessment of pupils' attainments in the Arts, Arts teachers' competence and ability in teaching inventively and monitoring, assessing and recording pupils' achievement is second to none. There may still be some continuing difficulty on some occasions with the subjectivism with which Best has dealt so clearly and on which he has guided Arts teachers (Best, 1992). The extreme subjectivism which was a feature of the 'impression marking' of early CSE consortia meetings is thankfully a thing of the past.

In general, rationales for the Arts in education now most often appear considered, coherent and articulately communicated, often gaining for the Arts a rightful place in secondary school subject option arrangements, for example, and a strong role in the Key Stage 1 and Key Stage 2 curriculum in the best primary schools as indicated by Clay *et al* (1998).

A cluster of factors appears to have facilitated these advances. Certainly the advent of the GCSE offered Arts teachers' expertise a way forward, affording them a central role in value statements, criterion design and referencing, and in developing related teaching and learning strategies. These strategies in themselves offered more appropriate ways of working in the Arts:

> when asked by a visitor what he thought the art course at Crofton was about, a year 10 student replied, 'making sense of life through making art myself, looking at art made by others and thinking about the whole lot.'
>
> (Kennedy, 1995: 7)

The introduction of the National Curriculum, the nature of which attracted serious and thoughtful criticism in the field of the Arts (Ross, 1995) and elsewhere (Brighouse, 1996), nevertheless offered a focus for constructive debate and development largely about subject nature, context and implementation, from which further professional development stemmed. The requirement for composing in music and for critical/contextual studies in Art both tended to encourage reflective thinking and creative planning, albeit as the result of imposition rather than choice. As many OFSTED reports show, the Arts have been recognized as making worthwhile contributions to whole-school efforts and achievements, in environmental work, literacy and numeracy, for example, while still retaining the unique and distinctive identities noted above.

This is not to say that the critics are mistaken or foolishly at fault, but it seems wholly negative not to recognize Arts teachers' achievements. More so if this has happened under an allegedly repressive regime whose effect is likely to be the 'evisceration of art education' (Hughes, 1997: 117) or to reinforce the assessment-led nature of Arts work in schools to a point where the establishment of a 'single linear orthodoxy' sets targets easily attained but 'to the exclusion of excitement, adventure, and a sense of ownership.' (Binch, 1994: 118).

This pessimistic picture does not match many colleagues' experiences, where, for example, residencies in schools by practising artists have generated excitement, a heightened sense of ownership and, often, links between schools and with the community (Sharp and Dust, 1990; Manser with Wilmot, 1995). There are, and always will be, controversies in the Arts in education. These often reflect the nature of the Arts in society as essentially contested dynamic concepts and it is very much the case that the ways in which these concepts are contested in the Arts lie parallel to those ways in which people evolve their concept of citizenship itself. This is a point which will be returned to below.

Although this is not the place for a full historical survey, it should be noted that one further factor may be seen in retrospect to have offered an opportunity for the professional development of Arts teachers and that was the Technical and Vocational Educational Initiative (TVEI). Although there was some confusion about the exact purpose of TVEI in schools (Dale, 1990), this chance of additional funding and support for curriculum development was taken enthusiastically by some Arts teachers. What was not always realized was the positive impact of TVEI on teaching and learning in the Arts in those participating schools and departments. In small-scale projects with schools and universities working in partnership (for example, Kempe, 1980; Finney and Hendy, 1990; Smith, 1990) the general framework of the initiative was defined and extended. For example, eight aims and themes were defined by an art syndicate (Smith, 1990) and these can be seen to underpin aspects of contemporary good practice across the Arts:

- equal opportunity and access to provision;
- development of competence and progression;
- development of knowledge, skills and experience;
- personal development, especially through realistic appraisal of achievement and potential;
- relevance and flexibility;
- equal regard for different outcomes;
- negotiation of content, form and style of response;
- facilitation of self-esteem.

A note of what were termed 'dichotomous values' was evolved and the items used as indicators or a rough checklist of better and less good elements in Arts education.

Dichotomous values for Arts education:

Positive +	Negative −
a) learner-centred/directed	other-centred/directed;
b) creative	imitative;
c) sequential	disparate/episodic;
d) divergent	convergent;
e) open	closed;
f) education and training	training only;
g) skills transfer	skills non-transfer;
h) decision-making	problem-solving;
i) risk-taking	safe havens;
j) innovative	reproductive;
k) continuity	closure.

It will be useful to add some explanation of these. Each opposing (dichotomous) pair of items or values attempted to indicate ends of a spectrum along which aspects of art projects, units of work, and teaching and learning values were situated. There was substantial discussion about whether some items could constitute values at all. For example, is 'sequential' a value? How many positives make for good practice? And so on. It was agreed at the time that these items might better be thought of as 'process or activity values', describing behaviour, predominantly in learning, handling of feeling, impulse, concept, media, space, tools, etc. while some applied more in helping consider distinctions in teaching approaches. For example, were pupils invited to respond to a starting point (theme, topic, issue, subject) determined by the teacher or to one evolved with the teacher through prior notice, individual thought and group discussion? With hindsight, this list might better now be termed 'binary oppositions' implying more of a spectrum than the term 'dichotomous'.

Other questions were resolved in various ways which would review and re-shape items, possibly quite radically. However, this was essentially a working document which indicated the collective arts activity or process values of the group at a given point in the life of the project.

As this section is concerned with noting the development and establishment of professionalism among teachers of the Arts, it seems reasonable to suggest that the developments fostered in Arts education by TVEI and the introduction of GCSE and some new A level syllabuses resulted not only in personal professional development but also in helping to achieve the establishment of a fruitful teaching and learning ethos. Much of that early ethos has been further developed in the intervening time and may currently be sensed not only as a set of effective strategies in Arts education but as contributions to a certain style of educative relationships and values concomitant with those of citizenship education.

The professionalism of Arts teachers is appropriately reflected in *The Arts Inspected: Good Teaching in Art, Dance, Drama, Music* (Clay *et al*, 1998). This account is illustrated with first-class examples of work in schools which demonstrate not simply the range of work but also exemplify some of those values, benefits and skills implicit in worthwhile Arts education which are embodied and displayed in the outcomes whether in the form of performances or objects. It makes an excellent source of information and issues for continuing teacher development.

Education and the discipline of the Arts

A number of sources (among them Best, 1992, and Swanwick, 1988) examine and make clear what every good Arts teacher knows tacitly, that the Arts educate the person and mind together in a healthy and dynamic equilibrium. Perhaps also some of us intuit that:

> Person and mind, however, are not identical terms. Person is a word to do with conduct as well as mental possessions, whereas mind stresses the latter and is vague about the former. Mind is the subsidiary word, for it is something only attributed to persons and as a concept is parasitic upon the concept of a person. Person, however, implies mind and more than mind.
>
> (Perry, 1973: 109)

Secondly, the good Arts teacher recognizes that pupils, in order to become educated in the Arts, need to be trained not only or necessarily to achieve the equilibrium which is referred to above, but so that, freed from day-to-day constraint, their learning may proceed. This learning, which might consist of investigating, spontaneous experimenting or legitimized play, can only be hindered for pupils who lack training in, for example, the effective use of materials or instruments. Pupils are unlikely to benefit from undisciplined, thoughtless approaches to the uses of silence or spaces. Well-trained young people not only support the ethos of the Arts but are enabled to achieve focus and absorption in genuine experience of what Abbs (1982) termed the 'pattern of artmaking'. It is worth paying attention to Abbs's schema and the propositions from which it stems, for it discloses five essential phases which can be schematically delineated in spiral motion as follows:

> The phases placed in such a schematic spiral relationship represent an idealized sequence. It has not been my intention to plot the separate itineraries of each artform (the differences emerging from the marked differences between the media) but rather to point to the common nature of the journey.
>
> (Abbs, 1982: 45)

For each phase, Abbs offers a founding proposition derived from a series of analyses of the Arts and the nature of creativity disclosed through critical expertise. As the title of his book suggested, Abbs's main intention was to propose a radical revision of the place of English in the curriculum. This model may be used, as his text shows, to analyse examples of Art projects in middle schools, but it also serves as a design tool for the construction of Arts curriculum. Abbs provides in his schematic representation a close link with Gestalt theory which, partly by way of the Bauhaus, was developed into the foundations of an extensive psychological theory of perception by Arnheim (1966,1970) which will be familiar to some Arts teachers. What perhaps is most helpful of Abbs is to offer a diagram of parts to be brought into the equilibrium referred to above, not, in my view, as a spiral but as a series of

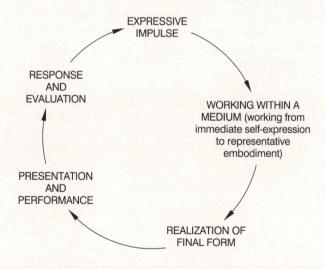

Figure 3.1 Pattern of artmaking *(Abbs, 1982: 45)*

oscillating cycles. Each is a full cycle while, at the same time forming with others the whole (gestalt) which is the genuinely educative experience of the Arts.

Thus we have two linked concepts of the discipline of the Arts. First, there is that form of discipline readily identified and achieved by experienced and successful teachers, the training of pupils in the knowledge and use of media, materials, space, gesture, phrase, sequence or body in such a way that the learning does not canalize, in the sense of Binch's 'single linear orthodoxy' (Binch, 1994: 118), but forms necessary thresholds to further confidence and freedom in arts practice, performance and presentation.

Secondly, there is the discipline of unified wholes, a recognition that potent arts forms have a rightness, an aptness, a concept of fitness which has little or nothing to do with fashion or style, or even necessarily with such established concepts as truth to materials or to the conventions of craft skills. Discipline is, in this sense, a liberating realisation that there is nothing new about the Arts except artists.

Returning to citizenship, it may be seen that a sense of real achievement in the Arts, of deeply felt knowledge of an entity in fully reciprocating harmony through the effects of human creative endeavour, is potent experience on which some intrinsic elements of citizenship might be founded. The more so if that experience, as in Abbs' propositions, has community at its heart, for Arts pupils, students and teachers are embedded, not only in the school but in a series of wider communities too. There is an argument here for the Arts having a central, even seminal role in communitarian concepts of education. (see, for example, Arthur, with Bailey, 2000).

Adventure, negotiation, decisions and judgements

It is unlikely that many of us will have the opportunity to paddle up the Orinoco, negotiate a place in a seal-fishing expedition with an Inuit band, or need to decide the course to set in navigating a new sea passage in the South China Seas. On the other hand, if we are genuinely involved in the Arts, as soon as we take brush in hand or join with others in composing a piece of music, evolving a play or working out dance moves, we may truly be adventuring. As Perry proposes:

> Adventure (though) must be found within the framework of society if it is necessary. It is always open to those on the boundaries of the things they have mastered, but perhaps most universally offered in the Arts. For the situation central to them is just such an opportunity of confronting problems with one's own resources, which brings it about that the artist can adventure in his own garden.
>
> (Perry, 1973: 121)

As I suggested above, there is nothing new about the Arts except artists, meaning that each fresh impulse or problem requires a new set of decisions or solutions. If Arts teachers are to engage with the best practice then the boundaries of mastery, as Perry puts it, the present condition of pupils' skills and learning must be confronted with new challenges before artistic growth can occur. This is why the hackneyed, stereotyped or standardized starting points and methods insisted upon by poor Arts teachers will bring about routine, stereotypical, standardized outcomes of little value to teacher, learner or future citizen. But newness is not the same as novelty for its own sake. No doubt novel ways of adventuring would be to throw away the paddles on the Orinoco, attempt to negotiate with Inuit hunters in Swahili or throw a dice to navigate the South China Sea. We cannot jettison, in a search for novelty, those traditions of procedure and methodological knowledge that enable us to recognize that the arts impose a discipline of wholeness. Regardless of level of achievement, none of us would wish to be up the Orinoco without a paddle. Without this key acknowledgement, that tradition binds but also gives freedom in Arts in education, legitimate adventures cannot be had. Real freedom will be denied us as either routine and standard solutions or wild, undisciplined outpourings come, inevitably, to be seen as tedious and incapable of lifting the spirit.

The part played by negotiation is central, both in importance and in practice in Arts education. There are several ways in which this can be seen to be the case. There will be forms of internal negotiation as an individual pupil considers ways of responding to a starting point, which with older pupils may have been negotiated by a group or with the teacher. A further form of negotiation lies in working within the medium, as Abbs called it (1982). These negotiations uncover and reveal the constraints as well as the range of opportunities and decisions invited by artistic problems. For example, 'How can we represent the sea this time? How long is the performance? Will the clay support itself? Can you see her hat from here? If you move in a crabby way it'll contrast with the gliding golden girl, won't it?'

It is this form of negotiation, by exploring the constraints on our freedom of response, that defines the nature and quality in the Arts. There is no free for all, anything does not go, as well taught pupils discover: 'I used to think that today's Art was just an excuse not to do any serious work, but now I believe it forces the person to understand by using their imagination' (*Pupil after Opt for Art Project*, NACCCE Report 1999: 122).

Negotiations within a group work context are familiar not simply in performance contexts but also in bringing together individual outcomes to form a collective visual or 3D form. Roles within the groups may be given or taken by negotiation and final outcomes will embody negotiation as well as meaning through feeling. If the Arts teachers are involved, they may have a variety of roles, as technical advisor, aesthetic consultant or as referee. This is consistent with the concepts of 'reflecting-in-action' and 'conversations with the situation' (Schon, 1983). As higher order teaching skills, these are to be seen in many Arts in education contexts as negotiations with the pupils as artists. Indeed, conversations in negotiating boundaries and judgements are very much what I had in mind when I wrote: 'We need more conversations in art appreciation. One of their functions might be to draw out and examine the substantially objective nature of aesthetic knowing and understanding.' (Smith, 1983: 85)

Understanding may take the form of what Taylor (1988, 1992) called, 'fruitful conjecture' and Broudy (1987) termed, 'enlightened cherishing'. In either case, judgements become elaborated and refined through reflective negotiation. These reflections are essentially critical ones on the part of the pupils and, like all worthwhile criticism, Eisner (1985) seeks to disclose and communicate those elements, aspects and qualities of our lives within the pupils' art objects, presentations and performances.

These three factors, decision-making and judgement, varieties of negotiation and critical disclosure are three prominent elements in any case to be made for the Arts in education to be taken seriously. The values inherent in knowledge, adventure, understanding and practical skills gained through engagement in the Arts will also however, predispose pupils and young people towards forming the concepts and prescribing to the ideals which active citizenship requires. The position taken here, therefore, is that the more genuinely the ways in which the Arts in education are true to themselves, and this section has attempted to convey some criteria for establishing this truthfulness, then the more important and supportive they will be in forming such a disposition in the pupils.

Transfer and transformation

The conclusion to the last section increases in importance, in direct proportion to efforts made to weaken this truthfulness in Arts education by introducing or forcing a role on the Arts, as instrumental in leading to better performance in other areas of the curriculum. Arts HMI report that: 'Some might justify the place of the Arts in the curriculum on the grounds that involvement in the Arts can lead to higher attainment in other subjects. This is a rationale that deserves serious consideration' (Clay *et al*, 1998: 3). Both Eisner (1998) and Staines (1999) have dealt conclusively with this putative rationale. Eisner, after an exhaustive review of all the published research concluded that: 'There is some (evidence), but it is very limited. The effects of the Arts appear to be greatest when the Arts are intentionally used to raise academic achievement in reading and writing', (1998: 59). In the case of music, Staines concludes:

> The overall thrust of this article has been to suggest that (i) the formulation of an overarching theory of transfer remains a distant vision; (ii) the results of research on general transfer of musical learning have so far shown inconsistency; and (iii) the claims being made by some people about the effects of learning music on non-musical areas should be treated with circumspection.
>
> (Staines, 1999: 134)

If the strong suggestion is that there is little or no evidence for transfer, how will Arts teachers sustain a belief or represent to others that the Arts, genuinely pursued by them with their pupils, will provide what was earlier termed a predisposition towards the values, concepts and ideals of citizenship? For a response to this question, we should turn to Crick:

> . . . an education that creates a disposition to active citizenship is a necessary condition of free societies. Education is training and learning towards freedom, and freedom is closely linked to an understanding of the concept of the political as a matter of peaceful compromises of values and interests. Understanding of general concepts fortified by practical activity is essential. It is suggested that any democratic political education (as in the present UK Government proposals) presupposes five 'procedural values': Freedom, toleration, fairness, respect for truth, respect for reasoning.
>
> (Crick, 1999: 337)

In the absence of conclusive evidence for direct transfer, which might in any case dilute or have deleterious effects on the Arts in education, we can see in Crick's suggestion close correspondences and connections between the 'procedural values' to which he refers and those at the core or heart of the Arts in education. In contributing to the 'presuppositions' of citizenship education, the Arts make a vital contribution. Moreover, they do so from the strengths of their intrinsic procedures and values rather than through the utilitarian application of extrinsic, ancillary benefits. We should also appreciate the implications of Crick's endorsement of an understanding of general concepts being fortified by practical activity as being 'essential'. This is not to say that all practical activity has the same intrinsic outcomes but it is to say that the parallels and connections between the Arts and citizenship in education are further extended by this commonality of the values of experiential and active learning.

In his chapter, Chris Wilkins argues strongly for his third approach to citizenship education, that of transformatory education. This he describes as aiming, '. . . not at prejudice reduction and understanding, but empowering pupils to change their material circumstances'. And he suggests later that: 'This might seem like a provocative conclusion to an overview of citizenship education. I make no apologies for this. All educators require a vision which infused their educational goals and practices, this is nothing new.'

Although Arts teachers in schools have not been noted for a specific concern with pupils' material circumstances, they should not be slow to connect with Wilkins in recognising that the transformatory powers accessible to pupils through the Arts may have a part to play. As Richards expresses it:

> Everybody knows the feeling of freedom, of relief, of increased competence and sanity that follows any reading in which more than usual order and coherence has been given to our responses. We seem to feel that our command of life, our insight into it and our discrimination of its possibilities, is enhanced. . .
>
> (Richards, 1960: 85)

I am not so sure that 'everybody' does know that feeling, although there is no doubt that everybody should have the opportunity to do so, but not just so they can 'make a start on the garage'.

4 Values, citizenship and English

Eve Bearne

Introduction

> ... there is no aspect of practice in the English classroom which is not laden with social significance.
>
> (Kress, 1995: 6)

On the face of it, English seems the perfect vehicle for teaching values and citizenship. It is recognized as a means of introducing children and young people to the social, cultural, moral and political values of the nation through the texts used and the discussion of issues arising from them. The key concepts listed in the Crick Report (QCA/DfEE, 1998) were:

- democracy and autocracy;
- co-operation and conflict;
- equality and diversity;
- fairness, justice, the rule of law;
- law and human rights;
- freedom and order;
- the relationship between the individual and society;
- power and authority;
- rights and responsibilities.

These are all familiar elements in the English curriculum. Until the late 1800s, however, these issues were often dealt with through the classics. English as a subject including both the study of texts and the study of language, grew from an urgent appeal to introduce newly literate groups in society to more than everyday or popular forms of text. With the rise of an affluent middle class:

> ... what the people – the newly enfranchised, newly literate people – needed was 'political culture,' instruction in their duties as citizens, and to be 'impressed sentimentally' by examples of heroic and patriotic action 'brought vividly and attractively before them'.
>
> (Churton Collins in *Bottoms*, 1999: 19)

The Newbolt Report of 1921 devoted its main argument to the importance of English for the nation, seeing 'pride and joy in the national literature' as a means of unifying people across classes (1921: 22). Most importantly, English as a subject would be more relevant and less 'remote from life' than the classics. This report signalled a shift towards English being based on a canon of texts and a standard spoken language which might be expected to 'humanize', civilize and unite the nation (Mathieson, 1975).

English as a subject on the school curriculum began, then, with political intent and has had its political and social consequences. In the 1930s and 1940s, academics such as F.R. Leavis and the Cambridge school saw the study of literature as a key to individual moral and cultural improvement. By the time of the Newsom Report in 1963, literature was seen explicitly as a tool for the development of civic values: 'all pupils, including those of very limited attainments, need the civilising experience of contact with great literature. . .' (1963: 5). Just a little later, in 1975, the Bullock Report questioned the validity of such claims, balancing these with the importance of 'imaginative insight' and literature as a 'personal resource' (1975: 124). In challenging the idea of English as an instrument of social change, the Bullock Committee was seeking to define just what 'English' should mean. The Report locates one of the tensions of teaching English – the competing claims of a 'personal growth' view of a subject where literature, can particularly contribute towards the individual's inner development and the socio-cultural view which seeks to place the texts within the historical contexts of their making. Since its development as a subject in the school curriculum, English has been a contested site (Jones, K, 1999; Brindley, 1994; Marum, 1996).

One of the key concepts in the Crick Report, 'individual and community', hits the nail on the head (QCA/DfEE, 1998: 44). In English teaching, as in values education as a whole, an education for entitlement requires attention both to the development of personal autonomy and to what it means to be a citizen in a democracy. These balancing principles apply as much to the classroom practices of English teachers as to the texts and their content. The questions are not so much about whether English should or should not contribute to education in values and citizenship, but what those values might be, whose values are being promoted and how they are approached in the classroom.

In this chapter, I want to consider some of the more problematic aspects of English and values education. Debates about values education in English are as much to do with attitudes as about the texts – spoken, written, heard, seen or read – that make up the curriculum. This includes the value given to learners' own ways of seeing the world. Values education in English cuts several ways: examining values which are evident in the cultural world we live in; promoting certain values through teaching approaches; giving value to the language and literacy experience of the children, young people and communities that teachers meet every day. However, no tidy summary like this can aptly capture the messiness of everyday teaching – the kinds of decisions that have to be made, often on the hoof, about how teachers can best present – and enact – the values they want to promote whilst encouraging pupils to develop reflective and critical approaches to learning. It is not an easy matter.

Thinking of the undertones

It is often assumed that the texts themselves carry messages considered valuable for young people to explore. Narrative, usually in the shape of an imaginative story, is seen as an ideal vehicle. It is the most obvious and widely used form of text that springs to mind when considering how to tackle issues of rights and responsibilities, power and authority, cooperation and conflict (Earl, 1999; Winston, 1998). Most societies and communities have used narrative as a means of passing on the mores of the group, teaching the community just what fairness and justice, the rule of law and the relationship between the individual and a community implies and involves. Narrative texts, with their in-built capacity to carry such messages, make up a good proportion of the English curriculum. However, it would be a mistake to think that narrative can be used easily to teach young people what to think, believe and do for the harmony of their community or society; the messages carried by stories are by no means straightforward. As an example, the following comes from the Dervish tradition of the Middle East; it was composed (orally at first) as a teaching story:

The Ancient Coffer of Nuri Bey
Nuri Bey was a reflective and respected Albanian who had married a wife much younger than himself. One evening, when he had returned home earlier than usual, a faithful servant came to him and said:
'Your wife, our mistress, is acting suspiciously. She is in her apartments with a huge trunk, large enough to hold a man, which belonged to your grandmother. It should contain only a few ancient embroideries. I believe that there may now be much more in it. She will not allow me, your oldest retainer, to look inside.'
Nuri went to his wife's room and found her sitting disconsolately beside a massive wooden box.
'Will you show me what is in the trunk?' he asked.
'Because of the suspicions of a servant, or because you do not trust me?'
'Would it not be easier to open it, without thinking of the undertones?' asked Nuri.
'I do not think it is possible.'
'Is it locked?'
'Yes.'
'Where is the key?'
She held it up. 'Dismiss the servant and I will give it to you.'
The servant was dismissed. The woman handed over the key and herself withdrew, obviously troubled in mind. Nuri Bey thought for a long time. Then he called four gardeners from his estate. Together they carried out the trunk by night, unopened, to a distant part of the grounds, and buried it. The matter was never referred to again.

The story of Nuri Bey epitomizes the complexity of using narrative to teach about right and wrong, rights and responsibilities, honour and betrayal. It is meant to teach, but is ambiguous; it is capable of many interpretations; it springs from a particular culture but has relevance beyond that culture. It raises questions worth debating: the obvious one is 'What *was* in the trunk?'– and we'll never know the answer to that one! But some of the other questions can genuinely lead to debates over values:

- Why might the servant have informed on the wife? What might the implications these days be for a 'whistleblower'?
- Does 'dismiss the servant' mean a permanent loss of job or just an exclusion from the room? Would it have been just if the servant had been sacked?
- Why did Nuri Bey decide on that course of action? What might the implications be for the future relationship between husband and wife?

These questions raise matters of responsibility to authority and the need for that authority to act justly towards those whom it employs. Seen in terms of responsible citizenship, the uncomfortable issues about whether to tell or not to tell, and whom to tell, are just as relevant today as they were when this story was first told. Nuri Bey's final decision is either the action of a very wise and mentally strong person or of a cruel despot. Comparable ambiguities can easily be found by studying modern leaders and their powers.

As it is so enigmatic, *The Ancient Coffer of Nuri Bey* offers just the right kind of lessons. It is not didactic; it does not tell us what to think, but poses a series of mysteries and perplexities that we have to think out for ourselves or ponder over with others. The Nuri Bey story is a reminder both of the role of narrative in exploring values and of the dangers of seeing narrative as a way of passing on the morals or beliefs of a culture.

The 'meaning' of any text lies not simply in the text itself, written or spoken, but in the interaction between the tale and its hearer/reader. In the past, English teaching often relied on the exposition of the 'right' version of a text. Not so now. Post-structuralist and post-modern theorists have helped us to revise our notions of 'meaning'. However, in this move towards a more open and diverse approach to texts, greater responsibility is put on the teacher to guide readers through texts. Whilst it may not be possible to ascribe one definitive version to a text, it is equally misleading to assert that any interpretation is as good as another. What needs to be recognized about any text is that it is a product, coloured by the historical, social and cultural currents surrounding its making. Any text is, therefore, necessarily saturated with the values of its time. At the very least, a developing reader/hearer needs to be helped to see that 'meaning' is not necessarily fixed. This statement itself needs some care. There are, of course, children who come from homes where their sacred texts are seen as expressing an unvarying truth. In classrooms, this means awareness and sensitivity is needed on the part of the teacher.

Innocence and experience

The shifting and refractive nature of stories is particularly evident in versions of myths, legends, folk and fairy tales. Western fairy tales, for example, have been through a series of theorists' hands, proposing them variously as morally instructive, disrespectful of women, subversive, reflective of the period in which they were first told – and now as the objects of playful retelling. Anyone reading Jacqueline Wilson's delicate retelling of *Rapunzel*, for example, will find not only the familiar tale about a young girl held captive by a witch in a castle, but a gently understated and sympathetic view of a childless couple who desperately want to be parents. Since traditional tales spring from the oral tradition, they are open to more diverse retellings. The reteller of a known tale often reflects a contemporary – and, perhaps, publicly discussed – concern.

Despite their sometimes gruesome content, traditional stories can be comforting in their familiarity, following known narrative patterns, distant from ourselves and our own lives. When brought up to date they can sometimes be shocking. Anthony Browne's picture book of *Hansel and Gretel*, with its contemporary illustrations, is a chilling tale of child abuse and murder, with no concessions to the young reader. The Crick Report lists as an aim for Key Stage 1, the ability to 'understand different types of behaviour using moral categories such as *kind* or *unkind*, *good* or *bad*, *right* and *wrong*; know about the results of anti-social behaviour. . .' (QCA/DFEE, 1998: 47). Anthony Browne, and other authors who make books for young children, know that it is not as straightforward as that. On one page, Gretel is depicted as a frail child pushing a grandmotherly character, who is wearing comfy, familiar slippers, into a burning fire whilst the cat screeches off to avoid the action. The resolution of the story is difficult even in the traditional setting, but is accepted because of the veil of historical distance. Browne's final double page spread in this contemporary version shows a joyful reconciliation with a modern father who had been complicit in abandoning the children. The stepmother has disappeared without explanation. In the current climate of high profile attention to child abuse and neglect, what decisions might a child reader make about right and wrong here? By his modern depiction, Anthony Browne quite rightly has decided that a young reader can grapple with some of the moral problems presented by such a text.

One of the contentious aspects of values education in English is the concern that children may need to be protected from harmful influences in the content or themes of texts which they meet. This is particularly sharply felt when thinking about the influence of film and video or popular cultural texts. The value ascribed to texts is often deeply related to concepts of children's innocence (Watson, 1996). Over the last century there has been public concern about the potentially harmful effects of just about every form of new text – particularly popular texts; 'penny dreadfuls'; early cinema; radio; comics and pop music magazines, and now television, film and video games are often a site for debates about what texts are of value to young people and which ones are harmful. Even the ancient Greeks thought that stories should be banned because of their harmful effects on the development of rationality in young minds. This is not to denigrate or deny proper concerns about the texts we should introduce to children – particularly in schools. It is important, however, to acknowledge that since 'meaning' does not just reside in the texts, as outlined earlier, but is shaped more in the meeting place between reader and text, then the relationship between young people's behaviour and the books, comics and videos they read or view, is a complex one.

In a research study into children's television, video and computer viewing which offers a thorough and balanced examination of all these issues, Jack Sanger reports on his team's research findings:

> . . . we found very little evidence thus far, that children are being particularly affected by the fictions of computer games or videos. The evidence was that, apart from a few individuals, whose life histories already contained evidence of emotional disturbance and who found expression or catharsis through screen entertainment, children were able to differentiate between fact and fiction.
>
> (Sanger *et al*, 1997: 176)

In a remarkably detailed and illuminating case study of 'H', aged 9, one of the team of researchers was asking him about material that might be called 'unsuitable'. H was able to experience the frisson of fear or horror without confusing it with real life. This is common with many children who find news and documentary more frightening than gruesome videos. H was also able to distinguish between the different conventions that adults and children have in entertainment. In school he is seen as able, individualistic and very keen to work on the computer composing his own scripts and stories. H may be a particular case, but his ability to manage, subvert and transform the texts he encounters can be seen in many other children. Young writers often use their own writing as a means of controlling an unruly or perplexing universe. Violence and killing, trust, friendship and reconciliation, falling in love, marriage, children, death of a loved person are common themes as they attempt to resolve some of the 'social, moral and political challenges faced by individuals and communities' (QCA/DFEE, 1998: 44). The English curriculum has long played a role in allowing the rehearsal of experience.

Reading, particularly, has occupied a central place in values education in English but it is clear that young readers equally use their reading for their own purposes. In an extensive study of teenagers' reading, Charles Sarland argues that alongside the canon of literature, promoted and given value by English teachers in secondary schools, runs an alternative canon (1996: 67). Where adults hotly debate qualities of value in the texts they think should be presented to young readers, so young readers also debate the quality of the books and films they enjoy. Sarland points out the recurrent tendency for academics and governments to produce their own canons of valuable literature, from Leavis in 1947 through to the 1993 National Curriculum for English. Each of these lists is a social, cultural and historical construct, not necessarily representing the features of reading which young people value. The 12-year-old pupils who shared their enthusiasms with Sarland were not only able to comment on the plot structure, characterization and themes of the books, but indicated that they could distinguish between gratuitous elements of, for example, violence and bad language and those incidents that were true to the integrity of the text (Sarland, 1996: 69). Despite the fears of some adults, these young people were perfectly capable of reading the texts they enjoy with a critical eye. They were certainly not victims of unhealthy texts.

Whilst recognising the importance of hearing young people's voices, however, it would be wrong to take a completely open and inviting view which suggests that anything goes. Jack Sanger identifies a lack of adult intervention in children's video and computer watching as a significant factor. The research group found that: 'There was an overall feeling that children are being left to drift in a world of growing technological sophistication, where realism is increasing and boundaries between fact and fiction diminishing' (Sanger *et al*, 1997: 3–4).

In order to help children to become 'critical consumers capable of managing this aspect of their lives', Sanger concludes that there will need to be adult mediation in order that children may develop critical thinking skills (1997: 172). The Crick Report identifies the 'ability to use modern media and technology critically to gather information' and develop a 'critical approach to evidence' as well as recognising 'forms of manipulation and persuasion' (QCA/DfEE, 1998: 44). Whilst young people can be very astute critics of the screen texts they watch, they will need to be accompanied in their watching by adults who can help them develop critical approaches. In her study of children's literacy development and televisual texts, Naima Browne similarly identifies the importance of teachers 'watching television with children, talking about what is seen, helping children to make sense of what they see' in order to develop their ability to become 'adaptable and creative thinkers. . . necessary attributes during periods of rapid change' (1999: 170).

Adult interventions

Perhaps the commonest form of adult mediation in English is the role teachers play in selecting the texts which they think are worthwhile for young readers. As Sarland (1996) pointed out, this necessarily involves judgements of value by the adults whose role is to promote reading – and the consideration of social and cultural issues prompted by texts. In terms of values and citizenship education, however, novels, picture books, poetry, plays or information texts can be problematic for several reasons. One of these may be because of changes in ideology since the time of writing; a much loved book from childhood may be shocking when re-read now. Other texts are written specifically to shake up complacent or established ideas. As social, political and cultural perspectives shift, both types of text give cause for concern, raising the tricky issue of censorship – or at least decisions about the perceived 'suitability' of some texts in schools and classrooms. New cultural populations arrive in schools to jog our elbows about the kinds of texts presented to young learners.

There are always new challenges for teachers who want to be culturally courteous to the groups they teach:

- What should teachers do about books which are overtly racist or sexist or which take a deficit view of one-parent families, the homeless or the dispossessed?
- How do we – or should we – tackle texts which deal with HIV and Aids, brutal murder, drug use, incest, death, divorce. . .?

And it is not only a matter of the texts already available: What about the gaps? How do we find texts that reflect the cultures and ethnic groups of the young people we work with?

The literature of war has long been a chosen area for young people's reading in English lessons. As Carol Fox points out:

> many of these books provide children with a rich and challenging way to learn about the past, the present and the future, to discover the characteristics of different genres to learn about the stories of ordinary people, to consider ethical issues of all kinds, to explore different cultures and histories, and to find out how nations and groups characterize themselves.
>
> (Fox, 1999: 130)

However, Fox identifies significant gaps in the literature presented to children in the UK. Very little is included about the 'colonial' troops who took part in the Second World War, particularly if they were black, omissions which must have implications for the descendants of those groups to be found in British schools today (Fox, 1999: 127). Values and citizenship education needs to be inclusive as well as culturally sensitive. English teaching and values education themselves are influenced by the shifting cultural, social and political climates in which teachers work; the instability of texts themselves and teachers' own sensitivities, preferences and preconceptions need to be considered.

Past and future

Writing Our Past, a Key Stage 2 community study from Birmingham, gives rich examples of some of the ways in which English might address some of the issues – and gaps – of values and citizenship education. Four schools worked with the University of Central England and the Development Education Centre, Birmingham, as part of a Birmingham LEA project to promote positive achievement in African Caribbean children.

The booklet giving an account of the work explains: 'The class teachers and others who took part in this project are inspired by the idea of mutual respect between people, from local level in neighbourhoods and classrooms, to global level between peoples and countries. This mutual respect was seen as essentially including children's self-esteem 'based on recognition of the value and importance of their homes and a belief in their own ability to learn and achieve' (Graham and Ballin, 1999: 4). The pupils studied the structure of different genres of writing, used writing frames to research and compile biographies, poetry, diaries, letters. Role-play deepened their understanding of the human issues they were researching. They shared their work with parents, families and other members of their communities. This project drew on personal and community experience to examine values, difference, rights, responsibilities and moral choice and it was tough and demanding work for the young people involved.

The foreword to the resource booklet outlining the project sums up the approach to adult mediation which informed the work: 'In our experience, children learn best when they are engaged by the content, when they feel it relates to their own lives, including their home background and their peer group relationships. Most importantly, they need to trust their teachers to respect them and the families of which they are a part' (Graham and Ballin, 1999: 1).

Such an approach not only made it possible for children to research, analyse and present the texts they wrote and read, but also gave the adults involved a chance to bridge home and school experience of language and texts. In the different ways of approaching texts, the project acknowledged the diversity of cultural contexts in which texts are read and produced.

In the secondary school, media studies in English lessons offers the chance to give consciously critical attention to the values carried by texts. However, issues of value or responsibility are evident not just within the texts, but in the methods used to create media images and copy. *Talking Rights; Taking Responsibility*, a set of materials designed specifically for secondary English and citizenship, suggests activities for debating legal rights and the responsibilities (and power) of parents and governments over the young (Jarvis and Midwinter, 1999).

Table 4.1 Writing Our Past projects (planning and preparation)

Aim	*Aim*	*Aim*
To support children as researchers	To encourage children as independent writers in a range of genres	To engage children with issues of global awareness, development education, human rights and the nature of history
Current understanding and previous experience	*Current understanding and previous experience*	*Current understanding and previous experience*
Children are familiar with a range of resources, but may copy undigested texts	Children are willing to write and respond to imaginative stimuli, but need help with the revising and redrafting processes. They also need help with the style and characteristics of different genres.	Children may pose questions and/or have a range of personal/family experiences. They may bring to school an awareness derived from the media; however, understanding may be limited and disconnected.
Strategy	*Strategy*	*Strategy*
To model, demonstrate and support children in learning how to: 1. set their own research questions; 2. skim read to pick up key points; 3. scan texts for specific information; 4. sequence information in a logical order; 5. record information; 6. get it 'written' first, getting it 'right' later.	To model, demonstrate and support children in learning how to: 1. assemble ideas using research grids; 2. work on drafts using writing frames; 3. use writing frames appropriate to specific genres.	To find and use resources and plan activities for children which: 1. enable them to make sense of experiences in their own neighbourhood, and relate these to wider issues of human rights at a global level; 2. promote empathy with other people's experience; 3. promote recognition of the commonality of human experience.

In *Talking Rights; Taking Responsibility* there is a section on the ethics of making the news, with questions which might be asked of a news photographer who has to take photographs of people suffering from illness, malnutrition, the effects of war or homelessness:

- What are you aiming to do when taking your photographs?
- What does it feel like when you are there in the midst of people?
- How do you feel about taking photographs of people?
- How do the people react to you?
- How do you get the information you need?
- What makes a good photograph?
- What difficulties do you face?

(Jarvis and Midwinter, 1999: 122)

The material does not duck any uncomfortable issues, neither does it offer solutions; it is directed towards helping young people identify a personal view which has been thought through in a process of discussion, debate, justification and negotiation of ideas.

An English curriculum which can genuinely embrace issues of value will be founded on a theory of teaching and learning which acknowledges that language and literacy are always linked with ideology; they are not innocent, nor can they ever be neutral. This means developing classroom approaches that recognize and value the learners' existing experiences of language and texts and build on them. It may at times involve dispute and agreements to differ. In order to create an environment of both trust and risk-taking, teachers need to be shored up by a sense of what they want the children to learn – about texts and about life – whilst not seeking closure or neat answers. The variety of values expressed through texts of all kinds – from the subversion of comics to the tragedy of young people's love in Baz Luhrman's film of *Romeo and Juliet* – offer a chance for learners to take an active part in constructing their own learning. Whilst English is not just a vehicle for values education, as Robert Scholes points out: 'Texts are places where power and weakness become visible and discussable, where learning and ignorance manifest themselves, where the structures that enable and constrain our thoughts and actions become palpable' (Scholes, 1985: xi). Collaboration, reflection and evaluation, the friction of debate, help children and young people develop a metalanguage through which they can make links between the different areas of their experience – literary, social and cultural – and learn how to take their ideas further.

All these matters need to be seen with a clear eye. It would be foolish to suppose that an intellectual grasp of a particular set of values might result in behaviour that is consistent with those views. Agreeing in the classroom that taking and driving away a vehicle is anti-social, dangerous and worthy of punishment will not lower the TDA rate. Besides this, what we believe to be right may at times go against the law of the land or conflict with a particular religious view. It is everyday practice to use English as a forum for discussion of green issues. How far can this be seen as accounting for young people tree-sitting or tunneling under contested building sites? Whilst much of the practice of English teaching sits easily alongside much in the Crick Report, it is not the duty of the English curriculum, nor its teachers, to inculcate values agreed and presented in even the most humane documents. It is, however, the responsibility of English to present the complexities, diversity, paradoxes, tough issues, harsh realities and ambiguities of life as reflected in texts, both spoken and written. These will be realized through classroom practice which acknowledges and welcomes difference, helping young people find ways of articulating their informed, reasoned, critical views.

> . . . English is the subject in which ethics, questions of social, public morality are constantly at issue: not in terms of giving children the 'right' way of thinking, but in terms of giving children the means of dealing with the ethical, moral issues on the one hand and by absorbing, and perhaps this is the most important, the ethos developed in the classroom.
>
> (Kress, 1995: 6)

5 Geography, values education and citizenship

Helen Walkington

Introduction

This chapter, drawing on new research findings, outlines and evaluates the way in which teachers can contribute to values education and citizenship education through their teaching of Geography. It aims to raise teachers' awareness of the values curriculum that they already provide through Geography teaching and to reflect upon the potential that Geography as a subject provides for future practice in values and citizenship education. The first section considers the potential contribution of Geography to issues in values education and citizenship education. This chapter provides examples from my own research which might provide a picture of the types of practice, most notably the teaching strategies, that contribute to good values and citizenship education, emphasising the way in which these link to geographical outcomes. The chapter also focuses upon drawing out principles for good practice in the teaching of values and citizenship education through Geography, and outlines reflective activities which may contribute to teachers' professional development. Finally the discussion considers the importance of current areas of geographical debate to values and citizenship education.

The contribution of Geography in values and citizenship education

Asking people what they perceive geographical learning to be can reveal a whole range of differing interpretations, from simplistic notions such as being able to use maps, globes and atlases and knowing the capitals of the world, to a more sophisticated understanding of human–environment interactions and the relationships between spatial patterns and processes. Much less frequently is a definition of Geography education associated explicitly with the teaching of geographical values, moral education or indeed citizenship. Education always takes place in a social context and this context is inherently value laden. Geography, as with any other subject, can therefore be viewed as a vehicle for values education. Geography, however, cannot be seen as a single approach to the teaching of values. Indeed within Geography there are many different approaches available to the teacher and many different ideologies within which it is possible to teach. The concept of a common values curriculum within Geography is therefore redundant. Nevertheless it can be argued that learners should have a values entitlement, and the provision of citizenship education is one example. Definitions of values education and citizenship education in the context of Geography teaching are considered next.

Catling (1992: 17) listed key dimensions of geographical experience for pupils which included 'building an appreciation of the role of values and attitudes in issues related to people, places and the environment', echoing Slater's (1994) concern that Geography education should develop both reason and feeling. Values are the standards and ideals for which we strive (Reich and Adcock, 1976) and are therefore composed of both emotional and motivational components. Values education is interpreted here as the opportunities provided by teachers which help learners to:

- understand and compare values and beliefs they hold and others hold, look at evidence, form opinions and conclusions;
- discuss differences and manage conflicts in non-violent ways;
- discuss and consider different solutions to personal, social and moral dilemmas;
- recognize the complexities of defining right and wrong and discussing elements of power and the role of decision makers in the community;
- communicate their values and understandings in discussion and through their behaviour;
- reflect on how their actions may affect others;
- demonstrate responsibility and initiative.

(Cooper *et al*, 1998: 165)

This definition of values education, when applied in a geographical context, clearly highlights the importance of an issue-based approach to Geography which promotes discussion between pupils. The definition also covers some aspects of citizenship education where values are considered in a social context.

The Crick Report (QCA/DfEE, 1998: 11) defined effective citizenship education as 'social and moral responsibility, community involvement and political literacy'. Minimal recognition of the global context, particularly pertinent to geographers, was provided. At Key Stage 2, for example, although the document recommended that pupils should 'know about the world as a global community,' this was associated with understanding 'the meaning of terms such as *poverty, famine, disease, charity, aid* and *human rights*' (QCA/DFEE, 1998: 48), signalling a negative focus to engaging with the global dimension. While there is room for Geography teaching to connect with each of the three facets of citizenship as defined in the Crick Report, a much closer connection exists between the study of Geography and global notions of citizenship. The following descriptors, many of which reflect the subject matter of Geography, outline Oxfam's definition of a global citizen, who:

- is aware of the wider world and has a sense of their own role as a world citizen;
- respects and values diversity;
- has an understanding of how the world works economically, politically, socially, culturally, technologically and environmentally;
- is outraged by social injustice;
- participates in and contributes to the community at a range of levels from the local to the global;
- is willing to act to make the world a more equitable and sustainable place;
- takes responsibility for their actions.

(Oxfam, 1997: 2)

Global Citizenship education, within this definition, provides learners with the knowledge, skills and attitudes to understand their rights and responsibilities as global citizens. It also emphasizes the importance of translating this understanding into considered behaviour, at a level appropriate to the individual, which can be practised within an educational setting. The following quote further emphasizes the links between Geography and a global conception of citizenship:

> Indeed the ever growing magnitude of environmental problems in recent times has raised fundamental issues of human kind's relationship with the biosphere and lithosphere, including human impact on the quality and quantity of human life. These issues permeate. . . citizenship.
>
> (Lynch, 1992: 13)

Local–global interactions are central to citizenship, a point echoed in the Oxfam definition, which highlighted local action in view of a global perspective. While Oxfam's definition has some degree of overlap with values education, for instance, in engendering respect for a diversity of cultures, the latter three elements emphasize the importance of action. This is reflected in Gilbert's (1992) notion of citizenship as *participation*. Actions provide a basis for linking the local and global scales which have given rise to the well used phrase 'think globally, act locally.'

The practice suggested by the chosen definition of values education is based around discussion which may be extended in global citizenship education to focus upon experiential learning and action projects. I have suggested that values education can most readily be integrated with the aim to promote issues-based approaches to Geography education where there is an emphasis upon participatory learning, the facilitation of discussion and the development of learners' reflective and critical skills. However, some commentators have highlighted a 'hidden values curriculum' (for example, Gatto, 1992) related to the personal values of teachers, which is revealed subtly in many ways, including the content of lessons, the classroom methods and the teacher's relationships with pupils and colleagues. Together both the hidden and formal values curricula relate to the belief system or world view of the teacher, what Slater (1992) describes as an educational ideology.

The hidden values curriculum

A teacher who adopts an information-centred approach in the classroom, displaying an encyclopaedic knowledge of the world, will clearly convey different values to one who takes an issue-centred approach, where understanding geographical processes forms the basis for learners to explore their own feelings and attitudes. These different approaches may be indicative of the educational philosophy held by the teacher. Values have been linked by Slater (1992) to four main educational ideologies (child-centred, liberal, reconstructionist and utilitarian). There appears to be some degree of association between teaching approach and educational ideology, although teachers do not always hold one view or adopt one approach consistently. The values associated with each ideology are outlined below.

Educational ideologies are closely related to a teacher's underlying aims, which inform values in Geography. These may include:

- a child-centred stance which values the child's development and thus the role of Geography is to help the child to self-understanding;
- a liberal /academic stance which values intellectual growth;
- a utilitarian view which values vocational skills;
- a reconstructionist view which values change to a more just society and emphasizes spatial injustices and imbalances in society, develops social and environmental concern in pupils and opens up the discussion of values and feelings.

(Slater, 1992; Walford, 1981).

Using the above classification of ideologies in Geography education, a teacher might try to consider the following questions:

- In which cases (for what topics, in what teaching situation, with which group of learners) does your teaching fall into one of these ideological positions?
- What values are you aware of conveying in each case?
- What underlying beliefs are driving your commitment to a particular position and how might these translate into a hidden values curriculum?
- Would a change in approach lead to greater potential for values education?

Values are conveyed through the adoption of a specific approach. The descriptions above seem to indicate that holding views consistent with the child-centred or reconstructionist ideology may provide the greatest opportunities for values education as interpreted above. The reconstructionist ideology in particular has great relevance for citizenship education where this focuses upon participating in change.

Geography resources are a further means of conveying a hidden curriculum. Both visual (eg photographs, video, CD ROM, etc) and textual resources (eg text books, teaching packs) can have an air of objectivity and authority which frequently remains unquestioned. However, any resource to some extent promotes a particular world view and can therefore be considered ideological. It is possible to identify these embedded ideologies, an important skill for the teacher conscious of the values she promotes in school.

Taking a resource you commonly use which contains visual materials (such as a book, photo pack, video, etc.) try to identify the dominant ideology as proposed in the earlier discussion. The following questions are suggestions to structure your own enquiry:

- What are the key concepts, topics or ideas that structure the resource?
- Whose opinions are articulated?
- What is missing? Are there theories or opinions that are ignored?
- What assumptions are made in the course of explanations provided?
- What are the literal and more subtle aims of the resource?
- How might the ideologies be balanced by the way in which the resource is used with learners?

Whether through the hidden or formal values curriculum, a teacher's chosen methodology is of fundamental importance in promoting democratic and participative values. Even in an apparently neutral area such as Physical Geography (where this is taught through a scientific approach), the way in which pupils are encouraged to learn can convey a values message. This is particularly so in relation to the degree of learner participation planned, and as Lynch notes, 'these modes [methods] are powerful socialising media and they are probably more potent in inculcating values and attitudes than are curricular knowledge or materials. They express the real underlying purposes of educators' (Lynch, 1992: 34). The classroom methodology not only relates to a teacher's underlying aims, it also provides the foundation for either active or passive learning, the critical or superficial investigation of issues and either action for change or tokenistic participation.

The key values, concepts and skills which link Geography to global citizenship education (Walkington, 1999a) are shown below. These are linked by a teaching approach which places an emphasis upon challenging or combating preconceived ideas, searching for the underlying processes and taking an holistic approach to enquiry. The approach is of fundamental importance in developing cooperative learning strategies and enables the use of issues to structure learning, for example environmental issues or those concerning justice and equity.

Global citizenship and values education through Geography

The research presented next provides examples that describe both values education and global citizenship education taking place through the teaching of Geography. The data

Table 5.1 Links between Geography and global citizenship education

Values	Concepts	Skills
a sense of place	sustainability	comparison (eg being able to
	interdependence	see differences and similarities)
a sense of community	change	critical thinking
empathy	place	decision making
	cultural diversity	

comes from my own research of the teaching of a 'developing' locality in Geography at Key Stage 2: '... a contrasting locality in a country in Africa, Asia (excluding Japan), South America or Central America (including the Caribbean)' (DfE, 1995: 89). However, the findings are highly relevant to all phases of Geography education.

Two groups of Key Stage 2 teachers were involved in the research. Teachers in the first group had all lived and worked in a 'developing' locality, so were teaching on the basis of personal experience. Teachers in the second group had no direct experience in the developing world and were teaching using commercially produced locality packs. The teachers were asked about their aims when teaching about the developing locality and their classroom practice for this topic, through questionnaires and individual interviews. The main differences between the two groups of primary school teachers were with respect to the teaching of values and citizenship education as revealed in the educational aims and classroom methods they described.

Teaching aims

All the teachers who participated in the research were asked to describe the key aim underlying their classroom practice for this topic, which formed a spectrum ranging from knowledge outcomes at one end to Global citizenship education at the other:

The aims raised mainly by teachers with no direct experience of the developing world focused upon fulfilling the National Curriculum, which included encouraging pupils to see both similarities and differences between the locality being studied and their home area (**a** and **b** in Figure 5.2). The aims shared by both groups of teachers, regardless of their experience in the developing world, were increasing global and cultural awareness and giving pupils a positive image of the locality (**c** and **d**). Aims stated more exclusively by teachers with direct experience were critical thinking skills and global citizenship education (**e** and **f**).

Table 5.2 Global-citizenship teaching aims

a. To know	b. To compare	c. To increase awareness	d. To value	e. To critically evaluate	f. To develop one's own citizenship

These results showed that while all teachers had geographical aims, some wished to combine these with values and global citizenship education learning outcomes.
Teachers' aims focusing upon values education included:

- valuing diversity;
- combating stereotypes;
- stressing the commonality of humanity (ie the similarities are of more importance than the differences);
- empathy.

Teachers' aims that focused upon the development of pupils' global citizenship included:

- encouraging the recognition of the interconnected nature of places and people;
- engendering within the pupils a sense of responsibility for their own actions;
- increasing the pupils' self-esteem, especially that of English as a Second Language learners;
- teaching the skills of critical thinking and evaluation;
- employing active participatory approaches to learning;
- allowing pupils to work collaboratively.

These aims for global citizenship are mutually supportive.

Teaching methods

The methods which teachers adopted are represented again on a spectrum. The two ends of this continuum are described as 'How' type and 'Why' type education. The 'How' type approach is a content-oriented, descriptive approach. In relation to a developing locality it might include information about *how* people live, *how* the place appears, *how* the people make their living. Most of the information is within the cognitive realm representing an 'education as transmission' model. 'Why' type education, in contrast, focuses upon enquiry. There is an underlying aim to develop critical thinking and the affective, as well as cognitive, dimension is addressed. The approach, therefore, questions *why* the place appears the way it does and *why* people make their living in the way that they do. Learning is active rather than passive, representing a participatory 'education as transformation' model.

Table 5.3 'Education as transformation' model

Information Gathering	Discussion	Experiential Activities
The teacher and pupils gather information about this place. This research is directed by the teacher.	Pupils share and discuss ideas and act out roles. Activities are designed to promote a positive image of the place. A school link may exist. If pupils have experience it is drawn out.	Pupils engage actively with the issues of the place. Their critical skills are developed. The approaches have a citizenship aim.

The way in which teachers were clustered on this continuum can be exemplified in relation to just one theme which arose in teachers' descriptions of their practice: the way in which stereotyping was approached. Four different strategies were described which ranged from a *'How'* type responsive approach to a *'Why'* type enquiry approach.

Only combat stereotyping if it occurs
Some teachers made use of the knowledge of pupils in their class or school to combat stereotyping. For example, in response to racist attitudes arising in her class one teacher asked pupils from a different class in the school to lead a lesson on their religion.

> I asked Meriam and Hassim to come into the classroom. Hassim started speaking in Arabic. They could both read in Arabic and he put his cap on and Meriam put her shawl on and all they did was look at each other. They went through the prayer ritual. . . the other children were just overwhelmed.

Teachers set out to combat stereotypes before they occur
This challenging form of education aimed to counteract negative images and ranged from giving only positive images (acknowledged as stereotypes in themselves) to teachers who tried to give a range of images of a country, to combat the narrow image of the locality from being generalized beyond its confines. Both of these response types were teacher directed, and, therefore, represent a *'How'* type approach, as exemplified by this teacher:

> I try to convey to the children that its a vibrant place full of exciting, jolly, laughing people... I only do positive stuff. I don't tell them about the wars, although I do talk about the disadvantages they've suffered, but I try to emphasize how well they cope and how well they improvise.

Provide a forum for discussion with the role of the teacher as a facilitator
Such teachers did not shy away from the negative images that pupils may already have but instead encouraged pupils to debate and justify their images through discussion. Teachers using this technique often made use of 'circle time,' (Fountain, 1994) where pupils are encouraged to speak when they are given a designated 'talking object' such as an artefact from the locality which is used to ensure everyone has contributed. Others mentioned the use of challenging moral issues so pupils can consider their own ideas in the light of a range of others. One teacher gave an example of this, he described making use of the pupils' interest in East African game parks and wildlife.

> . . . you've got a lead in there . . . but then you can bring in the interaction more. 'If you were a Tanzanian and you were trying to grow food and there were elephants outside – *what would you feel about this?'* So you can challenge them on things like that.

Clearly this is within the realm of values education as revealed in the aim to empathize and consider conflicting values; the need for food and the desire for wildlife conservation.

Give pupils the skills of critical evaluation, enabling them to interrogate information and their own attitudes
This fell within the realm of global citizenship education because it considers the social context of personal attitudes and values. Teachers were able to design activities that led pupils to challenge their own pre-existing images and ideas. One teacher described such an activity:

> OK, the initial input is the map of India, write in three words [to describe India]. Then we get loads of travel brochures and they cut out pictures of India (not the hotels)... then they have to say 'what are these pictures telling me India is like?' I find that is very successful in challenging this *very dry, dusty, poor* country. It comes over as being *very colourful, attractive, beautiful* beaches, (they have no idea that the beaches are so lovely there). . . beautiful buildings, lots of history. . .

The four approaches formed a continuum from teacher-directed to teacher-facilitated strategies. The teacher-directed approach tended to be content focused, while the facilitative approach was based on a strong commitment to pupils being actively involved in their own learning. Fien and Slater (1991) argued that values education does not take place unless the teaching approach is matched by a values objective. The research findings from this study revealed the converse also to be true. Two teachers shared a common aim: to discourage pupils from making judgements about people on the basis of appearances. For one teacher this was approached in the classroom by her telling the pupils not to make such judgements. In contrast another teacher showed slides of people from the locality in which she had worked and then used these to redress the pupils' first impressions through a structured class discussion.

A combination of aims and classroom methods can be used to locate each teacher on a *How-Why* continuum shown below:

The dotted line at the centre represents an even balance between *How* and *Why* type teaching. With increasing distance from the dotted line teaching is dominated by *How* type aims and approaches (to the left) and *Why* type aims and approaches (to the right). The

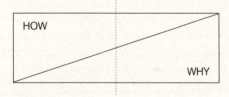

Figure 5.1 A How–Why continuum

teachers who participated in the research all positioned themselves on the *How–Why* model. Although teachers with direct experience of the developing world were clustered closer to the *Why* pole than those without, all teachers reported the desire to increase the *Why* type element of their practice. It was found that the *How–Why* model provided a robust tool for reflecting upon practice, a theme developed below.

Principles for good practice

Mercer, Wegerif and Dawes (1999) proposed 'exploratory talk' founded on a social view of intellectual development as an approach to improve pupils' reasoning. They found their approach helped pupils to work collaboratively on tasks, improving the quality of both group and individual work. The clear implication of such collaborative group work tasks is their potential contribution towards values and citizenship education. In this model of exploratory talk it is the group's responsibility to discuss alternatives, to ensure that all members of the group have contributed, then to reach agreement and take decisions. In so doing, reasons behind opinions given are expected by the group and challenges are accepted by individuals. The ground rules that support 'exploratory talk' are underlain by educational principles which have relevance for values and citizenship education. They focus upon the importance of participation, listening to and valuing the views of others as well as being self critical and reflective. My own research revealed that democratic principles were of great importance in creating a sensitive environment for values to be discussed. Furthermore, increased levels of self-esteem also contributed to pupils taking responsibility to encourage each other to be critical and reflective and to stimulate further enquiry.

The definition of global citizenship promoted by Oxfam (1997) clearly stressed the importance of active participation in citizenship. Indeed how else can we demonstrate effectively to students that their own actions can make a difference? An effective way to evaluate the extent to which action projects represent real citizenship or 'tokenism' is by using Hart's (1992) ladder of learner participation.

Hart (1992) proposed a ladder of participation with the first three rungs ('manipulation', 'decoration' and 'tokenism') classed as non-participatory, in contrast to rungs four to eight which showed a gradual increase in pupils' autonomy, learning potential and educational value. Findings from my own research exemplify these forms of participation. Stage four was termed 'assigned but informed.' For instance, one teacher's class had carried out research among their families (96 per cent of Pakistani origin) about life in localities in Pakistan. In stage five learners are 'consulted and informed,' for example another teacher had worked with his class to produce a play on land rights set in a Sierra Leonean locality that toured neighbouring primary schools. At stage six the action project is 'adult initiated, decisions shared with pupils.' A teacher and her pupil who had travelled to a locality in Nepal produced an assembly together where they presented artefacts, stories and feelings about the locality. At stage seven ('Child initiated and directed') Hart suggested that where pupils have complete control the action is likely to be marginalized. No examples of such participation were evident from my research. Finally stage eight, where the action project is 'child initiated, decisions shared with adults,' was exemplified by a further teacher's class who had asked whether they could do anything to help with the development projects that she had described taking place in a Ghanaian locality. The pupils had organized a sponsored race to raise money towards a specific project. It is possible to use Hart's ladder of participation to evaluate pupil participation in citizenship.

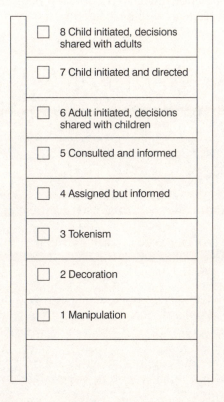

Figure 5.2 Hart's ladder of learner participation

Task 5.1: Using Hart's ladder

Using Hart's ladder of participation to evaluate pupil involvement in global citizenship education:

1. Make a list of any activities you have carried out which have extended beyond the classroom or which involved active learning approaches.
2. Consider how each of these relate to the stages on Hart's ladder of participation.
3. How far up the ladder would you be able to go?
4. Try to consider the benefits to the pupils in terms of citizenship and values education as well as the constraints that may be present in your own teaching context.

Sometimes the higher levels of the ladder require more planning in order to build the pupils' confidence in their own action projects. Hart's ladder can also be a useful tool for considering how action projects may progress through the school. Figure 5.4 showed a model acknowledging the complementary relationship between *How* and *Why* types of education. For specific subject areas within Geography, this model can be used to structure reflection on practice as indicated below.

Task 5.2: Reflecting on practice using the 'How–Why' model

The first step is to brainstorm *How* and *Why* descriptors for a given topic. Descriptors relating to globalization have been suggested below:

How:
- Our main focus is to accurately describe the process of globalization.
- I try to raise the pupils' awareness of globalization by telling them how it affects them.
- I share my knowledge of globalization with the pupils through a range of resources (stories, slides, pictures, video, artefacts).

Why:
- I encourage pupils to critically evaluate the concept of globalization.
- We look at why geographical areas are affected differently by globalization and why the process of globalization often raises the issue of inequalities in wealth and power.
- I use a lot of active learning approaches such as role play and simulation so the pupils are able to see for themselves how issues are interconnected and interdependent.

Using these descriptors:
1. Mark with a vertical line the place where you believe your practice lies on the model.
2. With a second line mark the position you would like your practice to be ideally.
3. Write down any changes you would have to make in order to fulfil your goals.

These changes can now form the basis of a personal development plan. Alternatively, this can be done as a department or planning team.

Discussion

Current issues in Geography have great relevance for the teaching of global citizenship and values. Indeed globalization, sustainability and interdependence are no longer considered only by geographers, they are important throughout education. However, the important perspective which geographers bring to these terms relate to their impact upon people, places and environments.

The process of globalization is frequently used to explain away features as diverse as the distribution of McDonalds outlets in the developing world and small businesses closing in the UK. Globalization as an explanatory process is rarely the subject of scrutiny. It has been argued that this 'powerful' and 'inescapable' force affects all of us, meaning that we can travel faster, communicate with people across the world more easily and eat a diet composed of dishes which derive from a multitude of differing localities. It would even seem that our values are becoming more globally oriented. Indeed the presence of diverse cultures creates a richness of values and traditions we otherwise might not enjoy. However, this is only one side of the process. The developing world's experience of globalization has essentially been one of exploitation. Instead of interdependence, many countries have become dependent. One's experience of the effects of globalization on a personal level is very different according to where you live and your position in society. Arising from this are clear implications for the teaching of Geography, as moral questions about our unequal position in a developed country are raised. It makes us question our rights and responsibilities as global citizens. We can begin to question the values that have speeded the process of increasing interdependence between nations and our commitment to participation in transforming our lifestyles. As educators we have a moral responsibility to consider the impacts of the different ways in which a force such as globalization is presented to learners. If globalization is presented as a dehumanized force over which we have no control, learners are unlikely to engage in action for change. From a reconstructionist perspective globalization can be conveyed as a human process which can be engaged with. This position is far more likely to enable the values involved to be discussed and citizenship education to take place.

A sense of place has been a guiding concept in Geography, which links values and life experience to a specific locality. However, this concept is essentially introspective, considering only one's own values. The concept of a global sense of place, which has grown in tandem with the concept of globalization, is newer (Massey, 1991), using a place as a 'window' on the wider world. This encourages learners to consider their own values in the light of others. A global sense of place ties Geography more closely to citizenship through the interplay of local and global dimensions in both geographical learning and citizenship behaviour.

Conclusion

Geography is a subject of huge potential in alerting learners to the interdependent nature of our planet. It also synthesizes many disciplines and therefore at primary level can provide the foundation for cross-curricular learning where much values and citizenship education takes place. At secondary level, Geography exposes pupils to global issues and to the processes that contribute to a politically, economically and ecologically interdependent world. Thus the role of the Geography teacher is of fundamental importance in describing and explaining patterns and processes and helping each individual learner to understand his or her role within this complex and dynamic system. The role of the individual in the world is the focus of global citizenship education. The individual inhabits many social groupings and, therefore, citizenship education and values education are important in placing an individual in the global sphere. This was echoed in Tuan's (1971: 181) phenomenological discussion on the nature of Geography, where the metaphor of Geography as the mirror of man was introduced: 'the root meaning of "world" (wer) is in fact man: to know the world is to know oneself.' This notion unites Geography, values and citizenship education. It also provides a justification for carefully designed aims and approaches in classroom teaching which allow learners to discover more about themselves through their learning of a subject. Not least it implies that teachers themselves have a role in reflecting on these issues first.

6 History: values in the diversity of human experience

William Stow

Introduction

It could be argued that no single subject in the current curriculum in England and Wales has stronger links with citizenship and values education than History. History's subject matter is the study of human society and citizenry in the past, and it is inevitable that students and children will learn lessons and be provoked into thought about human behaviour from its study. The lessons learned may not always be desirable ones, and they may indeed be learned on false premise or misinterpretation. But any student of History will have his or her understanding of humanity extended by time spent thinking, reading and writing about the past. Indeed the term 'the Humanities', of which area of learning History is an integral part, indicates in the most simple terms the connection described above.

Curriculum debate in the 1970s and 1980s seemed to indicate that History was most likely in the future to become a subset of humanities. The increasing emphasis, especially in Primary Education, on the child's immediate environment or on local studies indicated a shift towards justifying History in terms of its ability to help children define their *personal* identity and to learn about themselves (Phillips, 1998). On the other hand, 'traditionalists' in the curriculum debate of the 1980s deplored the lack of knowledge of landmarks in British History as a phenomenon that denied the child the right to establishing a greater sense of *national* identity. This debate continues today, with national newspapers' letters columns being festooned with outrage every time the curriculum is revised. A recent example demonstrates this:

> The landmarks of British History have become optional parts of the National Curriculum. They appear only as italicized examples of what is permissible to teach. . . However there is no such equivocation about teaching History through a host of politically correct social themes. . . Even good schools therefore will find it difficult to pass on to children a sense of national identity.
> (Letters to the Editor, *The Daily Telegraph*, 11 September, 1999)

Aims and purposes of History

Debates over the aims and purposes of History must be the starting point for any discussion of values and citizenship education, and the ways in which these are linked to the subject. There are a variety of rationales for History: some have characterized them as extrinsic or intrinsic justifications for the subject, while others (Lee, 1993; White, 1993) have discounted the value of such a distinction. Most see the History curriculum as fulfilling both extrinsic and intrinsic purposes. Thus, intrinsically, the outcome of learning History will be the acquisition of the skills required to study it. In the past, History has been used explicitly in various societies to inculcate children with certain attitudes and values. In Britain in the early 20th century, History was part of developing particular qualities of patriotism and loyalty to the Empire (Board of Education, 1905). More recent examination of History curriculum debates shows the subject being justified for extrinsic purposes. Beattie (1987), Thatcher (1993), Scruton (1986), Deuchar (1989) and Tate (1994) have all proposed History as an essential means of induction into the dominant culture of the nation. However, others support other notions of History as performing social functions. Pankhania (1994) sees History as an essential means to combating racism; White (1993: 15) and Slater (1993: 50) see it as assisting the 'promotion of students' well-being as an autonomous person within a liberal democratic community', and enabling 'a more effective participation in a liberal-democratic society'; Walsh (1993) prefers History to instil in children a love of the past; and Rogers (1987) would like History to enable children to understand the present better in its historical context.

Lee (1993: 24) claims that his justification – the transformative aim – is neither extrinsic nor intrinsic, but that it represents a type of learning, which enables children to 'handle the whole of human experience in a particular way'. He claims (1993: 24) that History 'offers a way of seeing almost any. . . issue in human affairs, subject to certain procedures and standards, whatever feelings one may have.'

The original aims for the National Curriculum (DES, 1991: 1–2) predictably contain a mixture of social and intellectual aims. They include:

- to help understand the present in the context of the past (Rogers, 1987);
- to arouse interest in the past (Walsh, 1993);
- to help give pupils a sense of identity;
- to help to give pupils an understanding of their cultural roots and shared inheritances (Tate, 1994; Pankhania; 1994, Deuchar, 1989; Thatcher, 1993);
- to train the mind by means of disciplined study; to introduce pupils to the distinctive methodology of historians (Lee, 1993; Thomson, 1970);
- to prepare pupils for adult life (White, 1993; Slater, 1993; Pankhania, 1994; Tate, 1994).

The consultation materials for the most recent curriculum review (QCA, 1999: 132) have resurrected the emphasis on values:

> Pupils develop their individual and collective sense of identity and learn to appreciate the diversity of human experience by understanding and valuing their own and others' inheritance. . .they are able to clarify their own life choices, attitudes and values in context, through considering the ways in which the past influences the present.

The different understandings of History represented by these varying views have clear implications for the teaching and learning styles within the subject, which in turn may convey certain values to children. For those who subscribe to a 'traditional', or 'positivist' (as defined by Copeland, 1998) view of historical knowledge and deny the importance of viewing the subject from a variety of perspectives, the learning that takes place is likely to be passive (Copeland, 1998). Teaching will tend to be didactic, and emphasis will be laid on the acquisition of knowledge by pupils, rather than on enquiry and investigation. The outcomes of this approach will include:

- an awareness or knowledge of the dominant cultural and moral values of society in the past;
- a knowledge of a corpus of historical facts, and an understanding of History as a 'fixed' subject;
- an understanding of what has traditionally been regarded as culturally, politically and morally important by societies in the past;
- an understanding of some of the diversity of human experience.

These aspects of historical knowledge and understanding *may* have other benefits, such as a clearer sense of civic responsibility and duty, a sense of national heritage, and a heightened sense of patriotism. The extent to which these are developed will depend on the selection of content of History syllabi.

For those who see History as 'a continuous process of interaction between the historian and his facts, an unending dialogue between the present and the past' (Carr, 1963: 30), learning will be an active process. Pupils will be encouraged to view a range of evidence and come to their own conclusions about the past. The curriculum model that accompanies this view will be one in which the process of historical investigation is clearly emphasized, and could be described as 'constructivist' (Copeland, 1998). The outcomes of such an approach should include the development of:

- an understanding of the primacy of evidence;
- an understanding of the uncertain nature of historical knowledge;
- an understanding of the diversity of human experience;
- an awareness of the variety of points of view which inform different versions of History.

As with the 'traditional approach', these aspects of historical knowledge and understanding may have other benefits, such as a clearer understanding of political and social current affairs, a greater tolerance of a variety of perspectives and range of opinions, and a clearer sense of individual and community identity. These, however, cannot be taken for granted. Factors, which will affect the development of these benefits, are discussed in the next section under a number of key questions. In the case of either approach, studying the subject will also provide children with knowledge, which has always been, and will most likely continue to be, valued by society. The urge to investigate the past is an almost universal aspect of human consciousness.

Values and History

What are the values dimensions to History?

Knight (1987) has identified three strands of the values dimension to History: values clarification, procedural values and substantive values. Values clarification in history implies offering opportunities for pupils to clarify their own values by thinking through moral and value-based issues in History. Knight suggests that such an approach could be charged with moral relativism, and that the examination of pupils' own present-day values through History negates the historical aspect of the study. Procedural values are defined by Knight as values which are implicitly modelled for children, such as tolerance, respect for evidence and reasoning and respect for the individual and the particular, through the methodology of History. This has echoes of the ways in which the Key Elements (DfEE, 1995) tie in with some of the Crick Report's (QCA, 1998) proposed skills, values and attitudes in citizenship. Substantive values are described as key cultural values that are represented in certain societies or groups in History. Knight (1987) proposes that children should be introduced (through what he calls 'values information') to values issues in the past, as a way of enabling more informed decision-making in the present. Straughan (1988) discusses three main approaches in which moral education is covered: values transmission – in which values are transmitted through teacher and institutional behaviour; values neutrality – in which the teacher takes a neutral stance as children examine social situations and the issues they raise; and values clarification. Heater (1990) considers that schools actually convey values in three ways: selection of materials, deliberate identification of certain objectives to provide a certain moral outcome, and the hidden curriculum. Aspects of this framework are useful, but a most significant factor, which Heater has omitted is the curriculum itself. This, therefore, is the first of the questions under which the issues will be considered.

What is conveyed (implicitly and explicitly) by the selection of content in a syllabus?
This is perhaps the most significant factor in determining the values that the curriculum embodies. Slater (1993: 45) states that, 'Selection involves a value-judgement which gives public importance and status to those who are selected and implicitly, sometimes deliberately, denies it to those who are not. History is not a value-free enterprise.' There has always been a degree of flexibility allowed for choice of content within the curriculum, although published materials have tended to push teachers towards certain content and emphases. Thus it would be perfectly possible within the current framework to select as subjects for study events, people and changes that explicitly emphasize the pluralist nature of society (Pankhania, 1994; Claire, 1996), or challenge the implicit racism (Pankhania, 1994) which lay in the old Study Units (DES, 1991). On the other hand, there are those (Tate, 1994; Clark, 1997) who advocate that the curriculum should emphasize 'high culture' by teaching about 'the best we have inherited' (Tate, 1994: 67). This emphasis could be characterized by some as 'elitist'. Others advocate the inclusion of particular subject matter to emphasize Britain's relationship to Europe, in order to promote a clearer sense of European Citizenship (Osler and Starkey: 1999).

In any case the precise content of the selection that schools make from the Programme of Study would be dictated by these underlying beliefs. Pupils could be learning *explicitly* about people or groups of people who represented certain values in society, or whose treatment by that society teaches pupils about attitudes and values of the time. *Implicitly*, the choices made by government, schools or individual teachers, about what content to emphasize, give messages to children and society about prevailing cultural and moral values (Slater, 1993). If the History curriculum is focused strongly on the disadvantaged in society, it could be regarded as having a socialist, Marxist or even anti-English bias (Phillips, 1996). If it emphasizes the military exploits and territorial, cultural, religious and economic conquests of the nation over other nations, it could be regarded as jingoistic, militaristic and even prejudiced (Pankhania, 1994).

What are the teacher's own values and those of the school/department, and do these link to particular models of teaching History?
The philosophy of the individual teacher will consciously and unconsciously affect the values role model that they represent to pupils. It also affects the way in which they regard the importance of children's own contributions to their learning in History. It is vital, therefore, for teachers to examine their own positions on the nature of History, and to be aware of their own political values and viewpoints.

Copeland (1998) proposes that the National Curriculum presents a mixture of values models, in that the emphasis on skills and understanding in the Key Elements supports constructivist ways of working, while the knowledge represented by the study units is a link to positivist traditions. The constructivist extreme of classroom practice would be the democratic History classroom, where the values of democracy are modelled through the relationships between staff and pupils, and where pupils have a clear say in choice of content and method.

What messages does the learning environment convey about the subject, or about particular values?
The use of the learning environment in History in its widest sense will convey particular messages about the underlying philosophy of the teacher, or the whole department at Key Stage Three. Resources and display material which represent the cultures studied as 'fairly homogeneous' will indicate that the experiences in History of other cultural groups were either less important or non-existent. Further than this, if the content of the History syllabus stresses democratic values, but the style of teaching employed creates an 'autocratic' classroom, there may be an inherent contradiction (Griffith, 1998). Display and resource material which emphasizes diversity and pluralism (Claire, 1996; Sherwood, 1996) and encourages interpretation of evidence, will contribute to a wider sense that History should reflect the experiences of all sections of society.

Should the values dimension to History be a focus for assessment?
The extent to which objectives for learning in History should be explicitly couched as values, citizenship or moral outcomes is open to question. As yet there are no really clear signals from the current Government as to whether citizenship will be taught discretely or as a cross-curricular element within subjects. If it is to be an integral cross-curricular aspect of History teaching, then teaching objectives and assessment outcomes would need to be

focused in part on citizenship and values. *Knowledge* about values in the past, or values information as Knight (1987) describes it, could be assessed fairly easily. *Attitudes,* of respect for reasoning and evidence, and of curiosity about the past would be much more difficult to measure. However, if any real importance is to be placed on this dimension to the subject, then it must feature in the intended assessment focus.

Mapping citizenship and PSHE onto the National Curriculum for History

The final report of the advisory group on citizenship education (QCA, 1998) highlighted three main areas of understanding and learning in citizenship: social and moral responsibility, community involvement, and political literacy. History is particularly suited to developing political literacy, as the subject matter of the curriculum at Key Stages 2 and 3 is implicitly and explicitly political. There are also many aspects of the area of social and moral responsibility which History will touch on, in the sense of providing children with 'values information' (Knight, 1987) and developing their ability to form and tolerate a range of opinions. Community Involvement has weaker connections with History, but there are obvious opportunities for links even here, when children at any stage are studying the History of the locality and should be interviewing local people or visiting local sites. In any case, the Local Study Unit will provide them with knowledge of their local communities.

The tables below map out the more explicit connections between the History curriculum at Key Stages 1, 2 and 3. There are slight variations in the format used: the reasons for this are described below. All tables omit the non-statutory examples given in the proposals (QCA, 1998). The Key Stage 1 table sets out the clear connections between History and citizenship and PSHE, as proposed to the Secretary of State (QCA, 1998). Examples are necessarily non-specific, as the History curriculum at this stage allows for a great deal of flexibility (despite the restricted diet offered by mainstream publishers).

The table for Key Stage 2 necessarily takes on a slightly different form, as there are so many instances of historical content which can provide opportunities for citizenship education. Examples are given as key questions (in relation to knowledge and understanding) and illustrated by reference (in italics) to different study units. When looking at skills, the National Curriculum column takes on the form of discussion of key ideas. References are made here to the key aspects of knowledge, skills and understanding – the Key Elements, (DfEE, 1995). The table could be used as a source of suitable key questions, but with substituted examples of content, or as a source of specific examples of links to particular study units. The Skills and Aptitudes section has examples of types of teaching and learning strategies. These could help to develop the particular skills and aptitudes of Citizenship and PSHE.

The table for Key Stage 3 is briefer than the previous one, as there are many examples of overlap with Key Stage 2, both in terms of the skills and aptitudes, and the knowledge and understanding of citizenship. Obviously the level at which these questions or strategies will be tackled, is significantly higher than at Key Stage 2. With increasing rigour, moral issues must be looked at in the social and values context of the time, and as far as possible without direct comparison to today.

Table 6.1 Key Stage 1 History curriculum

Citizenship Reference	National Curriculum Content
Knowledge and understanding:	
Know where they live/understand that there are different types and groups of people living in their local community.	Local study work – people around us, and change in the community: *interviewing people from the community about changes in their lives, including people who have moved to the UK. Discuss how many people move to new places in their lives.*
Know about differences and similarities between people in terms of their rights, needs, responsibilities, wants, likes/dislikes, values and beliefs.	Comparing experiences of life of families from different parts of the world: *Looking at ways of life in the past, and how people managed without modern technologies.*
Understand different kinds of behaviour using moral categories such as kind/unkind, good or bad, right or wrong.	Using stories of famous people in the past: *discuss their motivation for actions:* *'What do you think x was trying to do?'* *NB: caution is required when judging historical actions in contemporary moral terms.*
Skills and aptitudes	
Express and justify orally a personal opinion relevant to an issue.	Describe and explain their thinking behind some 'detective' work with artefacts or pictures.
Contribute to paired and class discussion.	Collaborative planning and response to objects and artefacts, or to buildings and places in fieldwork. Work in drama, taking on a different persona and putting forward a point of view for a mini-debate, or being asked questions while in freeze frame.
Use imagination considering the experience of others.	Stories of famous people: *Drama work, engaging in roleplay, or creative written or pictorial work connected to the stories.*
Reflect on issues of social or moral concern.	Ways of life of people in Britain in the past beyond living memory: *Discuss child poverty in Victorian times, through looking at visual evidence. Reflect on such issues through stories of famous people, especially Victorians who helped others in society.*
Take part in a simple debate and vote on an issue.	Children investigate a historical dilemma (such as a choice faced by a historical character) and vote as a group to recommend action.

Table 6.2 Key Stage 2 History curriculum

Citizenship Reference	National Curriculum Content
Knowledge and understanding:	
Know at a simple level how rules and laws are made and the varying purposes they serve.	**How have societies formed law?** *Egyptian laws from Pharaoh; Greek from Assemblies; Roman from Senate; Anglo Saxon from kings and church; Tudor from king and parliament, influenced by church; Victorian and 20th century from parliament (therefore, indirectly from will of people).* **How have changes in laws been brought about?** *Legal and illegal attempts to change law, including breaking the law for moral purposes: the Chartists and Luddites in Victorian times, or Boudicca's rebellion against the Romans.* **How did people's rights differ in the past?** *Contexts in historical drama (Wilson and Woodhouse, 1990) could include Tudor enclosure, Victorian child labour, or immigrant communities in Britain since 1930.*
Understand the need for laws and their enforcement in shaping behaviour and tackling crimes, and why certain behaviour is prohibited; the role of the police.	**How has the law affected people's behaviour in the past? How were people punished in the past?** *Laws, punishments and rules in Aztec society; Anglo-Saxon laws: what offences were people punished for, and what were the punishments? Rules and punishment in Victorian schools; the treatment of criminals and beggars in Tudor times.* **General questions, such as: 'why do societies all over the world and throughout time have rules? How do these differ in time and place?'** **How have societies been policed?** *Self-policing state (Ancient Athens); military policing (Roman Britain); feudal obligation and law (Anglo-Saxons); private watchmen (Tudors); introduction of police force (Victorians); changes in policing methods and equipment since then.*
Know about the workings of local and national communities, including the main faiths and ethnic cultures, and how individuals relate to them.	**How have different communities contributed to society in the past?** *Multicultural nature of pre-Roman, Romano-British, Anglo-Saxon and Viking society; looking at how the different groups shaped each other, and the tensions between the groups; multicultural communities in Tudor and Victorian Britain.* **Why were individuals persecuted for their beliefs?** *Experiences of different religious groups in Tudor society; immigrant communities in Tudor and Victorian times – what evidence is there of this? Why are such groups under-represented in visual evidence from the time?* **How have different ethnic and religious groups shaped the society and the architecture of the locality in Britain since 1930?**

Table 6.2   continued

Citizenship Reference	National Curriculum Content
Understand that there can be different kinds of government such as democracies and dictatorships.	**How have people been represented in different times?** *Democratic and non-democratic societies (Athens and Sparta); Tudor Government (monarch and parliament); Victorian and 20th century parliament (partial to total democracy).* **How have people been governed in the past?** *Different kinds of democracy/autocracy/oligarchy, etc. Pharaohs (Egypt) and Great Speaker (Aztecs), Kings of Benin, Saxon lords.* **What was it like to be settled/invaded?** *Government by consent and government through invasion and occupation (how do tensions arise in these situations?). To what extent were people in a particular period able to express their opinions freely? To what extent did rulers listen to the points of view of the people?*
Know about voluntary and community bodies that work in their local community.	**Looking at local History, which groups have helped people in the locality? How have people in the past been helped by government or other agencies?** *Alms for the poor from monasteries; Tudor Poor Law; Victorian workhouses; Victorian philanthropists; the establishment of the NHS, and the Welfare State in Britain since 1930.*
Know that there are different economic systems; know that there are different ways of allocating scarce resources; understand the choices that have to be made in modern society and the impact on individuals and communities.	**How did people earn a living in the past? How did they pay taxes and to whom? What did people spend their money on in the past?** *Children should learn that the idea of disposable income is a fairly recent phenomenon for the majority in Britain since 1930.* When did Government take on responsibility for feeding and protecting the weak/hungry in society? *Poor Law (Tudors); the Great Famine in Victorian Ireland: harsh economic choices for both Government and individuals.*
	How do economic changes affect communities and individuals? *Tudor enclosure; payment of Danegeld to the Vikings by the Saxons; Roman taxation; second Industrial Revolution – the arrival of the railways in Victorian times; subsequent boom in towns. How were wages and standards of living affected?* **How have people dealt with shortages in the past?** *Primary reasons for migration and settlement of Anglo-Saxons and Vikings – exploring new land for trade/shortages at home; Rationing during and after WW2; dole money; the Depression; the formation of the Welfare State in the 1940s.*

Table 6.2 continued

Citizenship Reference	*National Curriculum Content*
Know about the world as a global community . . . similarities and differences between communities in terms of social, economic, cultural, political and environmental circumstances.	**How have people in the past established contact with other societies? How have people treated other communities and societies?** *Roman trading in a multicultural empire, and attempts to merge with aspects of foreign cultures; Viking traders; The Tudors – their encounters with other cultures, and the reactions of those cultures to them; world expansion in British trade in the 19th century; the global community in the 20th century especially cross-national organisations like the Commonwealth and the UN.*
Key Skills and Aptitudes: Express and justify a personal opinion relevant to an issue. Contribute to paired and small group discussion on matters of personal or general interest; and be prepared to present the outcome to a class.	This is the fundamental marker of good historical practice. The children should constantly be doing this, through artefacts, visual and documentary work and through role-play.
Work with others in a class and gather opinions in an attempt to meet a challenge of shared significance through negotiation, accommodation and agreed action.	Collaborative work and negotiation to meet a challenge can feature in whole-class role-play, where children explore a real historical issue. *Land enclosure in Tudor times.*
Use imagination when considering the experience of others and be able to reflect and hypothesise on issues of social, moral and political concern.	Responses to historical fiction can be very rich in this respect, as some of the political and social issues may otherwise be rather complex for young children
Discuss a range of moral dilemmas or problems, in which choices between alternatives, selected and justified, using appropriate language are discussed.	Consideration of any number of historical dilemmas confronts children with the moral choices that people in the past have had to make. This can be done through source work or role-play.
Participate in a question and answer session with a local expert in a given field	Interviewing local residents, or employers/ees, on historical aspects of their community provides opportunities for the development of these kind of skills.
Take part in simple debates and have opportunities to vote on issues.	Debates on historical issues can, with proper preparation, provide rich opportunities for the development of empathetic thinking, and for the understanding of the 'rules' of debate; listening to others' points of views, and taking turns to put forward points that are supported by evidence.

Table 6.3 Key Stage 3 History curriculum

Citizenship Reference	*National Curriculum Content*
Knowledge and understanding: Understand the significant aspects of topical and contemporary issues and events	Connections between historical events and their contemporary parallels can be illustrated both at a local and national level. Questions may also be raised in more general terms, about the extent to which knowledge and understanding of the past aids or hinders understanding of contemporary political and social issues.
Understand . . . the legal rights and responsibilities of young people with particular reference to the UN Convention on the Rights of the Child . . . understand the general nature of legal aspects and responsibilities of other citizens	This **must** feature strongly in any study of the 20th Century or World Study after 1900 (QCA, 1999), especially in relation to the Holocaust. Children should actually be introduced to the terms of the Convention, and should look at the context which led to its introduction.
Understand the rights and responsibilities underpinning a democratic society, with particular reference to the European Convention on Human Rights (ECHR) . . . the Universal Declaration of Human Rights	The political aspects of study at Key Stage 3 should provide children with a broad understanding of the way democracy has developed in this country, and they should see that the franchise has been extended gradually from a partial representation to a full one. The ECHR *might* be seen by some as a party political issue, so care should be taken to look at balanced perspectives. With this and the Universal Declaration, the historical contexts of the post-war world should be investigated, and instances of flouting these conventions should range across democratic and non-democratic Governments worldwide.
Know about aspects of the criminal justice system	The totality of the History curriculum at Key Stage 3 should give children a picture of the historical development of this. They should be encouraged to look at the changes in the system and how these have been brought about. Specific case studies and role-play in aspects of these provide excellent opportunities for developing deeper understanding of the underlying issues.
Know about local government, the services if offers and the opportunities to contribute at a local level	The development of the power, influence and levels of representation in local government will feature in studying Britain 1750–1900. Looking at, for example, *Joseph Chamberlain's work in Birmingham in the 1860s* provides opportunities to discuss different perspectives and examine the variety of motives at play in taking municipal responsibility for services and government in local communities.

Table 6.3 continued

Citizenship Reference	National Curriculum Content
Know about the work of Parliament.	The first three study units at Key Stage 3 should initiate and consolidate children's understanding of these terms and issues. In particular, any work on social History in Britain 1750–1900 must be set in the context of parliamentary legislation – examples will be chosen which interest children, such as Acts forbidding the use of child labour in factories.
Know about the UK as a political entity	An overview of the changes in the government of the British Isles will be an outcome of work in the first three study units. Emphasising the multi-national constitution should allow discussion of equal ethnic and political opportunities, and encourage looking at the History of the UK from non-English perspectives.
Understand the economic system with reference to . . . major economic issues . . . such as poverty and unemployment	The complexity of these areas is evident. It could be argued that there is a tendency to emphasise the ill-effects of the market economy on certain groups in society, and to neglect the illustration or investigation of the benefits to others. There should be an economic aspect to the study of all the units at Key Stage 3, as the economy is so instrumental to social, cultural and political aspects of History.
Know about the world as a global community and understand the political, economic and social disparities which exist	The importance of international trade, diplomacy and race relations is evident throughout the study units – from the extent of the trading contacts of the Norsemen, through the development of the slave trade, to the expansion of empires in the 19th century, and into the issues discussed above in the world after 1900. It is vital that issues in this area are looked at from a balanced point of view, but that pupils are encouraged not to take simplistic moral standpoints on issues very distant in time. The political, economic and social realities of the modern world are in many ways very different from those of past times.
Skills and aptitudes Garner information about an issue from a range of sources with some understanding of the role these sources play	All good source work at Key Stage 3 should lead to this outcome. This is the clearest of links between History and citizenship.
Demonstrate an understanding of the use of statistics	The use of census returns and other demographic information will inevitably be based on the use of statistics, and compiling or interrogating databases.

Conclusion

This has been an attempt to provide an overview of issues for debate, and to give possible directions to policy and planning in school History. Along with the other humanities subjects, it offers a particular opportunity to teach and learn within a values context, and contributes hugely to the all-round development of the citizen. The chapter has related the subject to the current ideas about citizenship within educational policy. However, it should be remembered that being a citizen and being able to take a full part in society relies on far more than a list of behavioural and cognitive attributes. It is precisely by being *broadly* educated that an individual can be rooted in many different ways in surrounding cultures.

For many schools and History teachers, adapting to the new emphasis in the curriculum will be a question of fine-tuning. Even if citizenship becomes a separate subject at Key Stage 3 from 2002, History will still play a vital part in inducting young people into meaningful discourses about human values. It is the combination of the rigorous application of evidence and the examination of social, cultural and moral issues that makes History such a complete intellectual discipline. Inquiry into the past is also a fundamental aspect of human nature. As Gardner (1999: 153) states, 'Nearly all humans are curious about their origins and their fate; and in that sense, the study of 'our story' requires little justification. However, an appreciation of the discipline of History transcends personal curiosity.' What is required of History departments and individual teachers is that, prompted by the arrival of different emphases in the curriculum, they examine anew the values context that they are providing for children learning History. They must also be fully aware of their own philosophy of History and how that may affect their teaching and learning environment. Any change in the curriculum provides a chance to reinvigorate the subject and their pupils' learning, in a subject that offers a rich context for learning about values, which are at the heart of human behaviour.

7 ICT and worldmindedness

John Gardner and Patrick Walsh

Introduction

In this chapter, we consider how information and communications technology (ICT) might contribute to values and citizenship education in schools. It is no easy task to tackle such major concepts in one chapter and the excellent treatments of them elsewhere in this book will prove valuable backdrops for the reader. In targeting this section at those who wish to integrate ICT into their values and citizenship teaching, we have tried to make it accessible both to experienced ICT teachers and non-ICT experts, primary and secondary. Most importantly, we are also aiming it at those who wish to avail of ICT to further their own knowledge and skills in values and citizenship education. The Internet sites, which are discussed later in the chapter, may act as useful sources of ideas for teaching and professional development in values and citizenship education – not only for ICT coordinators but also for teachers throughout the school.

A word of explanation on the title of this chapter will be useful at the outset. We have chosen *ICT and Worldmindedness* in recognition of one formidable aspect of ICT: the potential for the Internet to enable worldwide communications and information sharing. Whether between individuals or groups, the communications-related dimensions of the technology have the potential to break down the physical and cultural barriers that currently separate the peoples of the world. More so than either television or telephony alone, it truly opens up the world and its citizens to the concept of 'large group consciousness', enabling dialogue in a manner that simply was not possible before. But more of that later.

We take up another important challenge for ICT teachers in this chapter: the recognition, in the context of values and citizenship education, that ICT itself constitutes a social phenomenon with attendant values and social impact dimensions. Its very existence and the manner in which it is used have implications for many aspects of today's living, and its pervasive influence in the lives of citizens is set to grow.

Finally, in this introduction, a disclaimer! In an ICT chapter such as this, the use of Internet addresses for identifying the sources of teaching materials and ideas is almost obligatory as well as desirable. However, anyone who uses the Internet regularly will appreciate that unlike 'real' physical resources – of the kind available from publishers and libraries, for example – the 'cyber' resources of the Internet have the potential to be more transient. By this we mean that a resource that exists today on a computer in Berlin, easily accessible from any school computer in the UK, may not exist tomorrow if it is removed for whatever reason from that machine. We have, therefore, checked all of the sites given in the text and at the time of writing they are live.

Values education and citizenship

Of necessity, we will only be able to define briefly what we mean by values education and citizenship. We will not engage in the questions and debates surrounding values, for example, which values are most important? Are they shared by all? Suffice to say that education, in the form of schools and schooling, has long been considered to be society's second most important vehicle (after the family) for passing on commonly held values. In *The Republic*, for example, Plato scripts Socrates as telling Glaucon that education: '. . . would not be concerned to implant sight, but to ensure that someone who had it already was turned in the right direction and looking the right way' (Lee, 1955: 518). Perhaps it was not as important in the ancient world as much as it might be today, but what Plato did not script was Glaucon asking: 'Whose way is the right way?' All teaching is value-laden but it will not be for this chapter to ask Glaucon's questions!

ICT teachers however, like everyone else, need some kind of basis for designing their contributions to values and citizenship teaching. To begin with, then, we recognize the common sense of the view taken in the report by the National Advisory Group on *Preparing Young People for Adult Life* (DfEE, 1999a), that curriculum time '. . . for aspects of citizenship and PSHE can do 'double duty' particularly at primary school.' Much of what can be said for ICT supporting citizenship education can also be said for personal, social and health education (PSHE), albeit with different resources for different issues for different age-groups. Judgement on these pedagogic matters will always be made by the teachers on the basis of what they know of their pupils' needs.

For definitions of values in the social context of modern living, one of the main overlap areas between PSHE and citizenship, we also borrow from the *Preparing Young People for Adult Life* report. The statements of values, under the headings Society and Environment respectively, are helpful in making the link between values and citizenship for this chapter. They are: 'We value truth, freedom, justice, human rights, the rule of law and collective effort for the common good. . . We value the environment, both natural and shaped by humanity, as the basis of life and a source of wonder and inspiratio' (DfEE, 1999a: 8).

For the most part, then, we will assume that it is values in these areas, augmented with issues of democracy, globalization and so on, that underpin many of the themes that come under the umbrella term of citizenship. Examples of these underpinning values and dispositions from the Crick Report (QCA/DfEE, 1998):

- concern for the common good;
- belief in human dignity and equality;

- concern to resolve conflicts;
- a disposition to work with and for others with sympathetic understanding.

For citizenship education, specifically, we add the definition from this report as being '. . . an entitlement in schools that will empower them to participate in society effectively as active, informed, critical and responsible citizens' (QCA/DfEE, 1998: 9).

Values education and citizenship: an ICT context

The Crick Report (QCA/DfEE 1998), while comprehensive, is relatively restricted in its treatment of how various subjects can contribute to citizenship education. Not so with ICT though! In a special appendix (Appendix B: 67–71), Stephen Coleman sets out the argument that ICT is '. . . growing fast as an educational tool, especially among young people' and that it would increasingly provide opportunities '. . . to participate in democratic discussion' and for '. . . invigorating citizenship education'. To consolidate his point he provides details of a variety of sources that cover aspects of political literacy, including the Internet addresses of UK Government, independent and party-political information sources.

That ICT is growing fast as an educational tool cannot be disputed but what Coleman is focusing on especially is the Internet. This provides both a means of communication between people and sources of information for them. The Internet is the global network of inter-connected computers that enables worldwide communications between people. Access to the Internet is possible from almost anywhere on earth using the tele-communications network that encompasses the globe. All conventional telephone systems, cellular microwave systems (eg mobile phone), digital television cabling networks and the broadcasting 'footprints' of orbiting satellites provide means of access to the Internet. The Internet can, therefore, be enjoyed by anyone with access through any of these means, whether they are in a major city, in the middle of a desert or in the deepest jungle.

While nowhere near approaching the volume of people connected by telephone, Coleman offers figures to show that in the 18 months between December 1995 and June 1997, the number of UK Internet users grew from 1.1 to 3 million. In the period since then, the growth can only be described as phenomenal. Internet service providers (ISPs), which do not charge for access to the Internet and which provide free e-mail facilities and a variety of free software for downloading, have proven a tremendous lure for new users. The provision of such facilities is not in any manner altruistic, of course, rather it is self-serving. The ISPs generate their income from advertising on the Internet and/or from the telephone charges levied for the actual contact.

The largest development within the Internet to date has been the burgeoning of information and resources available to its users through the World Wide Web. The Web was a long-predicted phenomenon, particularly in an educational context, for example:

> With vast libraries of data available to him [sic] via computerized information retrieval systems
> . . . and his own electronically equipped study carrel, [the student] will be freed for much of the
> time. . . of the restrictions and unpleasantness that dogged him in the lockstep classroom.
>
> (Toffler, 1970: 244)

As a vast virtual library it offers the second part of Coleman's focus: the provision of information for a global readership. Over the four decades or so since the first interconnection between globally distributed computers was accomplished (ie the rudimentary Internet of the 1960s), the format of electronically communicated information has gone from ticker-tape and largely numerical output to sophisticated, three-dimensional graphics, high quality audio and full motion, high resolution video. The visual quality of materials currently available to schools from museums, etc is, therefore, outstanding.

The business community has rapidly embraced the almost limitless possibilities for e-commerce (the selling of products from interactive Internet 'catalogues') in recent years. In contrast, the development of learning and teaching through the Internet is suffering from a lack of investment and, it must be said, a lack of knowledge of how best to exploit the educational potential. Nevertheless, there are some major examples of sound foundations being laid for the future. In the UK, for example, the National Grid for Learning (NGfL) continues to develop, with ever increasing numbers of schools 'connecting' to it and, through its links, to the huge resources of the Web. As more and more homes join the global net, it is inevitable that its use in an educational context must also grow.

This accessibility of the Internet – potentially in every home – precludes any exclusive ownership of its educational potential falling to schools. Access to such a global system will, therefore, increase exposure to value systems that may not be consonant with our own. Since this access will occur in the home, the shopping mall and the youth club, schools should not be surprised to hear unusual or even unpalatable views being expressed in class; opinions derived perhaps from largely unmonitored Web sites or Internet 'chat-rooms'. In the same manner that television has for many years played an active role in the development of society's, and particularly young peoples', value systems, so too will the Internet. It must be said, in the same manner that such a role for television has been considered in some quarters to be unwelcome, unregulated or inappropriate, the current and future role for the Internet as an educative medium also faces potentially hostile scrutiny. This scrutiny must be engaged in schools in the same manner as any other issue in citizenship or values education.

Issues in citizenship education: the role of ICT

The Crick Report sets out what the Advisory Group considered compulsory schooling should address in a citizenship context, and many of the concepts and issues they focus upon would find resonance with citizenship curricula around the world. They identify a series of key concepts, often mutually dependent but requiring different approaches according to the teaching context and pupil age-group. Examples of these include democracy, the rule of law, human rights and community-based volunteering. How may

ICT contribute to the development, in these areas, of 'active, informed, critical and responsible citizens'? It is here that the Internet rules supreme above all other aspects of ICT. Through the Internet, and its global library the Web, teachers and their pupils have the opportunity:

- to communicate with a variety of widely dispersed people and groups throughout the world;
- to access and share immeasurable quantities of information, of all kinds, with people and groups distributed all around the world.

Communication and information sharing

Communication, for example, discussion and debate on ideas, and the accessing and sharing of information (and experiences) form the central citizenship activities that are facilitated by ICT, in such a unique way. Using the Internet, pupils are not only citizens in their own local and national community but have the opportunity to become citizens of the world. They are able to use ordinary school computers to engage the ideas, cultures and values of their peer group throughout the world; exchanging information and developing an increased awareness, knowledge and understanding of global society and issues. The development of this 'large group consciousness' has now become a global pursuit – worldmindedness – where once it was essentially a nationally based concept.

The quality of communication that the Internet can facilitate between pupils varies according to the resources available to a school (or indeed in the pupils' homes). It can be 'live' (both ways simultaneously) either as full audio-visual (eg person-to-person in videoconferencing) or audio only (computer to computer interaction with voice transfer). More simply, it can be staggered and in text form, for example, alternative 'speakers' in a 'chatroom' or discussion group. Simplest of all, it can be an exchange of messages in conventional e-mail whenever the person sending or receiving is 'on-line'. Whatever the nature of the communication, the sense of 'talking' with new friends is a clear motivation for many pupils and reluctance to engage in the interaction, at least initially, is rare. However, sustaining interest may be more problematic if the context of the 'discussions' loses its way and becomes repetitive and boring. Browsing the Web can similarly become unproductive in a learning sense. As Guy Claxton puts it: 'Surfing can be creative but it can easily become facile and disconnected, a jumble of baubles and trinkets that grab the attention fleetingly and are gone' (1999: 224). No different from any other participative activity, Internet work in the classroom, therefore, needs continuous priming by the teachers concerned to ensure it does not become dilatory and ineffective.

A 'brokerage' facility to enable schools to find partners for collaborative projects (pupils to pupils) has become an established feature of many educational Web sites and a variety of school networks on the Internet now exist. The Windows on the World Web site (http://www.wotw.org.uk) is an example that provides a forum for schools to find and link up with international partners for collaborative projects. Another, the European Schoolnet (http://www.eun.org), offers a civics section in its 'Virtual School'. This part of the site hosts a discussion forum for teachers on citizenship matters and periodically enables contacts with members of the European parliament.

The information sources available for access and sharing on the Web would defy any attempt at quantification. The global convergence of telecommunications networks with deskstop computer technology means that any information source, from the humblest small town library, or indeed school, pupil or ordinary citizen, through to the most famous of national museums and libraries, is amenable to those who can access the Internet. Very many of the more sophisticated sources have designed their Web sites to facilitate educational usage, often providing ideas and resources for project work, or from time to time promoting competitions or collaborative initiatives. Most Web sites allow printing or downloading of their materials (for storage in the school's own computers), which can then be used by teachers and pupils away from the computer, if so desired. Of course many schools now have their own Web sites where they post up information about themselves, their activities and their pupil interests.

But how does 'communication' support citizenship education? If you have not been involved in this type of activity before, the use of ICT to foster collaborative work between pupils in your school and those in another, perhaps many thousands of miles way, may take a bit of imagination.

Consider a class that wishes to explore the type of culture or government in a country far away. Perhaps it is a society experiencing conflict (eg Kosovo) or facing a major social or governmental development (eg the Australian referendum on constitutional change). Short of organizing a visit to investigate the issues, the pre-Internet opportunities were more or less restricted to letter writing exchanges and the exchange of newspapers or perhaps audio and video tapes covering the aspects under investigation. The nearest thing to 'real-time' dialogue – discussion, explanation, etc – would have involved relatively, perhaps prohibitively, expensive telephone conferences. With ICT, however, e-mail and video conferencing opportunities put the pupils directly in touch with their counterparts in the far off country from their own school desks – assuming, of course, that the pupils in that country have access to the Internet. Whether the activities involve a fixed set of objectives (eg for a planned project) or an open forum for discussion and exchange of ideas or materials, is up to the teachers and the pupils.

Once a collaborating partner school is found, a number of options are possible for extending the interaction beyond the mere exchange of e-mails. These include the provision of a chat-room or discussion forum for pupils to discuss matters that interest them, including (but not always!) the topic they are collaborating on. This is not to say that teachers do not join in the discussions, which in most cases they do, but it is important to give the pupils their 'own space' as well. A similar forum is normally made available for the teachers to engage in discussion and to share resources, lesson plans, reflections on approaches taken to different topics, etc. A 'publishing' area may also be available for teachers (and pupils) to publish their thoughts, pieces of work and discussion papers. Links to Web sites and other key contacts, which have relevance to the collaborative project area, are a feature of most sites and are updated regularly by the participating teachers and pupils. Very often, in addition to e-mail facilities or 'publishing' areas, a simple bulletin board may be provided to enable ad hoc messages and notices of events or meetings to be posted.

Clearly the most important resource in any collaborative citizenship project between schools is the sharing and discussion of ideas by the pupils concerned. The next most important activity, in the ICT context, is the sourcing of information and materials on the Web. For up-to-date discussion material, it is difficult to beat the immediacy of newspapers and one site (http://www.webwombat.com.au/intercom/newsprs/index.htm) offers links to over 4,000 newspaper and news magazine Web sites around the world. Table 7.1 gives some examples (all English language) from this huge source:

'Conventional' ICT resources also deserve a mention at this point. CD ROM and computer-based learning materials, for example, can offer significant support to the teacher wishing to promote aspects of values and citizenship education. Encyclopaedia CD ROMs (eg Encarta, Grolier) offer the most accessible opportunities for stimulating discussion or assisting with project work, providing text digests and pictorial resources for a wide variety of topics. For many schools, struggling for resources and funds, the short-term integration of ICT in citizenship education will be well-served by these relatively inexpensive resources.

Sources of ideas for teaching and learning

What should be clear from this brief discussion is that the principles of Internet/World Wide Web integration into values and citizenship education centre on two overlapping processes: communication and the accessing/sharing of information. While the former depends on the quality of connection, for example, slow computers with slow Internet links will quickly stultify any attempts at interactive communication, the latter depends on identifying good sources for the information needed for the project. 'Search engines' and 'browsers' exist to help users to find what they want but sometimes the process can be tedious. Very often a continuous and protracted refinement of search criteria is needed to get to specific types of sources, assuming they exist. In the area of values education and citizenship, however, several agencies provide Web site links to support teachers and pupils in schools. Many of these offer ideas for lessons, downloadable resources for classwork and opportunities for pupils (and teachers) to contribute to the resource base. In the next section we consider several of these Web sites.

Table 7.1 A selection of International Newspaper Web sites

Country	News medium	Web site	Archive of past articles?
Denmark	Copenhagen Post	www.cphpost.dk/index.asp	✓
South Africa	Natal Witness	www.witness.co.za	✓
Bosnia Herzegovina	Bosnia Report	www.bosnia.org.uk/bosrep	✓
Vietnam	Nhan Dan	www.nhandan.org.vn	✗
Jamaica	Daily Gleaner	www.jamaica-gleaner.com	✓
India	Kashmir Times	www.kashmirtimes.com	✗
Russia	St Petersburg Times	www.sptimes.ru	✓
New Zealand	New Zealand Herald	www.nzherald.co.nz/nzherald99/index.cfm	✓
Albania	Albanian Daily News	www.albaniannews.com	✓

Sites of interest

There are many sites that can provide materials for values and citizenship education and this chapter clearly could not address all of them. Many of the large corporations, particularly the BBC, for example, have major educational Web sites and these can be sourced fairly easily from their printed promotional materials or from browsing. What follows is our selection of sites and we encourage you to avail of them as appropriate. However, with the sheer volume of accessible material that will exist on other sites, you should always take the opportunity to browse the Web in a wider search for them.

A variety of Government-backed and independent Web sites exist, which support democracy, human rights, law and order and other aspects of citizenship education. A few of the most notable will be considered here. The Crick Report mentions the Foreign and Commonwealth Office site (http://www.fco.gov.uk). This site provides information (and guidance) for the UK citizen contemplating going abroad or simply studying overseas cultures in, for example, citizenship education. It gives up-to-the-minute assessment of conflict situations, digests of UK foreign policy and texts of ministerial speeches dealing with all aspects of the UK's external relations. As a source for discussion on international issues, it is comprehensive and accessible.

The first non-Government site of interest which we have chosen, described in the Crick Report (1998: 68) as excellent, is the One World site, '. . . dedicated to promoting human rights and sustainable development by harnessing the democratic power of the Internet' (http://www.oneworld.org). Covering both natural disasters and those arising from conflict and human rights problems, the site offers discussion materials on international crises. Details of the prevailing circumstances, any humanitarian or other interventions, ongoing or proposed processes of resolution and the outlook for the future are among the information offerings available. The provision of parts of the site in French, Dutch, Italian and German translations gives further meaning to the global 'oneworld' flavour of the site.

Charter88 (http://www.charter88.org.uk) is a site that campaigns for 'a modern and fair democracy in the UK'. It offers sections dealing with alternative types of voting systems (first-past-the-post, single transferable vote, alternative vote, etc), parliamentary reform, who's who in Government, freedom of information and so on. By virtue of its 'mission', it is largely a UK-relevant site but does draw on international experience in various aspects of democracy and government. For citizenship education per se, it offers the Citizen21 Web site (http://www.citizen21.org.uk), an 'on-line resource for educators' with the facility to download resources or to acquire materials in print form. The site provides a comprehensive set of links to other relevant organizations including the Citizen Foundation (http://citfou.org.uk), the Institute for Citizenship (http://www.citizen.org.uk) and the Community Service Volunteers (http://www.csv.org.uk).

The Citizen Foundation, supported by the Law Society, provides several offerings of immediate interest to teachers wishing to contribute to citizenship education and particularly to their own professional development. In the Curriculum Development section, internal links provide sources of information, and classroom and in-service training materials, under the headings: Rights, Responsibilities and the Law; Citizenship in Primary Schools; the Moral Education in Secondary Schools Project and the Primary Citizenship In-service Project. The Citizenship in Primary Schools section points to resources offering stories for 6–11 year olds on Friendship; Laws and Rules; Respecting Differences; Property and Power; and Community and Environment. For secondary schools, there is a link to the Young Citizen's Passport which offers a booklet approach (with chapters covering family, money, policing, law, travel, work, safety, etc) to support citizenship and PSHE teaching.

The Institute for Citizenship site quotes its mission as promoting '. . . informed, active citizenship and greater participation in democracy and society'. It offers details of projects it supports in local communities and nationally, and provides links to external sites for information. One of the most useful of these is the MORI poll site with access to a wide selection of public attitude polls in the UK since 1996. The Public Attitudes to Citizenship survey of 1998 (http://www.mori.com/ polls/1998/citizsens.htm), for example, makes interesting reading for citizenship discussions. The questions were designed to collect data on such matters as the respondents' views on what made a good or a bad citizen and whether they considered themselves good citizens. The site gives a summary of the findings.

The Community Service Volunteers' site promotes the concept of volunteering for the common good: 'We believe that everyone has something to offer' and in 1998, according to their site, they facilitated the volunteering of some 100,000 people in UK and worldwide projects. The site offers support for piloting local volunteering schemes and provides details of ongoing projects, including major environmental projects around the UK.

The 'common good' has been mentioned as an underlying concept in citizenship and values education and a site of this name, *The Common Good*, is run by the Australian Broadcasting Corporation (http://www.abc.net.au/civics). This wide ranging site offers support for teachers '. . . in developing strategies that will prepare students to play their part as active and informed citizens', offering citizenship and values education for primary and secondary classes. There are details of ongoing school projects on citizenship (primary and secondary), a bulletin board for recording peace quotations for the International Year for the Culture of Peace (2000) and advice on how to deal with contemporary issues. Curriculum resources, syllabus links, teacher forums, discussion papers, key contacts and external Web site links are all available. One of the latter is to a British Council (Australia) sponsored site called Montage (http://www.bc.org.au/montage). Montage provides a '. . . series of interactive curriculum projects for use by teachers around the globe. The projects are designed to develop and maintain international collaboration between students and teachers using the latest communications technologies'. Schools, teachers and pupils are kept up-to-date on a variety of projects and are facilitated in finding partners and joining projects with other schools nationally and internationally. Projects include inter-school discussions on cultural celebrations and commemorations, environmental work on life in the oceans and a novel Internet-based mock trial. In this project two schools, under the stewardship of a senior member of the law profession, conduct the prosecution and defence of a trial through a 'real-time' text-based discussion system. Another interesting project links schools in Wales with schools in New South Wales '. . . exploring the nature of government, democracy and the rights and responsibilities of citizens. They are sharing their findings and understandings, and exploring their differences. . .' (http://www.abc.net.au./civics/walses_nsw/).

Further browsing across the Web will undoubtedly reward the determined searcher with many ideas and possible partnerships for project activities.

ICT as an issue in values and citizenship education

As discussed in the introduction, the impact of ICT itself on society must also be considered as a citizenship-related matter and we turn to this issue now. Here again our brief is to be brief! However, there are a number of 'big' issues in relation to the role of ICT in today's world and in its use in education. ICT itself is changing society in a manner that is in some respects obvious and in others more subtle. We are reminded of John Dewey's words of a century ago:

> I make no apology for not dwelling at length upon the social changes in question. Those I shall mention are writ so large that he who runs may read. The change that comes to mind, the one that overshadows and even controls all others, is the industrial one – the application of science resulting in the great inventions that have utilized the forces of nature on a vast and inexpensive scale: the growth of a world-wide market. . . of cheap and rapid means of communication and distribution between all its parts. . . one can hardly believe there has been a revolution in history so rapid, so extensive, so complete. . . political boundaries are wiped out and moved about, as if they were indeed only lines on a paper map. . . habits of living are altered with startling abruptness and thoroughness. . . that this evolution should not affect education. . . is inconceivable.
>
> (Dewey, 1900: 5–6)

Indeed we will not dwell on the changes either but we acknowledge the resonance that this statement from yesteryear has today. The globalization and the cultural and political changes that have taken place in recent times are very much the result of the communication and information sharing which telecommunications provide for more and more people. Tom Stonier, for example, (cited in Evans, 1979: 209) considered this lateral communication *between people* rather than *to people*, by governments, etc to be a major dimension of the strides being made in electronic communications in the late 1970s. He projected that it would destabilize autocracies by promoting an open society and, indeed, on that basis he predicted the disintegration of the Soviet Union. The Internet, and its Web resources, is essentially an open system allowing access to anyone who has the necessary hardware and communications media (eg telephone, satellite). Arguably, therefore, it is inherently democratic. Therein lies another discussion point for the ICT class. The counter-argument is that those with the wherewithal for access are privileged. Owing to social circumstances, individuals, communities and whole peoples will remain disenfranchised from access to it for perhaps many years to come. What effect or importance this has for the world cannot be addressed here but is certainly an issue about ICT that could be appropriate for discussion in a values discussion (eg equity, opportunity) in class.

In terms of promoting democracy as a world ideal, still an aspiration in some places and perhaps only in a restricted variant in others, the Internet may also be found guilty of preaching largely to the converted, in other words, pupils in western democracies. Those who govern in a less than democratic way are unlikely to find the challenging freedoms of the Web attractive but Stonier's words may well continue to echo for them: 'No dictator can survive for any length of time in communicative society as the flow of information can no longer be controlled from the centre' (1983: 203). On the other hand, there are those who see the coming to pass of the Orwellian scenario for technology: an insidious means of invading the privacies and freedoms of the individual through state monitoring of e-mail and Internet communications.

Stephen Coleman (QCA, 1998: Appendix B) raises a number of sensible cautions (including the divide between information-rich and information-poor societies above) and these are well worth bearing in mind in the ICT classroom. The development of critical skills, skills that enable outdated, trivial or biased information to be identified and appropriate judgements made, in much the same way as conventional library resources might be used, is clearly necessary. In providing on-line discussion forums teachers may also need to foster simple debating skills by introducing protocols based on listening to others before responding, tolerance of counter-viewpoints and so on.

Importantly, a degree of monitoring of the Internet Web sites being used is necessary. Pupils are generally very responsible but accidental straying into areas that are unsavoury is always possible. Controversial topics will inevitably arise in class discussions on citizenship, values and morals, for example, racism, pornography, substance abuse, violence, extreme politics, and any unsupervised follow-up Web site searches may produce sites that are offensive and perhaps illegal. Equally they could produce sites that are legal but insensitive or upsetting, or which treat important events and issues in supercilious and sensationalist ways. Such sites would include some of the on-line news services which rush camera teams to the locations of disasters or other tragedies to beam on-the-spot video footage around the world on-line. No different, of course from the broadcast satellite versions but they at least are not as accessible as the Internet is on a classroom desk. The existence of such sites, and their creators' values, or lack of them, may well find a place in a discussion of values in the media. A helpful guidance document in relation to schools' Internet usage has recently been issued by the British Education and Communications Technology Agency and Department for Education and Employment (BECTa, 1999; (vtc.ngfl.gov.uk/vtc/library/pub.html).

Conclusion

Throughout this chapter we have attempted to address the use of ICT to support values education and citizenship, and we have broached the issue of ICT itself having an impact on these by virtue of its own all-pervasive impact on society. The Internet is not just facilitating the exploration of alternative value systems and various dimensions of citizenship throughout the world, for example, democracy, human rights and law and order, it is in many respects contributing to change as its almost limitless potential for globalizing the issues enables our young, upcoming citizens to become more worldminded. In closing this chapter, we should, therefore, like to focus briefly on the responsibilities facing teachers in the provision of an education that is becoming more 'information' oriented. In an echo of Coleman's cautionary comments about the quality of information on the Internet and the use it is put to, we leave the last words to Guy Claxton:

The most widespread applications of information technology powerfully and insidiously invite us to think of learning in terms of the acquisition and manipulation of information. . . Yet, if it is true that everything comes to look like a nail to a man who only has a hammer, it is equally the case that everything will come to look like information to a person who only has (or predominantly relies upon) a laptop. . .Access to avalanches of information loosely connected by threads of casual associations, does not of itself bring about the transformation of that information into knowledge or wise judgement, nor the development of the requisite skills and dispositions for doing so. It is the business of education to foster the development of the ability to select, integrate and evaluate theories and opinions, not to drown in information – however glitzy.

(Claxton, 1999: 224–225)

8 Mathematics, values and citizenship

David Malvern

Mathematics and values?

To many people mathematics is so obviously value free that to find it included in a book of values is at least surprising and perhaps even nonsensical. The argument goes: mathematical statements such as $2 + 2 = 4$ are simple matters of fact, utterly incorrigible and not open to any debate depending on values. Mathematical arguments, to be acceptable mathematics, are presentations of logic with which all must agree and they cannot, therefore, be value laden. It will come as a further surprise, then, to be confronted with the following quotation from St Augustine:

> The good Christian should beware of mathematicians, and all those who make empty prophecies. The danger already exists that the mathematicians have made a covenant with the devil to darken the spirit and to confine man in the bonds of Hell.
>
> (Augustine, 1982)

Read today, this is a dramatic and alarming view of mathematicians. As written, however, it becomes more reasonable to the modern eye when it is understood that by mathematicians here Augustine was referring to those who 'feign the power of divination and foretell what they themselves intend to do' and at least one modern translation calls them 'astrologers'. The point is that, at least in how it is applied, mathematics can be evil or good, as he stresses elsewhere:

> ... we must not despise the science of numbers, which, in many passages of holy Scripture, is found to be of eminent service to the careful interpreter. Neither has it been without reason numbered among God's praises, 'Thou hast ordered all things in number, and measure, and weight.
>
> (Augustine, 1998)

It is possible to dismiss this as antique and hardly relevant to today, but the power numbers seem to hold over people and the strong reaction they cause are evident in things like the significance given to 1999 changing to 2000. Clearly the response to such an apparently trivial matter is cultural. There is little mathematical reason for such interest, 2000 is not a particularly interesting number in itself. More interesting but unnoticed was 1980 ($1980 - 089 = 1089$, one of only five incidences of when subtracting the reversal of a four digit number from the number, results in an answer with the same digits rearranged – the others are 2961, 3870, 5823 and 9108). Even more interesting will be 2025 which is a Kaprekar number ($2025 = 45^2$ and $20 + 25 = 45$), but it is 2000 which catches the public's imagination. In spite of this, there is no universal liking for mathematics and in her report on mathematical literacy, Brigit Sewell (1981) tells of grown adults running off when asked to answer questions about simple mathematics for the survey.

Moreover, disputes among mathematicians continue. At the second International Congress of Mathematics Education in 1972, the talk 'Modern Mathematics: Does it exist?' by Rene Thom, the celebrated French mathematician, was hissed and booed by one section of the audience and cheered on by others. The French delegation walked out! As this chapter is being written, a vitriolic war goes on over the Internet in the USA between Federal reformers of mathematics education and a resistant group called 'Mathematically Correct'.

Over four score and seven decades ago philosophers brought forth into this world a new mathematics, conceived in correct computational formulae and dedicated to the proposition that two plus two equals four. Now we are engaged in a great educational war, testing whether algebra I or any form of mathematics so conceived and so dedicated can long endure. We are met on a great virtual battlefield of that war. We have come to dedicate a portion of that field to those who are giving up the quality of their education so that California's Math Framework might live. It is altogether fitting and proper that we should do this.

(Mathematically Correct, 2000: unpaged)

In large part this comes about because mathematics is the victim of its own success. At the very beginning of the tradition of mathematics as we know it, mathematics and science were intertwined. Thales (624–546 BC) was generally considered the founder of both Greek science and mathematics and perhaps the most popularly known early mathematicians, Pythagoras and Euclid, also worked, apparently seamlessly, in the sciences. Euclid systematized geometry axiomatically but also treated optics as part of geometry. Pythagoras's analysis of sound, which remains unaltered today, was at one with his theories of numbers and of astronomy. According to Pythagoras, numbers were *the ultimate essence of reality*: '. . . Harmony, expressed in mathematical ratios and means, was the controlling force of the cosmos. . . These interlocking disciplines provided a means of comprehending the true nature of the universe' (Gouk, 1988: 103–04).

For centuries, mathematics gained success after success in explaining the world and empowering human kind within it. Explanations of building, music, navigation and so on, were intrinsic to the development of number theory, algebra and geometry and were overwhelmingly successful. With Newton, creative in both mathematics and physics, this success encompassed the solar system and universal laws. Maxwell extended mathematics' rule over light, electricity and magnetism and, following the mathematizing of Mendel's work on inheritance, it seemed as if there was nothing mathematics would not eventually dominate. Mathematics uncovered truth after truth and its method was the road to the truth.

Unfortunately, the very process that produced so much mathematics disguised the fact that much of it was flawed. Looking back on the canon of mathematics permitted an overview which showed, far from being developed logically, mathematics had more 'simply grown'. As Morris Kline puts it:

> The illogical development also involved inadequate understanding of concepts, a failure to recognize all the principles of logic required, and an inadequate rigour of proof; that is, intuition, physical arguments, and an appeal to geometric diagrams had taken the place of logical arguments.
>
> (Kline, 1991: 522)

Attention turned to making good these errors and focused on mathematics itself separate from any application it might have. Mathematics became more and more separate from its relationship with the real world. Rigour became an over-riding concern and the creation of a single, systematic logical structure the goal. In turn, this process created its own contradictions, or paradoxes, and attempts to resolve them produced not one mathematics but many and continued the divorce of mathematics from reality. Values lie, therefore, not only in what mathematics is used for but also in what it is and what kinds of truth it deals in.

What is mathematics?

It is common to distinguish four main schools of thought, which emerged from analysis of what mathematics is. The first is usually referred to as the Platonist view and sees mathematical entities, such as number, triangle, etc, as existing independently of human thought. Mathematics is, then, a process of discovery. Again, although today we might see it as fanciful, we can find in the writings of Augustine the point that things mathematical would exist even if the world (and with it human mathematicians) had never been.

> Six, which is made up of its aliquot parts, is a perfect number in itself, and not because God created all things in six days, rather the converse is true; God created all things in six days because the number is perfect, and would have been even if the work of the six days did not exist.
>
> (Augustine, 1998)

Gasking (1960) argues that there is a 'public' or 'over-individual' character to mathematics, which gives an incorrigible meaning to its statements. Mathematics is independent of individuals, their likes and dislikes, societal predilections, the language of the mathematician and so on. It has a universality and is embedded in nature, which explains why we have found it so useful. Consequently, of course, as we are products of nature, we ourselves share in this universality and like any other conceivable being in the cosmos are beings just as mathematical as nature. Intelligent aliens would be capable of understanding our mathematics if little else about us, and this independence of humanity apparently gives mathematical truth a primacy. It is the most objective truth we know, somehow 'pure'.

There is a contradiction at the heart of all this, however. The price paid for universality is abstraction. When we say $2 + 2 = 4$ is always true, we refer to highly abstracted twos and fours. If two people join two already in a room, we have to take a restricted view of them to say the result is four. If Jack and Jill are joined by Joan and John, for example, we do not have four Jacks or four women. We have to move away from the individual to a more abstracted level of generality (people) before $2 + 2 = 4$, and for universality to be gained $2 + 2 = 4$ cannot refer to a specific observation of a particular realization of it. Curiously, then, to gain the universality in truth, which convinces people that it represents the best objective reality we have, mathematics has to move more and more into the realm of the abstract.

The second school of mathematics, formalism, takes this view even further. It argues that we have, within mathematics, symbols and rules which connect them, but because the resulting statements are only universally true when they do not refer to any particular thing or things, they themselves have no meaning outside mathematics. Mathematics is entirely self-referential – a sort of game played with objects that have no meaning, by rules that are only defined within the game. The rules are strict and require effort and discipline to apply them. There is an undoubted fascination in what happens when you do this, and an aesthetic reward to be had in doing it well. There is, however, no external meaning there, and that others may find some of the results useful may be well and good, but it is not the business of mathematics itself (see box below). Like climbing a mountain, there is no motivation in utility to solve a mathematics problem; we solve it 'because it's there'. In this view, mathematics is an invention to meet the challenge and to find elegance in solutions – as Keat's poem has it: 'Beauty is truth, truth beauty'.

Task 8.1: Discuss the following:

1. 'A mathematical proposition such as $8 + 5 = 13$ . . . is incorrigible, because no future happenings whatsoever would ever prove the proposition false, or cause anyone to withdraw it. You can imagine any sort of fantastic chain of events you like, but nothing you can think of would ever, if it happened, disprove '$8 + 5 = 13$'. (Adapted from Gasking, 1960)

   - Do you agree?
   - Does $8 + 5$ always have to equal 13?

2. 'To expect (students) to learn mathematics in the process of applying it is preposterous. It is like trying to teach people to play water polo before they know how to swim. Nor do I believe that students are necessarily motivated to study mathematics because it is useful. Most will concede that it is useful – so are castor oil and other revolting forms of medication. Ultimate usefulness will not motivate study by a teenager – and it should not. . . The great mathematician, Marshall Stone, says, "I hold that utility alone is not a proper measure of value, and would even go so far as to say that it is, when strictly and shortsightedly applied, a dangerously false measure of value." (Stone, 1957) . . . I think that utility is being overemphasized at the expense of certain intrinsic values of school mathematics which would serve the student better in the long run. We never hear anymore about the beauty of mathematics or about its structure and internal consistency – or about mathematics

as an ideal arena for the application of logic to the thinking process – or indeed about any of the cultural values of mathematics that have been cherished by the race for generations. . .It implies, moreover, that mathematics in and of itself is pretty dismal stuff which can interest no one unless it is attached to some supposedly interesting situation in the 'real world'. If we make this attachment maybe some of the interest derived from these external situations will 'rub off' on the mathematics and thus render it more palatable to the student. This, I submit, is an example of the 'strict and shortsighted application' of the utility criteria which Professor Stone deplored. It is moreover a bizarre position for an organisation of mathematics teachers to take.'

(Allen, 1988)

- With what parts of this extract do you agree or disagree?
- Is it a bizarre position for an organisation of mathematics teachers?
- What should motivate teenagers to learn mathematics? What does?

Ormell (1980) represents this stance as seeing mathematics like an onion. As the rings are peeled away, more are revealed. Peel and peel away, no central core of meaning is reached, just more and more rings. While this may describe deeper mathematics, however, it both denies its history, which is very much connected with meanings in the real world, and mathematical activity, much of which is applied constantly to things with real meaning. He suggests it is a better picture to see the outer rings as mathematics in action connected to meaning, and the inner rings as getting more and more abstract and 'meaningless' the deeper you go. The 'mathematical onion', of course, is capable of growing by adding more applicable mathematics to the outside and by inventing inner rings for their own sake.

Intuitionism, the third school, is so called because it permits only the simplest intuitive ideas to be used. It, therefore, excludes certain logical steps, by not accepting, for example, that disproving that something is not true is a proof that it is true. In this, its logic is more that of the Scottish trials which can result in three verdicts: Guilty, Not Proven and Not Guilty, unlike English courts which only recognize Guilty and Not Guilty. By restricting what can be used, this approach requires much discipline in applying the strict logic needed. It also reinstates much of the usefulness of mathematics as its building blocks are precisely those simple notions, such as the real numbers and finite sets, which we find intuitively obvious from our experience. It does, however, considerably reduce the cannon of mathematics that it finds acceptable.

The idea of something being obvious to us can be extended to the fourth school of thought, commonly called conceptualism, which holds that mathematics being what mathematicians do is a product of human ingenuity and its truths are culturally determined. This is the complete opposite of Platonism, with no realm, however abstract, where universal truths exist. Moreover, if mathematics seems useful to our understanding of the real world, it is because in inventing mathematics we have shaped it to be so. This raises many interesting questions, such as whether or not universal constants are properties of nature or only 'universally' true within our model of nature, nor can it be taken for granted that we could use mathematics to talk to aliens who may have invented their own and different version.

It also brings into focus the issue of what is true regardless of human whim and what is decidable by humans by an act of will. It is important, for example, to realize that legal truths fall into the latter category, as can be exemplified by considering the logic of Solomon's judgement (see below). Legally, this is an acceptable solution and a way of identifying which woman is the more compassionate and, therefore, which we might prefer to bring up the child. It is not, however, a proof of which is the biological mother – a matter not open to being determined by justice, even as served by the wisest judge.

Task 8.2 Solomon's judgement

1. The following is taken from the transcript of a trial of a man accused of stealing a package from a parked car:

    Defence Council: 'But on the crucial point – have you or have you not proved my client broke into the car and took the package – will you agree with me you have not produced direct evidence of his guilt?'

    Police Witness: 'We don't have a witness to him actually smashing the window and grabbing the goods, if that is what you mean. But we have presented the evidence from the car park video cameras which identifies him entering the car park around the time the crime was committed and shows him leaving carrying a package. No one else is shown on the tape. No one else could have done it. So if it is not anyone else, he must have done it.'

    If you were a member of the jury, what verdict would you vote for?

    - in an English Court (Guilty or Not Guilty)?
    - in a Scottish Court (Guilty or Not Guilty or Not Proven)?

    If you were the accused:

    - What follow up questions would you want your council to ask the police witness?
    - What logical argument would you want her to make to the jury?

2. Solomon's classic judgement is that faced with two women both claiming to be the mother of a child, he suggested the child be cut in two and the women be given a half each. One woman protested and said that rather than having the child killed, she would withdraw her claim. Solomon declared her the real mother.

    - What is the logical basis of this judgement?
    - How might you argue that the opposite conclusion is just as logical?
    - Nonetheless, why might this be the best human judgement?

Mathematics education, values and citizenship

From the discussion of what mathematics is, it can be seen that it is riddled with values as to what kinds of truth it deals with, what is true and what is not, what kinds of purpose it serves, utilitarian or aesthetic, what is acceptable as proof, what has meaning, what is and what can be willed. How it is taught will determine the education in values it promotes. As Freudenthal puts it:

> ... the picture of mathematics also influences that of mathematics education in a direct way. Whoever cherishes a picture of mathematics outside the world – a deductive system or a catalogue of formulae – is likely to systematize or to interpret mathematics instruction in the same spirit. On the other hand, whoever experiences mathematics [as] something in the making, vibrating under the impulses of world and society, will be inclined to teach it in the same way – directly or as an educational developer.
>
> (Freudenthal, 1991: 131)

The mathematics teacher, then, has first to survey what mathematics has to offer and then determine where he or she stands with respect to mathematics and what society expects of a mathematics education.

In terms of mathematics, we have seen this means teachers not just sorting out their own views on whether or not mathematics has meaning in the real world, but determining how their pupils will respond to, and benefit from, alternative views. Ormell's onion contrasts his view, that applicability to real things lies all the way round on the outside and children are best inducted into mathematics through their experience of reality, with a formalist onion from which application (if it appears at all) is a secondary offshoot. It was this contrast which caused some of Thom's audience to walk out. Thom argued that teaching based on the abstraction and rigour of formalist mathematics was at the expense of meaning and would inhibit mathematical development and creativity in pupils: 'In the early development of a child, explicit and deductive learning play absolutely no part: when learning to walk, it would be more of a hindrance than a help to understand the anatomy of a leg' (Thom, 1973: 198).

Ernest (1991) has produced the most complete analysis of mathematics teachers' approaches. His model is a framework based on five primary and nine secondary elements. The primary ones are: Epistemology; Philosophy of Mathematics; Set of Moral Values; Theory of the Child; Theory of Society; Educational Aims (a simplified adaptation of the whole framework is given in the Appendix at the end of this chapter). By combining various alternatives for each element, he identifies five stances that represent consistent positions within a model of educational ideology for mathematics. Each stance is based on a particular view of what mathematics is, what the aims of mathematics education are, how the teacher views the child and which learning theory he or she adopts and so on.

Task 8.3: Mathematics education ideologies

If you had to pick only ONE of the following statements to represent your view, which would it be?
1. Mathematics is:
(a) a set of true, unquestionable facts, and rules;
(b) an unquestionable body of useful knowledge, consisting of two parts – pure and applied;

(c) a body of hierarchically structured, pure knowledge;

(d) a body of absolute and certain truth whose knowledge is useful for developing the whole being;

(e) created, tentative and grows with social realities.

2. The aims of mathematics education are:

(a) for the acquisition of basic functional numeracy;

(b) to provide useful skills at the appropriate level and to pass examinations;

(c) to provide mathematical knowledge to train future mathematicians;

(d) to develop the child's potential creativity, inquiring attitude to know mathematics;

(e) to develop a democratic spirit, critical thinking, and empower the child to be a confident poser and solver of mathematics.

3. The child:

(a) is someone who can easily be sidetracked and needs to be guided by strict authority;

(b) should be taught the skills needed if seen to be capable of handling such skills;

(c) is capable of deriving goodness from mathematics even though this might not be evident from birth. The child should be exposed to all the goodness of mathematics;

(d) has full rights and should be treated as an individual; he/she needs to be protected and enriched with experiences to enable him/her develop his/her full potential;

(e) is born with equal rights, gifts, and potentials but is influenced by the surrounding cultures.

4. The ability to learn mathematics is:

(a) innate and inherited so different programmes should be used for different children;

(b) innate and inherited, potential can be realized only through teaching;

(c) innate and inherited with genius at one extreme and the 'mathematically incapable' at the bottom;

(d) innate, inherited and individualistic, with each individual's ability needing an appropriate set of experiences to be fully realized;

(e) the same for all, it is only the impact of the society that introduces differences in the development of this ability.

5. The teaching of mathematics:

(a) should concentrate on the passing on of the body of knowledge; practice of skills and techniques should be encouraged, and calculators should be discouraged;

(b) should centre on the application of learned skills and techniques to relevant work situations;

(c) should be the transmission of knowledge from the teacher, the possessor of this knowledge, to the students using various approaches which will motivate and facilitate learning;

(d) should be by providing a carefully structured environment for the learner to exploit; the teacher should be both a resource and a facilitator for the learning;

(e) should be carried out by providing a wide variety of practical resources for creative and critical activities; the teacher should intervene only on controversial issues.

(Adapted from Babila-Njingum, 1995)

Ernest (1991) concluded from his study that there are five major mathematics education ideologies. The 'Industrial trainers' who see mathematics as a set of truths and rules which should be taught 'chalk and talk' to children who are empty vessels to be filled. The emphasis is on socially useful training, back to basics and practice. Children, who have a fixed mathematical ability and have to work hard to realize it, will gain moral values of industry, effort and self-help. 'Technological Pragmatists' believe in meritocracy, for them mathematics is an unquestioned body of useful knowledge, which should be taught as the acquisition of useful skills through practical experience. Children are like a blunt tool and need teaching to sharpen them and make them more useful to wealth creation and technological development. They will gain the values of utilitarianism and pragmatism, and come to see that honesty is important and that you get what you deserve. The third is the 'Old Humanists', who value 'blind' justice and objectivity and for whom mathematics is a body of pure knowledge. Teaching transmits this knowledge in a way that emphasizes mathematics as enlightening, a universal cultural good developing the intellect and building character, and requires the teacher to motivate and explain. Next, 'Progressive Educators' are altogether more romantic, person-centred and empathetic. For them the child comes first and is like a flower to be nurtured into self-realisation through mathematics taught in activity, exploration and play. Mathematics is a process and personalized and leads to caring and human values. Last, the 'Public Educators' who adopt conceptualism or a social relativist understanding of mathematics as a human invention. Here the child is a 'sleeping giant' who needs to be introduced to mathematical thought as a cultural product, not fixed, but mutable and open to their questioning and negotiation. Teaching should be open ended, promoting discussion, critical awareness and the socially relevant. Education is empowering and democratic with children gaining the values of social justice, liberty and equality.

Ernest's categories do not apply to all societies with equal force. They are more of a snapshot derived from a particular time and place. Babila-Njingum (1995), for example, showed that in Cameroon there is no such diversity in the views held about the child and assessment is seen more widely as a good in the interest of the pupil; the political labels used by Ernest belong to Western Europe, and so on. But this just serves to make even stronger the point that if mathematics is best left to mathematicians, mathematics education is far too important to do so. Being an educational enterprise it serves a wider constituency and is subject to societal and political demands. Part of the declaration of 'Mathematically Correct' is quoted above, and the following is adapted from their 'Towards a Cease-Fire in the Math War', a sort of manifesto published on the Web in 1998:

Task 8.4: Mathematics education guidelines

'...we hereby offer... the following guidelines designed to promote... a more efficacious mathematics education for all:

1. Demand greater mathematics knowledge for teachers.
2. Stress that standards of learning must have yearly benchmarks.
3. Refrain from promoting any theory of learning or method of teaching at the expense of any other.
4. Encourage frequent objective tests to monitor student progress.
5. Keep the focus on mathematics.
6. Refrain from promoting heterogeneous grouping or repudiating homogeneous grouping.
7. Admit that arithmetic and algebra are key elements of the early curriculum.
8. Include symbolic skill building, abstract mathematics and repeated practice.
9. Reinstate an emphasis on proof and mathematical justification.
10. Emphasize that algorithms should be taught, understood and used.
11. Indicate that calculators and computers should be used sparingly.

(Adapted from Mathematics Correct, 1998)

- Which do you agree with and with which do you disagree?
- Should society set such demands for mathematics teachers?
- Is it necessary for all the teachers in a school mathematics department to agree with each other about these kind of things?

Like most people, including the present author, you will probably find any such manifesto a curate's egg – it is good and bad in parts. Such controversy is an inevitable outcome of mathematics education being in the human arena, however, and is further evidence of mathematics' involvement with values. However controversial any particular stance may be, what is beyond doubt is that mathematics has its part to play in an education in values and a preparation for citizenship. At the very least it has much utility which is empowering. Not only does the citizen require some skill in mathematics when shopping to obtain happiness according to Mr. Micawber – to live so that income exceeds expenditure – but also to protect themselves from the unscrupulous. For instance, the interest on a credit card is often quoted monthly, 1.5 per cent per month, for example, and could fool the mathematically unwise to believe the annual rate is simply 12 times the monthly rate (18 per cent in this example), when in fact it is compounded month by month and actually is over 19.5 per cent per annum.

It is also a useful and necessary training in logic. It is necessary because not all logical rules are automatically grasped. It is easy to show that most children (and many adults) will make simple errors which a mathematics education ought to eliminate. As an illustration, imagine a simple card game in which the deck is dealt equally to two players. Each plays a card in turn with one rule: if player A puts down a diamond, player B must follow with a club. After a game as player B, most children answer 'A diamond' when asked 'When you put down a club, what card must I have played immediately before?' Not only is this logically wrong, it is often wrong in practice. The rule is that a diamond must be followed by a club, not that a club can only follow a diamond – a club can follow any suite. A mathematical education should teach that p implies q does not mean that q implies p. The error can be amusing in children, who cover their eyes and think they cannot be seen ('I can't see you' means 'you can't see me'), but more painful later, when 'I love you' does not always mean 'you love me'.

It is also a protection against partial truth so prevalent in political slogans. Take the case of the expansion of higher education. Thirty years ago, only about 7 per cent of the age range went to university compared to about 35 per cent now. This is a five-fold increase and, as obviously many more people receive a higher education than before, the overall standard of education in the age range must have risen. Also, the pass level of a degree now has to be set so that 35 per cent of the population can pass whereas before it could be set appropriately for only the top 7 per cent – it could reasonably be argued that the threshold standard for successful higher education has fallen. Nonetheless, the best are still the best and at the top probably do just as well as they have ever done, and their standard has not changed at all. So, when one political party taunts 'Standards have fallen' and the other shouts back 'Standards have risen', the mathematically educated citizen asks 'Which standard are you talking about ?' Obviously, studying some statistics helps here.

Having some knowledge of the results of mathematics, and a grasp of its principles, is useful to the citizen, enabling him or her to take control of those aspects of life where an ability with quantities is crucial or expands choice, and empowering where an awareness of logic frees him or her from indoctrination or prejudice. More deeply along with other disciplines, it has much to tell us of the human condition, in particular of how we stand with regard to the nature of different kinds of truth and the character of meanings, and in not taking either truth or meaning for granted. Mathematics is a significant part of human experience and for millennia has enthralled those with the skill to do it and fascinated those who can appreciate it. Without it, there will be no complete understanding of what we mean by being true and being proved true, nor will there be a full grasp of the range of aesthetic experiences open to humanity.

Appendix
Overview of the Five Educational Ideologies identified by Ernest (1991: 138–139).

Table 8.1 Key Stage 3 History curriculum

Social Group	Industrial Trainer	Technological Pragmatists	Old Humanist	Progressive Educator	Public Educator
Political Ideology	Radical right 'New Right'	Meritocratic conservative	Conservative/ liberal	Liberal	Democratic socialist
View of Mathematics	Set of truths and rules	Unquestioned body of useful knowledge	Body of structured pure knowledge	Process view: personalised maths	Conceptualism; Social constructivism
Moral Values	Authoritarian 'Victorian' values; choice; effort; self-help work; moral weakness; us-good, them-bad	Utilitarian; pragmatism expediency; 'wealth creation'; technological development	'Blind' justice; objectivity; rule-centred structure; hierarchy; paternalistic 'classical' view	Person-centred; caring; empathy; human values; nurturing maternalistic; 'romantic' view	Social justice; liberty; equality fraternity; social awareness engagement and citizenship
Theory of Society	Rigid hierarchy; market-place	Meritocratic hierarchy	Elitist; Class stratified	Soft hierarchy; welfare State	Inequitable hierarchy needing reform
Theory of the Child	Elementary school tradition child as 'fallen angel' and 'empty vessel'	Child 'empty vessel' and 'blunt tool'; future worker or manager	Dilute elementary school view; character building; culture tames	Child-centred; progressive view; child: 'growing flower' and 'innocent savage'	Social conditions view: 'clay moulded by environment and 'sleeping giant'
Theory of Ability	Fixed and inherited; realised by effort	Inherited ability	Inherited cast of mind	Varies, but needs cherishing	Cultural product: not fixed
Mathematical Aims	'Back-to-basics': numeracy and social training in obedience	Useful maths to appropriate level and certification (industry-centred)	Transmit body of mathematical knowledge (Maths-centred)	Creativity; self-realisation through mathematics (child-centred)	Critical awareness and democratic citizenship via mathematics
Theory of Learning	Hard work; effort; practice; rote	Skill acquisition; practical experience	Understanding and application	Acvitity; play; exploration	Questioning; decision making negotiation
Theory of Teaching Mathematics	Authoritarian transmission; drill; no 'frills'	Skill instructor; motivate through work-relevance	Explain; motivate; pass on structure	Facilitate personal exploration; prevent failure	Discussion conflict questioning of content and pedagogy
Theory of Resources	Chalk and talk; Anti-calculator	Hands-on and Microcomputers	Visual aids to motivate	Rich environment to explore	Socially relevant; authentic

Table 8.1 continued

Social Group	Industrial Trainer	Technological Pragmatists	Old Humanist	Progressive Educator	Public Educator
Theory of Assessment in Maths	External testing of simple basics	Avoid cheating; external tests and certification; skill profiling	External Examinations based on hierarchy	Teacher led internal assessment; avoid failure	Various modes; use of social issues and content
Theory of Social Diversity	Differentiated schooling by class; monoculturalist	Vary curriculum by future occupations	Vary curriculum by ability only (maths neutral)	Humanise neutral maths for all: use local culture	Accommodation of social and cultural diversity a necessity

9 The value and values of Physical Education and sport

Richard Bailey

Introduction

> Games conduce, not merely daring and endurance but better still temper, self-restraint, fairness, honour, unenvious approbation of another's success, and all that 'give and take' of life which stands a man in such good stead when he goes forth into the world and without which, indeed, his success is always maimed and partial.
>
> (Charles Kingsley, in Mangan, 1981: 148)

> If competitive sports build character, it is character fit for a criminal.
>
> (George Leonard, 1972: 77)

As these two quotes suggest, views of the relationship between Physical Education and what can broadly be termed values education have been passionate and frequently opposed. The debate, which can be traced back to the very beginnings of educational philosophy, cuts to the heart of the subject.

On the one side are those for whom sport and physical challenges represent ideal opportunities for young people to learn about success and failure, of overcoming obstacles, of restraining one's own selfish desires for the good of the team; those who, in a past time, might have cheered that 'the Battle of Waterloo was won on the playing fields of Eton'. On the other are those who complain that a great deal of the content of Physical Education enshrines a selfish antagonistic structure in which players attempt to defeat and show their superiority over others; values which are no longer appropriate to instil in our young; those who might retort that the Battle of Waterloo was probably *started* on the playing fields of Eton!

Questions of values and education are not merely of historical or philosophical interest. Recent policy and guidance documents (for example, SCAA, 1996b; QCA/DfEE, 1998; DfEE, 1999a; DfEE, 1999b) reiterate something that is self-evident for most teachers: formal education, and each of its constituent elements, should contribute systematically to all aspects of pupils' development, not least of which to their social and moral development, for their immediate value and for their value in preparing pupils to become active, capable and responsible members of society. Physical Education, like all subjects, must demonstrate what role it can play. If it cannot, in the increasingly overcrowded curriculum, it may find itself even more marginalized than at present. The threat is possibly greater for Physical Education than most other subjects as, more due to history than anything claimed by Physical Educationalists, 'it is the rationale of "character-building", of moral development, of citizenship development, of social development, that justifies the existence of physical education and athletics in educational institutions' (Stevenson, 1975: 287).

Physical Education as values education

The view that participation in physical activities can contribute to young people's developing values and 'characters' has a long and distinguished history. Plato warned of the consequences of an education that over-emphasizes the academic at the expense of the physical. In the *Republic*, he argues that what is needed is a balance, 'to produce a mind that is civilized and brave, as opposed to cowardly and uncivilized' (Lee, 1955: 145). Similar sentiments were expressed by Jean-Jacques Rousseau (Foxley, 1974) and many other educational writers (see Meakin, 1981, for a detailed discussion), leading to the so-called 'Muscular Christianity' of 19th century Britain, whose philosophy is summarized by the 1864 Royal Commission on Public Schools: 'The cricket and football fields. . . are not merely places of exercise or amusement; they help to form some of the most valuable social qualities and manly virtues. . .' (cited in MacIntosh, 1957: 178).

This 'cult of athleticism' (Mangan, 1981) had as its stated aim the production of individuals exemplifying the virtues felt useful to an expanding empire: bravery, self-confidence, discrimination, and so on. The emphasis was upon team sports that were frequently organized, managed and officiated by the pupils. Learning to lead on the playing field would translate, it was assumed, to leadership in industry, business, government and the military. This faith in team sports survived until after the First World War, during which generals still felt that soldiers would develop manliness, discipline, courage, loyalty and a capacity for self-sacrifice through team sports (Shields and Bredemeier, 1995).

More recently, a number of philosophers have sought to present physical activities, especially sporting activities, as inherently moral enterprises. Peter Arnold (1984) is representative of a view that Physical Education and organized games are not simply useful media for values education, but rather that they are fundamentally *about* values education. Since 'sport is inherently concerned with the moral' (1984: 280), participation in such activities offers players the opportunity to practice moral virtue. Arnold interprets sport as essentially concerned with fairness, with fairness seen as a confluence of freedom and equality. Sport embodies freedom since it is (at least outside of the school) engaged in voluntarily. It embodies equality as, in choosing to participate, players come together in full agreement that the game's rules impartially apply to all. Sport is fair because players willingly follow the rules even when there may be an advantage for them not to do so. The source of fairness in sport, therefore, does not lie with the referee, but with the players, and their motivation to conduct themselves in appropriate ways. Another advocate, David Aspin, has similarly argued that:

> It is possible for one to treat the whole topic of sport, not as means to promote the ends of moral education, but as being, in certain respects, activities necessarily underpinned by and shot through with presuppositions that are of an irreducibly ethical character. . . They may therefore, to some extent, be regarded as moral enterprises.
>
> (David Aspen 1975: 49–50)

According to this view, the teacher is presented with a marvellously accessible model of values education: 'simply by seriously engaging pupils in competitive games and athletics, a teacher is of necessity implicitly pursuing aims that embody moral values, for such values are enshrined in many of the rules which constitute these activities' (Meakin, 1982: 68).

Both Conservative and Labour governments in recent years have explicitly endorsed this position. John Major, in his introductory comments to *Sport: Raising the Game* (DNH, 1995: 2) enthuses:

> Competitive sport teaches valuable lessons which last for life. Every game delivers both a winner and a loser. Sports men must learn to be both. Sport only thrives if both parties play by the rules, and accept the results with good grace. *It is one of the best means of learning how to live alongside others and make a contribution as part of a team.*
>
> (emphasis added; cf. Labour Party, 1996)

This endorsement has been reflected in successive National Curriculum documentation. No other curriculum area has Programmes of Study so overtly linked to values and citizenship outcomes: 'develop an understanding of how to succeed in different activities and learn how to evaluate and recognize their own success' (Key Stage 2); 'learn to take the initiative and make decisions for themselves . . . take a variety of 'roles such as leader and official' (Key Stage 3). Evans and Penney (1995) highlight, such assumptions are profoundly political: as well as offer skills to pupils, Physical Education, and especially games, also socialize them. This view supposes that physical activities produce disciplined citizens of good character, thus helping to ameliorate our contemporary ills. 'In a society that is more diverse, pluralistic, fragmented and individualized, sport provides the social cement to restore and repair the cracks appearing on the social terrain' (1995: 188).

Before we are carried away with such enthusiasm, it is worthwhile sounding a note of caution. It is unlikely that those who follow the exploits of some of our most talented sports players will be easily convinced that participation *necessarily* enshrines moral values: intimidation of officials and aggression towards other players routinely take place in professional football; temper tantrums of elite tennis players are as memorable as their exquisite stroke play; corruption in boxing is now taken for granted. In light of modern sport, Arnold and Aspin's claims seem at best anachronistic and at worst hopelessly misguided. How can sport enshrine values when so many of our sporting greats are clearly morally vacuous?

Arnold (1984: 278) has claimed that the following of rules in sport is inextricably linked to the possession and development of values and 'character'. But surely this misinterprets the function of rules in sport, which simply serve to make the activity possible. They need have nothing to do with the moral conduct of the players. Indeed, as Lesley Wright (1987) has pointed out, it is quite conceivable that rules could be devised that specifically encourage injury or cruelty (which may be the case with unlicensed boxing and fox hunting). It would be ridiculous to suggest that these would be moral enterprises, and that participants would receive a values education simply by adhering to the rules.

It is always possible to apply moral criteria in an interpersonal situation. Humans, as purposeful agents living in a society, are always morally accountable for what they do. However, this does not mean that we are justified in describing every human action as moral. Driving a car requires adherence to the rules of the road, but there is no reason why it has to be understood as a moral activity, nor why driving should be understood as a 'vehicle' for values education.

It is quite possible for someone to play a game fairly (in that he or she follows the rules), and have no moral regard for his or her opponent. In discussions of values education in Physical Education, therefore, it is vital to consider questions of feelings and affection, and the development of particular attitudes, such as caring, tolerance, benevolence, loyalty, sympathy and compassion (Wright, 1987: 100). Since these qualities need not necessarily arise during Physical Education lessons, they must be the result of something more than the activities themselves. In order to understand what this additional factor might be, it might be useful to briefly review the empirical data related to Physical Education and Sport and social and values development.

The most comprehensive review of the literature on this subject is by David Shields and Brenda Bredemeier (1995). Their conclusion is that the research evidence neither corroborates nor falsifies the hypothesis that participation in physical activities develops appropriate values and behaviour traits (1995: 178). In fact, a more accurate summary would be that *some* studies suggest that participation can contribute to values and social development, and *others* suggest that it cannot (or worse, that it can actually be damaging). For example, many parents and teachers feel that organized physical activities encourage cooperation in children, but some studies found an increase in hostility to others and a decrease in generosity and altruism in some pupils. Likewise, it is well established that sports players are less likely than non-participants to engage in delinquent behaviour; however, some studies have found that regular players show less sportsmanlike attitudes and values than others do (Shields and Bredemeier, 1995).

The evidence seems to show that sport and physical activities can have either a positive or a negative effect on children's attitudes and behaviours. One possible reason for this apparent anomaly is flawed research methodology. However, another possible explanation is that researchers have usually focused on the activities in which children participated, rather than the way those activities were presented. Most of the empirical studies carried out in this area assume that learning outcomes in Physical Education are solely derived from the activity being taught. This is not the case. The way that the activity is being taught is at least as important (Macfadyen, 2000). This distinction between the *content* and the *context* of Physical Education lessons is of fundamental importance for the present discussion: values education will not happen by itself, simply as a result of the teacher organising a game and enforcing the rules.

Content and context in Physical Education

Len Almond (2000: 6–7) offers a useful distinction between educational values that focus on the content of lessons ('goods of accomplishment') and those that emphasize opportunities for interpersonal competencies, for friendships and community ('goods of relationships'). Of course, these values should not be considered independently. Rather, they are inextricably linked: the teacher ought to plan with both content and context in mind. Just as he or she would aim to offer opportunities for progression in the physical skills and techniques that are taught in Physical Education classes, so should he or she strive to develop pupils' social skills.

In planning for education into values and for citizenship, it is important that teachers do not conceive of their task in too technical a way: it is not simply a matter of training pupils into certain forms of behaviour. Perhaps most would agree with John Wright (1992: 124), that education should aim to nurture certain qualities widely deemed to be desirable and necessary for the continuation of a democratic society: 'self-confidence leavened by an agreeable humility, curiosity, courage, persistence, kindness, gentleness, a care for the less fortunate, and a care for other forms of life'.

However, it would be a mistake to move from an agreement that these might be necessary elements of an adequate values education to the assumption that they are sufficient. Ethical living requires something more than simply adhering to a set of principles that can be memorized and applied like an equation. Frequently, decisions have to be made between different kinds of good: between truth or loyalty, self or others, short or long-term benefit (Kidder, 1995). The recognition of this fact does not remove the need to establish and distil the principles upon which civilized society is premised, but it does stress the importance of augmenting such values education with reflection on the conflicting pressures and painful choices (sometimes between two rights) that are bound to confront each of us, at different times in our lives:

> The important point for learning morality and citizenship is to understand that making moral decisions is as much about making hard choices, and having the intellectual and emotional equipment to make them properly, as it is about knowing the rules of moral conduct. We can learn ground rules, and principles which we should try to follow, but there will always be cases in which the moral response is not automatic or obvious – cases where we are caught between conflicting principles, cases where diagnosis of the problem and practical interpretation of an abstract principle are difficult.
>
> (Bentley, 1998: 62)

There is evidence that Physical Education can provide a worthwhile environment for the sort of values education outlined above. One approach which has been found to be effective is the 'Built-In Dilemmas/Dialogue' (BIDD) (Romance, Weiss and Bockoven, 1986; Hellison and Templin, 1991), which is summarized in the box below. In the BIDD approach, pupils are routinely confronted by moral dilemmas arising from Physical Education lessons.

Task 9.1: Built-in dilemmas/dialogue strategies

1. Ask the pupils if the activity in which they have just taken part was fair: Did everybody take part? Did they all have fun? How do they decide what makes a game fair?
2. Plan tasks with built-in problems or omissions, and encourage pupils to change the rules as they wish.
3. Play games with and without a referee, and discuss the advantages and disadvantages of each.
4. Discuss issues such as sportsmanship, cooperation and trust as they arise in lessons.

Another, widely cited, example of values education through Physical Education is Donald Hellison's 'Responsibility Model' (Hellison and Templin, 1991). The focus of this approach is the promotion of pupils' sense of responsibility. Hellison hypothesized a series of levels and sub-levels, each reflecting goals towards which individuals aim to progress. There is no intention that these levels represent developmental stages through which pupils move (although they can be interpreted in this light; see Shields and Bredemeier, 1995). Rather, they articulate the kinds of responsibilities that pupils need to consider in everyday contexts:

> This educational process is intended to cause students to *feel* empowered and purposeful, to experience making responsible commitments to themselves and others, to strive to develop themselves despite external forces, to be willing to risk popularity to live by a set of principles, to understand their essential relatedness to others, and to distinguish between their own personal preferences and activities that impinge on their rights and welfare of others.
>
> (Hellison and Templin, 1991: 104)

Accordingly, these goals are shared and discussed with pupils, to offer a common vocabulary for the teacher and pupils. Likewise, certain strategies are suggested that can help pupils become more aware of, experience, make decisions about and reflect upon their goals: 'This model requires a conceptualisation of the teaching act that is different from more traditional models. If students are to become responsible, they must experience some responsibility' (Hellison and Templin, 1991: 108).

The 'Responsibility Model'

Levels:

Level 1: Self-control and respect for the rights and feelings of others:

- self-control;
- inclusion;
- negotiating conflicts;
- internalising respect.

Level 2: Participation and effort:

- going through the motions;
- exploring effort;
- redefining success.

Level 3: Self-direction:

- independence;
- goal-setting;
- knowledge base;
- plan and evaluate.

Level 4: Caring and helping:

- supporting others;
- helping others;
- group welfare.

Strategies:

- awareness;
- experience;
- choice;
- problem-solving/student sharing;
- self-reflection;
- counselling time;
- teaching qualities.

Source: Hellison and Templin (1991)

The virtue of Hellison's approach is that it offers a degree of progression and structure that is generally absent in the literature. A weakness, however, is that it seems rather individual-istic and too narrowly focused upon the behaviour of individual pupils. The emphasis throughout is *self*-responsibility (Shields and Bredemeier, 1995), and there is an absence of the development of a sense of *social* responsibility and community that is emphasized is much recent work (the most obvious being the Crick Report, QCA/DfEE, 1998). This need not invalidate the model, but it might suggest an extension is required.

Physical education and a sense of community

Bentley (1998) draws upon child psychology to construct a model of values and citizenship education in which the child's awareness grows from the self outwards.

Like Hellison's approach, Bentley's offers a clear and simple model of children's developing sense of responsibility. However, here the child is explicitly located within the wider contexts of community and society. Hellison's 'Responsibility Model' generally operates at the level of 'self', progressing only at the last stage to 'relationships'. In order for it to adequately address issues of community and society, perhaps an extension is required:

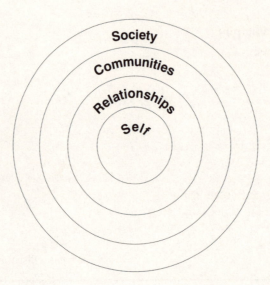

Figure 9.1 A child's growing awareness of values and society (after Bentley, 1998)

A 'social responsibility' model?

Level 5: Community:

● cooperation;
● mutual assistance;
● civic responsibility;
● citizenship.

Strategies:

● cooperative tasks and challenges;
● discussion/debate;
● community projects;
● voluntary work.

(*Source:* Author)

The idea of 'social responsibility' lies at the heart of a number of recent UK Government documents, especially the influential Crick Report (QCA/DfEE, 1998). This is evident in the selection of the three 'strands' that constitute what is taken for effective citizenship education:

- social and moral responsibility;
- community involvement;
- political literacy.

(QCA/DfEE, 1998: 40–41)

These strands form the basis of identified learning outcomes and indicate the sorts of skills and aptitudes, knowledge and understanding that pupils should acquire as they progress through school.

The Report suggests that schools consider combining elements of citizenship education with other subjects (QCA/DfEE, 1998: 22). It explicitly links this suggestion with History, whilst Geography, English and PSHE all received favourable reviews. Physical Education, however, is damned by feint reference: 'PE can encourage individual initiative and effort as well as teamwork skills' (QCA/DfEE, 1998: 49)! Surely this must be a mistake; despite its frequent references to 'learning through action' (QCA/DfEE, 1998: 37), there seems to be an inability to recognize the most obvious forum for such learning. Bentley, who was a member of the Advisory Group on Citizenship, has elsewhere outlined criteria for successful implementation of citizenship education:

- issues should matter to pupils;
- they should be rooted in the local environment and be encountered everyday;
- they should be active and practical.

(Bentley, 1998)

Physical activities are of central importance in the lives of many children: issues of morality, community and politics move from abstraction in classroom discussions, to meaningful and significant questions of the day in the context of sport.

The following tables suggest some ways in which the Physical Education curriculum can be utilized in support of citizenship education (as conceived by the Crick Report).

Conclusion

This chapter has attempted to articulate the contribution that Physical Education can make to the related areas of values and citizenship education. The historical view of sport as inherently involving the development of morality and character, whilst appealing, is not convincing. The teachers' role in planning for such development is of fundamental importance, and cannot be overstated. Once the importance of explicit and systematic planning is acknowledged, Physical Education stands out as the ideal medium for values and citizenship education. More than that, physical activities hold an unequalled place in children's development and attitudes. Since these activities are held in high regard and often can take place outside the school day, when conceived of appropriately in terms of both content and context, they provide a medium for lifelong values and citizenship education.

Table 9.1 Citizenship education and Physical Education – Learning Outcomes for Key Stage 3

By the end of Key Stage 3, pupils should be able to:

Skills and Aptitudes	*Example Physical Education Links*
• Express and justify, orally and in writing, a personal opinion relevant to an issue.	Discuss: cheating and drug-enhanced performance in athletics; racism in sport; ability and disability; nationalism and the Olympic Games; are there boys and girls games?
• Work with others to meet a challenge of shared significance through negotiation, accommodation and agreed action, and be able to reflect on the process.	Problem-solving activities in an outdoor setting; games-making; life-saving challenges; reflecting on tactics in team games; co-operating in the use of space or equipment in dance or gymnastics.
• Use imagination when considering the experience of others and be able to role-play, express plausibly and reflect on viewpoints contrary to their own.	Composing, performing and appreciating dances; exploring different perspectives on bullying; cultures/religions different than their own, etc.
• Analyse, discuss and reflect on significant issues and events encountered within the community.	Campaigning for playing fields; school sport/coaching links; surveying availability of local sports provision; dance performance for local Primary Schools on an environmental issue.
• Garner information about an issue from a range of sources . . . with some understanding of the different roles these sources play.	Research different ways that particular groups of sports players (women, disabled and ethnic minorities, etc), are represented in different media.

Table 9.2   Citizenship Education and Physical education – Learning outcomes for Key Stage 1

By the end of Key Stage 1, pupils should be able to:

Skills and Aptitudes	*Example Physical Education Links*
• Recognise how the concept of fairness can be applied in a reasoned and reflective way to aspects of their personal and social life.	Play a simple game in which the rules have not been fully worked out: What other rules are needed to play the game fairly? Why is it important for games to be fair?
• Understand the different kinds of responsibility that they take on, in helping others; respecting differences or looking after shared property.	Cooperation and privacy in changing for PE; helping set up gymnastic apparatus; assisting partner in dance composition; practising skill activities with a partner and offering simple suggestions for improvement.
• Know about the nature and basis of the rules in the classroom, at school and at home; also, whenever possible, know how to frame rules themselves; understand that different rules can apply in different contexts and can serve different purposes.	Pupils devise a set of simple safety rules for Gymnastics lessons: how are these rules different from class /school rules on behaviour? why do we need rules in games? adapt the rules of a small-sided game: how can we make sure everybody has fun? how can we encourage every player to join in? devise a Pupils' Charter for behaviour in PE.
• Understand the language used to describe feelings associated with aspects of relationships with others.	Pupils compose, perform and evaluate a short dance-drama on the theme of friends; discuss issues arising from partner or group work.
• Know about the different kinds of relationships which exist between pupils and between adults and pupils; also have some notion that the power in such relationship can be exercised responsibly and fairly or irresponsibly and unfairly.	Small groups play a simple game in which they take turns acting as referee or scorer; discuss the role of referees and scorers: why are they important? how can they be unfair?

10 Values education, citizenship and the contribution of RE

Lynne Broadbent

Introduction: setting the context

The publication of four documents, namely the Statement of Values published by QCA (1997), the Report by the National Advisory Group on Personal, Social and Health Education (DfEE, 1999a), the final report of the Advisory Group on Citizenship, otherwise known as the Crick Report (QCA/DfEE, 1998) and the recent National Curriculum document on Citizenship for Key Stages 3 and 4 (DfEE/QCA, 1999a), have sharpened public focus on values education and the teaching of citizenship. In many respects, the documents might be welcomed as offering a much needed framework for the curriculum, for the Education Reform Act of 1988 had identified the need for attention to be given to pupils' personal development, requiring the curriculum to be 'balanced and broadly based' and one which promotes the spiritual, moral, cultural, mental and physical development of pupils and of society, and prepares such pupils for the opportunities, responsibilities and experiences of adult life. However, the curriculum resulting from this Act became focused on assessing achievement in the firmly fragmented core and foundation subject areas and, despite valuable guidance on cross-curricular themes such as Citizenship, Health Education and the Environment (NCC, 1990), attention to personal and social education failed to make a significant contribution to the curriculum as a whole.

The four documents have implications for teaching and learning in Religious Education and indeed for the place of Religious Education within the school curriculum. First, the prime focus of Religious Education is the beliefs, values and consequent lifestyles of individuals and communities and is, therefore, inextricably linked to questions of values. Secondly, the expectation that citizenship education will become an entitlement for all pupils requires Religious Education to address, as a matter of urgency, how it might contribute to pupils' personal, social and health education and to citizenship education through its content, methodology and through the development of pupils' skills. Furthermore, the expectation that by 2004, full programmes of citizenship education requiring up to 5 per cent of curriculum time (QCA/DfEE, 1998: 22) will be established throughout the primary and secondary phases and could herald a time when RE, alongside other humanities subjects, finds itself jostling for space in a crowded curriculum.

Values are intrinsic to Religious Education, and the relationship between Religious Education, personal and social values and citizenship has long been debated. That there are natural links between the three areas is indisputable. However, as with any relationship, integration between these three areas should be explored with caution and not undertaken lightly, wantonly or without due consideration of the purposes for which each area was ordained! These are issues highlighted in this chapter.

Background to values education and citizenship education in Religious Education

The integration of values education, that is personal and social values, is embedded in the history of Religious Education. The 1944 Education Act was formulated as Britain emerged from the Second World War and from the threat of Naziism. The White Paper of 1943 had proclaimed the universality of a desire for a spiritual and moral revival and specified that such values should be imparted through Religious Education:

> There has been a very general wish not confined to representatives of the Churches, that religious education should be given a more defined place in the life and work of schools springing from the desire to revive the spiritual and personal values in our society and in our national tradition.
>
> (HMSO, 1943: 11)

Thus from the Education Act, which first established Religious Education as a compulsory subject on the school curriculum and which formalized the practise of locally agreed Religious Education syllabuses, the subject was harnessed in a national programme of spiritual, moral and social rearmament. In practice, pupils learnt the Bible stories, for syllabuses of the period comprised lists of biblical stories for both primary and secondary phases, with the intention that pupils would 'catch' the faith and there after live moral lives based upon Christian principles.

While such a vision for the education system and in particular for Religious Education might be understandable following a world war, by the 1960s, educationalists such as Harold Loukes, began questioning whether such an approach to curriculum design enabled the adolescent pupil 'to make sense of his [sic] own human condition' (Loukes, 1961: 9). Loukes identified the need for Religious Education to be 'conducted in an atmosphere of realism and relevance' (1961: 11). When his research identified adolescents' interests in problems of personal relations (namely issues of authority, friendship, sex and marriage), problems of personal responsibility (money, work, leisure and prayer) and problems of meaning (suffering, death and learning), Loukes devised a 'problem approach' to curriculum planning through which pupils would learn 'that thought and discussion are as methodical as any other means of learning, that problems in religion and morals can be approached as methodically as problems in any other field' (1961: 146) He insisted that, 'we are concerned in religious education, as in all education, with how to think' (1961:46). The legacy of Loukes lies in the identification of firstly, the personal and social issues which are of interest to pupils and upon which there is a religious as well as a secular perspective, and secondly, a methodology for approaching such issues.

The issues identified by Loukes are 'controversial' issues, for there 'is no one fixed or universally held point of view' (QCA/DfEE, 1998: 56), but diverse religious, as well as secular, perspectives. Controversial issues, such as wealth and poverty, prejudice and discrimination, the environment and the ideal society continue to form the basis for Religious Education programmes at Key Stage 3 and at examination level today. Religious Education teachers are experienced in preparing pupils to 'deal with such controversies knowledgeably, sensibly, tolerantly and morally' (QCA /DfEE, 1998: 56). Pupils are required to identify the nature of the 'controversial' issue, to investigate possible religious responses through reference to the teachings key figures such as the Buddha, or to scripture, and the interpretations of these sources by members of faith communities today. The resulting 'evidence' is evaluated and presented with clarity and understanding in oral or written form. There is thus a strong link between the skills to be developed through the Religious Education curriculum and those to be developed through programmes of citizenship education (QCA/ DfEE, 1998: 41).

Reference to issues such as wealth and poverty, prejudice and discrimination raises questions about the relationship between the individual and society, and here, the second strand in the new curriculum proposals, 'citizenship', can be traced through the history of Religious Education. The Swann Report (DES, 1985: 466) identified that a major task in preparing all pupils for life in a harmonious pluralist society 'must surely. . . be to enhance their understanding of a variety of religious beliefs and practices thus offering them an insight into the values and concerns of different communities'. Since the 1970s, locally agreed syllabuses for Religious Education have advocated the development of pupils' knowledge and understanding through encounters with the range of religious beliefs, values and practices represented in the local area. This has resulted in visits to local places of worship, to churches, mosques, and gurdwaras, and in invitations to representatives from local faith communities to visit schools to speak about their beliefs and practices. The Swann Report anticipated that such teaching could have significant implications both for pupils and for society. 'Bringing about a greater understanding of the diversity of faiths present in Britain today can also therefore we believe play a major role in challenging and overcoming racism', and furthermore 'could lead them to a greater understanding of the diversity of the global community' (DES, 1985: 518). Hence, since 1985, Religious Education has been identified as having a role in the preparation of pupils for life in a multifaith and multicultural society.

Whether the anticipated role for Religious Education has, or could have been realized in the intervening years is debatable. However, research has continued to struggle to refine its representation of religious communities in order to avoid over-simplistic and generalized statements about individuals' religious belief and practice. The Westhill Project (Read, Rudge and Howarth, 1986) adopted a triangular framework for the study of religion, noting that the interaction between traditional belief systems and shared human experience produced individual patterns of belief, while more recently, ethnographic research (Jackson, 1997, and Nesbitt, 1998) has highlighted the dynamic nature of faith traditions and the need to acknowledge differing patterns of practice within each religion. The production of educational resources based on individual case studies is an attempt to avoid the stereotyping which misrepresents individuals and communities.

Current aims for teaching and learning in Religious Education encapsulate the need to address areas of personal and social values and the area of citizenship as highlighted above. The SCAA Model Syllabuses (SCAA, 1994) have significantly influenced the development of new Agreed Syllabuses. The aims of Religious Education cited in the syllabuses may be taken to reflect a consensus about the subject's educational rationale. Paraphrased below, the aims state that religious education should help pupils to:

- develop their knowledge and understanding about Christianity and the other principal religions represented in Great Britain;
- develop their understanding of the influence of beliefs, values and traditions in individuals, communities, societies and cultures;
- develop their ability to make reasoned and informed judgements about religious and moral issues, with reference to the teachings of the principal religions represented in the UK;
- enhance their spiritual, moral, cultural and social development by:
  - developing awareness of the fundamental questions of life raised by human experience;
  - responding to such questions with reference to the teachings and practices of religions;
  - reflecting on their own beliefs, values and experiences.
- develop a positive attitude towards other people, respecting their right to hold different beliefs from their own, and towards living in a society of diverse religions.

The vision for Religious Education propounded in these aims is of a subject that seeks to develop pupils' knowledge and understanding of religious beliefs, values and practices, and to develop pupils' skills, both in intellectual terms (for example in responding to questions of life by reference to the teaching of religion) and in personal terms (by developing pupils' ability to reflect on their own beliefs and values). Moreover, Religious Education is seen as a subject that fosters respect for the right of individuals to hold diverse beliefs and seeks to promote respect for living in a society with diverse beliefs. Not only is this the vision for Religious Education, but the above are values explicit within the subject: that the development of knowledge and understanding of religious belief and practice, the development of skills and the fostering of respect for diversity within society, are worthy of promotion through Religious Education.

Key issues in the teaching of values and citizenship through Religious Education

A concern for personal and social values and for citizenship education has been traced through the history of Religious Education. However, how far can Religious Education seize the current initiatives for personal, social and health education and citizenship education and implement them through the Religious Education curriculum? The relationship between the three areas is harmonious and troublesome.

The Report on Personal, Social and Health Education recommends that revised National Curriculum subject orders should 'make explicit the role of each curriculum subject in promoting personal and social development' (DfEE, 1999a: 21) and suggests that the statement of values identified by the National Forum for Values (QCA, 1997) should provide the values underpinning the work of schools in relation to personal, social and health education. The values focus on four areas, the Self, Relationships, Society and the Environment, and reflect the concerns of both human experience and of religion. They thus present a potential framework for addressing the two attainment targets currently associated with Religious Education, 'Learning about ' and 'Learning from' religion (QCA, 1998). For example, the individual may be valued as a part of God's creation, and a human existence seen as an opportunity to secure release from the continual cycle of death and rebirth. The individual is particularly celebrated in life-cycle rituals where the individual's changing status in relation to the religious community is affirmed, whether welcomed as a child into the faith community, acknowledged as an adult member, or celebrated as a married person whose offspring will become the new generation of believers. In 'Learning from' religion, pupils will have opportunities to reflect on their life-cycle changes, their 'individual identity' (NCC, 1993: 4) and their religious or secular celebrations.

Religions are rich in parables about 'Relationships', 'Joseph and his brothers' and 'the Good Samaritan' being ideal for discussions on rights and responsibilities in the primary school, while at the secondary phase, pupils will debate the basis for choice of marriage partner and learn about the rituals and promises which characterize religious marriage ceremonies. 'Society', the third area of values, gives rise to questions of belonging to diverse communities, to the study of religious rules, or practices such as zakat charity, within the Muslim community, or the concept of a 'just society' in Judaism, while the 'Environment' raises ethical issues in both religious and secular contexts.

There are distinctions between the statement of values produced by the Forum and resulting teaching and learning in Religious Education. Thatcher (1999) identifies weaknesses both in the consultation process and in the values themselves. In Religious Education, the values have a history and context. They originate in the teachings of key figures and events in the history of the faith, and members of faith communities willingly engage in storytelling and ritual to transmit the values to future generations, so binding the faith community together within this value system. The religious community, therefore, takes on the role of inducting and nurturing the new generation into belief and practice. In Religious Education, clear and constant reference back to the source of the values and their function within the faith community both lends substance to the values themselves and protects the teacher from potential accusations of bias or even indoctrination, an issue which has challenged generations of Religious Education teachers! It is not the role of the Religious Education teacher to induct or nurture pupils into any belief or value system, even when the values themselves comprise a bland collection of seemingly irrefutable statements. We can encourage pupils to 'Learn about' religion by exploring religious values, and even to 'Learn from' religion, by reflecting on what they might learn from religion in the light of their own experiences, but the outcomes of that reflection must rest with the integrity of the individual pupil.

In the proposals for citizenship education, there are also strong degrees of commonality with Religious Education, notably through two of its three strands, namely social and moral responsibility, including skill development in relation to controversial issues, and community involvement, although its interpretation in relation to Religious Education might be somewhat broader than that presented in the proposals. The British Youth Council's case for citizenship education (QCA/DfEE, 1998: 19) suggests that the curriculum should 'enable children and young people to develop an awareness of community and cultural diversity' and 'should help them see where and how they fit into the community'. This resonates with LEA Agreed Syllabus requirements for Religious Education, which focus on the range of religious communities locally and nationally and engage pupils in the beliefs and values of those communities.

The Crick proposals identify key concepts for citizenship education (QCA/DfEE, 1998: 45) and many of these have a religious context through which pupils' knowledge and understanding of both national and global citizenship might be developed. The concept of 'Justice', for example, would lend itself to study of the Christian communities in Latin America struggling to find a means of survival in poor economic conditions under an oppressive political regime through programmes of Liberation Theology; the concepts of 'Authority' and 'Cooperation and Conflict' could be illustrated by reference to the Muslim ideal of a religious state or to the land rights of the Arabs and Israelis, while the concepts of 'Rights and Responsibilities' could address the food laws or Sabbath day observances which define a faith community. Thus the issue of citizenship education raises the significant question, 'citizenship of what?' for religious communities might well experience tensions between their allegiance as religious and 'secular' citizens. There is also considerable correlation between the Skills and Aptitudes for citizenship (QCA/DfEE, 1998: 46–51) and the Skills and Processes in Religious Education (SCAA, 1994: 7–8).

There are, however, two issues to be raised in terms of the Crick proposals and their relationship with Religious Education. Firstly, they state that citizenship education is not just about knowledge of citizenship and civic society but 'education for citizenship, behaving and acting as a citizen' (QCA/DfEE, 1998: 13). The difficulties for Religious Education of learning intentions which transcend the boundaries of developing knowledge and understanding and fostering an attitude of respect and move into areas of prescribed behaviour have been identified above. Such learning intentions are not consonant with the role of the Religious Education teacher. Secondly, while the British Youth Council clearly acknowledges the presence of community and cultural diversity and made this and the issues it raises a focus for learning, elsewhere the proposals stress notions of 'common citizenship' and 'common ground between different ethnic and religious identities' or even statements that 'majorities must respect, understand and tolerate minorities and minorities must learn and respect the laws, codes and conventions as much as the majority' (QCA/DfEE, 1998: 17). At best, this is over simplistic and patronising and at worst, verging on racism. Certainly, this tone runs counter to Religious Education where difference is identified and positively celebrated. In this way, pupils learn about the distinctiveness of each religion.

One further concern which relates to the proposals on Personal, Social and Health Education and those on Citizenship Education: both are based upon 'deficit models' in terms of curriculum intervention, the first document seeking to address the social ills of 'unintended teenage conceptions, drug misuse, and criminal activity' (DfEE, 1999a: 1) and the second seeking to address 'the weakness of civic discourse' and to 'avoid a further decline in the quality of our public life' (QCA/DfEE, 1998: 14). The aims are interesting in the light of an earlier OFSTED report (1994: 1) which stated that 'Education cannot. . . be expected to fill a moral vacuum'. Religious communities evolve as a result of, and continue to be supported by, a positive vision, a vision not necessarily of a supernatural kind but one relating to a sense of individual and community significance both in the present and in the future – hence the adherence to a code of community values and visions of the future kingdom of God or nirvana or moksha. Hicks (1995: 145) highlights the need for positive images for citizenship education: he states that 'images that citizens have of the future of their society directly affect what they feel it is worth doing in the present'; positive images 'can act as beacons to draw a society towards achievement of its aspirations'. Programmes of curriculum development should evolve from positive educational visions rather than a need to redress social and political ills. Maybe this is one instance whereby citizenship education might consider the potential benefits of modelling itself upon religious tradition!

Identifying a model for integrating values and citizenship education within Religious Education

If a 'hotch potch' of loosely connected concepts, knowledge and skills is to be avoided, then any model for integrating values and citizenship education within programmes of Religious Education must be preceded by a clearly structured framework. Such a framework might be based upon that suggested by Inman (1991) for the integrated delivery of the cross-curricular themes and might be presented as a national document to guide humanities teachers in the integration of values and citizenship education.

The framework itself would identify overarching concepts through which the subject content might be delivered and pupils' skills developed. The concepts themselves could well be those already identified within the Crick Report, since almost all find some direct correlation with concepts applicable to the Religious Education curriculum. The concepts would need to be accompanied by key questions which would serve to relate the concept firstly to the appropriate age phase and secondly to one or more of the four areas of values identified within the personal, social and health education report. For example, the concepts of the Individual and Community would be appropriate for Key Stage 1 or Key Stage 3 pupils but would be presented very differently, as demonstrated below:

Concept: Individual and Community			
Key Questions:	Key Stage 1:	To what communities do I belong?	
	Key Stage 3:	How does the teaching of the communities I belong to affect my lifestyle and my response to moral issues?	
Area of values:	Key Stage 1:	Self	
	Key Stage 3:	Society, or in religious terms, the religious community	

The next stage would involve a mapping exercise, mapping areas of Religious Education content and skills that might naturally correlate both with the concepts and skills and aptitudes proposed for citizenship education. For example, as identified elsewhere, teaching about Liberation Theology would fit easily within the concept of 'Justice' and values related to society, while 'Rights and Responsibilities' would embrace issues related to rites of passage and values related to the self. Both citizenship education and Religious Education share an intention to develop pupils' skills of reflection, their capacity to present a reasoned argument and their ability to gather information from a variety of sources. Finally the teacher would identify learning experiences and pupil tasks which would support the development of the selected concepts and skills. Examples of possible Religious Education programmes of study which integrate values and citizenship education might serve to illustrate the above:

Key Stage 1

Concept:	Fairness
Key Questions:	What does it mean to treat others fairly?
	How do people feel when they are treated unfairly?
Area of Value:	Self/Individual
RE Focus:	The Story of the Prodigal Son

Learning experiences to develop skills:
- read/tell the story;
- pupils describe how the son is treated by his so-called friends, his father and his brother;
- pupils identify the possible feelings experienced by the characters;
- pupils reflect on how they treat others and how they themselves are treated;
- an aspect of the story is expressed through art, writing or role play.

Key Stage 2

Concept:	Rules and Laws
Key Questions:	What rules and laws govern the way others behave?
	Who makes the rules and laws?
	Where are the rules and laws to be found?
Area of Value:	Society/in religious terms, the Community
RE Focus:	Holy Books: Jewish Scripture, The Torah

Learning experiences to develop skills:
- pupils use textbooks and videos in order to prepare a set of questions to ask the Rabbi/member of the Jewish community about the Jewish scripture;
- visit to the synagogue to look at the Torah scrolls and to interview the Rabbi about the origins of the Torah and its influence on his/her life;
- on return to the class, pupils discuss potential moral issues raised as a result of their investigations, eg the keeping of Shabbat and food laws;
- pupils devise a series of 'what if' scenarios as role-plays and discussion stimulus.

Key Stage 3

Concept:	Rights and Responsibilities
Key Questions:	What is the relationship between human beings and the natural world?
	How does human action affect the natural world in the present and for the future?
Area of Value:	Environment
RE Focus:	Jewish and Muslim attitudes to the Environment

Learning experiences to develop skills:

- explore contemporary responses to the natural world (this could include reference to sustainable development and the aims of environmental groups);
- use a wide range of sources, eg religious texts, videos, interviews with Muslims and Jews to identify Muslim and Jewish responses to the environment;
- following class and small group discussions, pupils should produce posters, leaflets or radio broadcasts from Muslim and Jewish perspectives advocating care for the environment.

Key Stage 4

Concept:	Individual and Community
Key Question:	How does the teaching of my community affect my response to moral issues?
Area of Value:	Self/Individual
RE Focus:	Attitudes to abortion in Christianity and Sikhism

Learning experiences to develop skills:

- the term abortion will be clearly defined;
- pupils explore the legal position regarding abortion;
- pupils identify the interests and aims of voluntary organizations;
- pupils investigate the attitudes of Christians and Sikhs to abortion, noting where appropriate, differing beliefs within each religion: the investigations will incorporate the use of a range of resources including statements from holy books, videos and the Internet;
- findings to be presented through debate and role-play scenarios.

It is envisaged that the results of such a mapping exercise would produce a range of programmes of study for Religious Education that could readily contribute to values and citizenship education. This departmental contribution could then be clearly identified in any OFSTED inspection while the assessment of pupils' developing knowledge and skills could be assessed through reference to the concepts, key questions and pupil tasks. However, not all aspects of Religious Education could be fitted into such a framework without compromising the subject's aims and integrity. Where this is the case, these aspects should remain firmly outside the framework to be taught solely for the purposes of fulfilling Religious Education aims and skills. Similarly, where aspects of values and citizenship education cannot be taught through the Religious Education curriculum, these too should remain firmly outside the framework and be taught in other contexts.

Conclusion

The chapter has tried to demonstrate that there are natural links between values and citizenship education and Religious Education. Religious Education plays a significant role in the area of values education and makes a significant contribution to citizenship education through its interactions with local religious communities, through its engagement with current and controversial issues and through its focus on the development of common concepts and skills.

However, the distinctions between the role of Religious Education and the proposals for values education and citizenship must be acknowledged. The Religious Education curriculum can be neither hijacked for the solution of social ills nor harnessed for a programme of training which ventures beyond the development of knowledge, understanding and skills. The way forward must be to move beyond the political posturing of the current proposals, acknowledge the boundaries of the subject areas, and to develop a framework of concepts and questions that will empower teachers to engage in curriculum development. Then we may well become people with 'vitality and direction', a society moving 'forwards towards achievement of its aspirations' (Hicks, 1995: 145).

11 Citizenship: the case of Science

Gill Nicholls

The context of Science

The aim of this chapter is to position the role of citizenship and values within the Science curriculum. This is no easy task as the Science curriculum itself has been, and still is in a constant state of flux. We only have to look at the numerous changes that the Science curriculum has gone through in the last decade to appreciate that Science educators and policy makers themselves do not have a cohesive approach to the constitution of a Science curriculum. Yet despite this, new and increased demands are made of the Science curriculum. Citizenship and values being just one of the components. The growing concern is summed up in the Nuffield Foundation Report, *Science 2000 and Beyond*. Its opening words state:

> This report is the product of a desire to provide a new vision of an education in science for our young people. It is driven by a sense of a growing disparity between the science education provided in our schools and the needs and interests of the young people who will be our future citizens. Education, at the end of the 20th century, no longer prepares individuals for secure, lifelong employment in local industry or services.
>
> (Nuffield Foundation, 1998: 1)

This gives an indication that, whatever, the Science curriculum's present shortfalls, it still is clearly associated with future citizens. The final quote on the introductory page demonstrates the importance of Science to future citizens: 'The ever-growing importance of scientific issues in our daily lives demands a populace who has sufficient knowledge and understanding to follow science and scientific debates' (Nuffield Foundation, 1998: 1).

With the above statement in mind it is important to place the significance of Science within the whole school curriculum in perspective, before a discussion of citizenship and Science education can be addressed. *Science Beyond 2000* highlights Science's role within the curriculum:

> The current significance of science is reflected in the fact that it now occupies the curriculum high table with literacy and numeracy as the essential core of the primary curriculum. In addition, science is also a core subject of the 11–16 curriculum, along with English and Mathematics.
>
> (Nuffield Foundation, 1998: 4)

Effectively, Science is high in the education stakes however, the changing curricular position of Science has not been accompanied by a corresponding change in the content of the Science curriculum, in particular at the secondary level. The Report suggests that: 'Contemporary analysis of the labour market would suggest that our future society would need a larger number of individuals with a broader understanding of science both for their work and to enable them to participate as citizens in a democratic society' (Nuffield Foundation, 1998: 4)

Why is this so important to Science and the role Science education can play with regards to citizenship and values? Over the last 30 years, the image of Science has changed with both negative and positive events. Science is often regarded as absolute truth, yet recent events such as Chernobyl, CFCs, depletion of the ozone layer, genetically modified foods and cloning have tarnished Science's profile; while successes in the medical world continue. How are pupils – our future citizens – to interpret such data and information?

The Crick Report (QCA/DfEE, 1998: 7) states as one of its primary aims for citizenship: 'For people to think of themselves as active citizens, willing, able and equipped to have an influence in public life and with the critical capacities to weight evidence before speaking and acting.' The report further enforces this by suggesting that: 'Individuals must be helped and prepared to shape the terms of such engagement by political understanding and action' (1998: 10). These statements imply that to sustain a healthy and vibrant democracy, such issues do not require an acquiescent (nor a hostile and suspicious) public, but one with a broad understanding of major scientific ideas who, whilst appreciating the value of Science and its contribution to our culture, can engage critically with issues and arguments which involve scientific knowledge (Nuffield Foundation, 1998: 4).

If Science educators are to attempt meeting such expectations we need to be able to provide our pupils with teaching and learning opportunities that allow them to actively explore issues and events in Science through a variety of contexts. This can include case studies within the local community, which can lead to critical discussion, and debate within the classroom. The main focus of these types of involvement is to challenge and stimulate pupils, to make Science relevant to their everyday lives and understand their role in society. As Heater (1990) suggests 'a citizen is a person furnished with knowledge of public affairs, instilled with attitudes of civic virtue and equipped with skills to participate in the political arena'.

In an attempt to define the knowledge, attitudes and skills that Science education can contribute to citizenship and values, the learning objectives set out below can help formulate the types of lessons that can be introduced to pupils of all ages.

When using the following table to help develop Science lessons with citizenship and values in mind, it must be remembered that the categories suggested are permeable. Knowledge about citizenship and values is only partially useful if it does not lead on to the

Table 11.1 Learning objectives

Knowledge	Attitudes	Skills
Facts	Self-understanding	Intellect and judgement
Interpretation	Respect for others	Communication
Personal role	Respect for values	Action

formulation of attitudes and the acquisition of skills. Attitudes are but prejudices unless grounded in a firm and clear understanding, and action is wanting direction without attitudes and is irresponsible and/or inefficient if born in ignorance. It is important to understand what is meant by each objective.

Knowledge, attitudes and skills.

Pupils need to know basic facts surrounding the scientific area for discussion or investigation. They need to understand how the status and role of the citizen has evolved in Science, particularly in their own community and the state at large. They need to be informed how citizenship and values is articulated through scientific institutions, and present day laws. Pupils also need to realize that citizenship and values operates in a context, one which deals with practical issues. As such they need to realize that as individuals they will be confronted with problems and issues that affect them both at a local and global level. In this context, scientific knowledge and information is only part of the pupil's requirements. The knowledge that is given to them has to be at an appropriate level and introduced in such a way that pupils can make sense of it and come to understand the implications of their decision making. Science has a key role to play in bringing the young citizen to understand his or her own potential personal role in the community and society in which they live. A clear understanding, for example, of CFCs might make the individuals choose not to purchase goods containing CFC.

Clearly the first task for the Science teacher is to motivate and stimulate their pupils' interest in the subject matter. Whether this is nuclear fuel, cloning or personal health issues. As a Science teacher it is essential that the pupils feel that current issues such as GM foods is of equal interest to the teacher as it is to the pupils themselves. Here the Science teacher must play a significant part in clarifying pupils anxieties and feelings with respect to the issues under discussion. Equally many of the issues that could and will be discussed in Science lessons are emotive and sensitive. Teachers must be aware of pupils' feelings, as well as appreciate that a pupil will have their own prejudices towards the subject. As such it is the teachers responsibility to lead the pupil into understanding his or her own prejudices.

Allowing pupils to develop rational and flexible thought is not a simple task, however, Science can and ought to play its part. Science is in a strong position to influence the way pupils can become critical, ask questions and seek information from a variety of sources as means to answering the questions posed. The way the Science curriculum functions demands that pupils draw conclusions from data collected. It expects pupils to argue their case based on evidence, what the teacher can influence is how pupils can be cultivated to realize that the judgements they make can influence the public arena.

The development of judgement is a vital aspect in citizenship. Beiner (1983: 163) suggests that: 'Judgement is... irreducible to algorithm. What is required is not a "decision procedure", but an education in hermeneutic insight, taste, and understanding'. What does this mean in terms of pedagogy for the Science teacher? The Science teacher's need to enable the student to understand the values, and bias he/she holds, and how they will be used in judgements that area made. The teacher must also allow the pupil room to explore the consequences of the action or inaction that a pupil might wish to take in certain circumstances. Here such issues as apathy and active demonstration may be considered, by allowing the pupil to appreciate other people's point of view. Good examples here are pollution and cloning:

Pollution
- Pupils could consider the issues related to pollution from a variety of angles.
- Why do Green Peace actively demonstrate and attack the state about pollution when individuals continually pollute their own environment?
- What effects do individuals polluting their environment have on the local community?
- What responsibility does the individual have to global pollution?

Cloning

Pupils should be encouraged to consider issues related to cloning. For example, Dolly the sheep. This could take the form of a research and debate exercise.

In the above examples, pupils should be actively encouraged to consider evidence and reflect on the decisions they make, both from an individual point of view and as a collective decision making force as a class. Teachers should adopt a teaching style that facilitates and actively encourages pupils to be critical in their thinking and analytical in their approach to problems. Science and scientific issues as expressed in the media can be used as a vehicle for such activities. For example, Genetically Modified (GM) crops are frequently discussed in the media without a clear explanation of what GM means, there is an implicit assumption that this is not only known but also understood. Yet, many pupils do not know what GM crops or foods are. As a consequence pupils' critical analysis and thinking related to such issues are impeded. Science teachers should think how the teaching of the scientific information could be integrated into the evaluation of issues related to GM crops and food.

Science education should play a part in future citizens being critical about the information they are given and the value that can be placed upon that information.

Task 11.1: GM foods and crops

Pupils in rural and urban areas can be encouraged to conduct a survey related to GM crops, by asking farmers and, or visiting their supermarkets to find out which products contain GM ingredients. The results can be brought back to the lesson, analysed, then presented to the class for discussion.

Trefed (1996) argues that when pupils encounter Science in their daily lives, it is rarely in the context of 'doing or engaging in science'. For example, here are two randomly selected headlines from a daily newspaper:

'War launched on killer bug'

'Use recycled paper blocks as a more environmentally friendly fuel'

Each has something to do with Science, and something else. The first example is about immunisation against meningitis and the other about fuel and the environment. In other words, Science presents itself to the pupil in the context of a problem or an issue, one that needs to be thought about systematically and critically. These types of stimulating activities allow pupils to engage in the arguments that show Science is not perfect, nor does it give us all the answers, and indeed, sometimes it gives the wrong answers. Carl Sagan (1996: 30) expresses this notion well:

'Science is far from a perfect instrument of knowledge. It's just the best we have. In this respect, as in many others, it's like democracy. Science by itself cannot advocate human action, but it can certainly illuminate the possible consequences of alternative courses of action.'

(Sagan 1996: 30)

What I am suggesting is that science is preoccupied with everyday, serious questions of values and citizenship. Therefore, values and citizenship education needs Science education in the curriculum, if pupils are to be able to discuss action, and understand the consequences of those actions in a more global world.

The Crick Report (QCA/DfEE 1988: 37) states that: 'School and its local community provide a perfect context for pupils to examine issues and events and to become involved in activities, participatory activities and experiences where emphasis is on learning through action'. Through this type of involvement, pupils can be helped and guided through the political, civic and social issues related to scientific information and knowledge. Engagement of this nature can lead to balanced decision-making, incorporating some of the requirements and expectations of citizenship and values. These include:

* the belief that individuals must be helped and prepared to shape the terms of such engagements by political understanding and action;
* some knowledge of what social problems affect them and even what different pressure groups and parties say about them;
* the knowledge that it will empower them (pupils) to participate in society effectively as active, informed, critical and responsible citizens.

(QCA/DfEE, 1998).

The above statements from the Crick Report and Nuffield Foundation, must and do have implications for the Science curriculum and citizenship and values education.

Implications for the Science curriculum

Citizenship is fundamentally concerned with social relationships between people, and relationships between people, and the institutional arrangements of complex industrial societies. Thus exploring citizenship and values within the Science curriculum requires an examination and consideration of both pupils and the institution (school and society as a whole). In Mills' (1970) terms, we are concerned with what kinds of persons we are able to be and the kinds of persons we might be. What kinds of opportunities and constraints confront pupils in terms of current institutional arrangements? Understanding the conception of citizenship and values in Science requires an understanding of the concept of 'self' and the manner in which institutional arrangements (in this case the school) may provide opportunities for, or place constraints upon, self-development (in this case the pupil).

Why is this important in Science education?

We can start from the perspective of the pupil as a human being, one that is influenced both biologically through genetic inheritance, but also socially where they require a social milieu to develop their recognisable human qualities. The nature of human beings is developmental, one would expect pupils to change and develop over a period of time. These changes will be in response to a variety of aspects such as economic, political and social contexts.

Equally as pupils develop and mature, their own actions and beliefs will affect the contexts they find themselves in. For example, exploring cloning of Dolly the sheep in year 3, 4 or 5 can be exciting and stimulating as it can be in years 9 and 10, but by years 11, 12 and beyond the individuals' overt actions could influence future debates on cloning. Where Science education is important to citizenship and values education, is in helping future individuals choose the course of action that could or might be taken. The key thing here for the classroom is that choices for action are different and opportunities to take action are also different. However, all are influenced by political, economic and social contexts.

What Science education can do, is to introduce pupils to such contexts through everyday examples that can be investigated through the community, environment and social/cultural elements of their lives. As Gould (1988: 40) suggests: 'Self-development refers to the freedom to develop oneself through one's own actions. . . a process of the development of the person over time.' He goes on to say: '. . . in order to effect such choices concretely a wide range of actual options need to be available to people. . . It is through making choices in their actions in particular situations over the course of time that people come to know who they are.' (1988: 41–46). If we apply this concept to the science classroom it allows us to conceptualize the notion of citizenship and values in our teaching. That of developing in pupils the capacity to make decisions related to Science issues, and what action they may choose to take.

The way the present curriculum is constructed does at times constrain what pupils might engage in. If pupils and teachers feel such constraints, alternatives are needed, alternatives that require forms of reasoning that enable pupils and teachers to make links between personal experience of Science and social structures. For many pupils, Science is done to them, and they feel they are subject to vast impersonal facts that they cannot understand, let alone control and act upon. What we need our pupils to achieve in Science is 'a quality of mind that will help them to use information and to develop reason in order to achieve lucid summations of what is going on in the world and of what may be happening within themselves' (Mills, 1970: 11).

It is this quality of understanding that Science education should be aiming for. It provides a framework for pupils to understand themselves and the relationship to the larger world of Science in terms of their civil, political and social rights. At present most pupils and young adults do not possess the quality of mind essential to grasp the interplay between man, science and society. For many, the world is experienced as one in which they are constantly subjected to forces and events that they do not understand, such as BSE, GM foods, cloning and nuclear fuel. It is often difficult for pupils and adults to relate their personal and scientific knowledge and expectations to the understanding of such complex issues. It is also difficult for them to appreciate the complexities of opportunities and the constraints that are on them from society in making their own choices and decisions about scientific issues.

Added to this, is the dimension of citizenship related to developing attitudes and values, which underpin rights, duties and obligations. These can be considered from two points of view when teaching Science: 1) what values and attitudes can or should the Science curriculum engender in pupils; or 2) what do we mean by duties and obligations within a Science context?

The very nature of Science and scientific enquiry encourages discussion and debate. Debate requires skills as well as knowledge. Science is in a key position to allow pupils of all ages to engage in debate related to scientific concepts and issues and contemporary problems. Within this context, debate allows for Science literacy to occur in the classroom. We live in a society increasingly dependent on science-based technologies, a society reliant on scientific research for new modes of production and communication, new materials for consumption. An understanding of the scientific ideas associated with such production is essential if pupils are to make decisions for themselves in the future – whether these decision are related to diet or the type of fuel that they will use, or car they will drive.

Debate and discussion surrounding such issues are of key importance to future citizens. The Science curriculum can accommodate such issues, and can be planned into normal lesson time. Often researching issues as a precursor for teaching require pupils to be collaborative and work as teams. These are crucial for citizenship and values education.

Alternative views of citizenship and the role of Science education

Alternative views of citizenship and values can be identified, what needs to be explored is the role Science education can play within these alternatives. The first consideration is that of the division between the individual and citizenship and values, and the importance of citizenship for society. MacIntyre (1982) suggests that 'the crucial moral opposition is between liberal individualism.' This refers to the liberal tradition whereby citizenship is largely considered in terms of individual rights. As Mills proposes the individual *qua* citizen has certain rights to be free of interference from, or oppression by, the state. The essential character of the citizen is consequently vigilance in defence of his or her rights and liberties. Morality consists in the full flowering of the individual person, and citizenship and values provides the necessary freedom for this to occur. The alternative to this is the Greek tradition, which places priority on the positive view of liberty – citizenship provided opportunities to serve the community. Morality consists of the conscientious discharge of one's civic duties and obligations.

The above perspectives can be taken account of within the Science curriculum. The role Science education can play, is to make the individual aware of both their individual rights to knowledge and decision making, as well as the individuals' commitment to the community. A good example of this is the case of nuclear fuel and power stations. How do pupils perceive these issues? Is there a difference between pupils who live near a power station and those who do not. Such a discussion can stimulate lively debate within a Science classroom, while bringing pupils' attention to their roles as citizens within such issues.

The second related approach towards citizenship and values, is that of the private and public citizen. It is a truism that the state impinges on the individual's life with so much greater pressure than at almost any other time in history. The demands and opportunities for the citizen to actively participate in this relationship have similarly never been greater. It can also be argued that the desire to simply switch off is equally powerful. The 'let them (Government) get on with it' approach. The demands here are those of the two kinds of freedom: the freedom from civic concerns in order to pursue a private, family life; and the need to participate democratically in order to preserve political freedom. Here too Science education has a role to play.

A good case for consideration here is that of the recent controversy surrounding fields of GM crops:

Genetically modified crops

Pupils even as young as years 3 and 4 in the primary school can be introduced to this topic. The questions can be posed in such a way that pupils have to consider the arguments about GM crops from the Government's perspective (that is, the need for more food at less cost) and the individual consumer's perspective (the choice of not having food contaminated or experimented with).

As has been indicated earlier, part of educating for citizenship and values, is cultivating the art of exchange of views, debate, communication and respect for others' points of view. The Science teacher can, with good planning, allow for such activities to happen in a constructive way within their classroom. However, implicit in such planning is the need to understand one's own feelings, prejudices and values.

To meet the learning objectives in Science for citizenship and values, the teacher must choose carefully the subject content and the relationships presented within the body of knowledge with which pupils are going to be involved.

Conclusion

This chapter has attempted to draw together current debates about the nature and context of the Science curriculum and the place citizenship and values have to play within that context. It has made explicit the view that Science is a key function of our present society and as such our pupils need to have a good understanding of the limitations and expectations of Science in their everyday life. However, within that understanding is a deeper and more pressing issue of how pupils, as individuals, can influence what may or may not happen as a consequence of Science in society. I have argued that Science and Science education has a key role to play in creating an environment of critical thinking and judgement-making for our pupils. Investigating, collecting data and evidence is an intrinsic part of the Science curriculum. Such skills can be used to facilitate some of the elements of citizenship and values our pupils need to acquire and understand, in order to play a full and active part as future citizens.

The Science teacher's pedagogic practice is key to establishing the types of learning objectives suggested. Incorporating the notion of self-understanding into Science lessons is a good way of encouraging citizenship and values, as it facilitates the need for pupils of all ages to confront their values, prejudices and biases, in an environment that has to consider others views as well as their own.

Part 3

Part 3

12 Spiritual education: what's it all about

Roger Straughan

Introduction

In this brave new educational world of 'management-speak', the notion of spiritual education seems to sit uncomfortably alongside the current sacred cows of quality control, performance indicators and school league tables. Yet Adrian Thatcher (1999: 1) has recently highlighted 'an upsurge of interest in spirituality' and the fact that 'the spiritual and moral development of children has received unparalleled attention among teachers, lecturers, curriculum-makers and theorists in the 1990s throughout the English-speaking world.' Moreover, although spiritual education may sound far removed from the present hard-nosed concerns of educational policy and practice, the fact remains that our schools are today being inspected and assessed on their ability to promote the spiritual, moral, social and cultural development of pupils.

The spiritual area cannot then be ignored in any investigation of values education, though the range of issues and problems which it raises cannot be adequately discussed in one limited chapter. Even in the previous opening paragraph, several fundamental questions suggest themselves, all deserving much more detailed and lengthy analysis than they will be able to receive in this chapter. What, for example, is 'spirituality' and does it provide the subject matter of spiritual education? Can one be *educated* in this subject, and is this the same as *developing* spiritually, whatever that may mean? How can success and failure possibly be assessed here? How, if at all, can the spiritual be distinguished from the moral, the social and the cultural – let alone the religious?

In trying to probe these questions and to follow what has been said about them in the current debate, we can quickly find ourselves in the same position as Stapleton in *The Hound of the Baskervilles* – floundering helplessly in a bog with no clear markers to guide us or solid ground to cling to. Philosophy is not usually thought of as offering practical help in such situations, but one way of trying to pick our way through this spiritual morass is to keep asking the two simple-sounding questions which have formed the core of the philosophic method ever since Socrates – what do you mean, and how do you know?

In this case, the scope for asking these questions is huge. What do we mean by spiritual, spiritual education, spiritual development – and indeed spirit itself? How do we know when spiritual education or development has taken place, or whether the spiritual is a suitable (or even possible) subject for education? The first part of this chapter will briefly examine these and other related questions, while the second part will try to make some practical, if controversial, suggestions in an attempt to advance the debate further.

Problems of definition

The 1988 Education Reform Act required schools to provide a balanced and broadly based curriculum which promoted the spiritual, moral, cultural, mental and physical development of pupils at school and of society. This reference to spiritual development was by no means new – the 1944 Education Act, for example, contained a similar statement – but it has served to stimulate a fresh interest in the subject, no doubt sustained by the involvement and practical requirements of the National Curriculum Council and of OFSTED. The result has been a flurry of policy documents, conference papers and academic publications, all struggling in various ways to define the contours of this mysterious terrain. This chapter will not attempt a detailed summary of this material, but will refer to some of it at times to illustrate the main issues.

The main impression gained from studying the debate is that there is only one safe and clear conclusion to be drawn: the virtual impossibility of reaching any meaningful consensus on the question of what is meant by spiritual education and development. An effective way of demonstrating this is to list a sample of definitions offered in one of the most comprehensive contributions to the debate. Best (1996) states that:

1. Education in spiritual growth is that which promotes apprehension of ultimate reality through fostering higher forms of human consciousness (1996: 33).
2. The term ('spiritual') needs to be seen as applying to something fundamental in the human condition. . .it has to do with the universal search for human identity (1996: 34).
3. The spiritual life is part of the human essence. It is a defining characteristic of human nature, without which human nature is not full human nature. It is part of the real self, of one's identity, of one's inner core, of one's specieshood, of full humanness (1996: 35).
4. Spiritual people are characterized, to a greater or lesser extent, by all or most of the following: awareness. . . breadth of outlook. . . a holistic attitude. . . integration. . . wonder. . . gratitude. . . hope. . . courage. . . energy. . . detachment. . . acceptance. . . love. . . gentleness (1996: 48–49).
5. Fundamentally spirituality has to do with becoming a person in the fullest sense. . . (and). . . this dynamic form . . . can be described as a capacity for going out of oneself and beyond oneself (1996: 51).
6. The word 'spiritual' will refer to anything which might be regarded as a source of inspiration to a person's life (1996: 77).
7. Spirituality is that quality of being, holistically conceived, made up of insight, beliefs, values, attitudes/emotions and behavioural dispositions, which both informs and may be informed by lived experience (1996: 78).

8. All spiritual development, which I understand as primarily the development of psychic self-identity, requires the composition of a continuous, coherent and creative life-narrative (1996: 94).
9. Current guidance on the inspection schedule describes spiritual development as relating 'to that aspect of inner life through which pupils acquire insights into their personal existence which are of enduring worth' (1996: 170).
10. Spiritualization is seen here as the process whereby teachers and pupils employ and develop unique combinations of positive qualities from within all the domains of being human (1996: 320).

What are we to say about such 'definitions', some of which appear in NCC and OFSTED documents? A first reaction, to borrow a famous philosopher's phrase, is to reach for one's conceptual gun. The language employed here transports us to such dizzy heights of abstraction, generality and obscurity that one longs for a Socrates to bring us down to earth as he did when speaking of moral education: 'when I see the subject in such utter confusion, I feel the liveliest desire to clear it up' (Guthrie, 1956: 99).

A second reaction is to feel extreme sympathy for the schools and teachers at whom these 'definitions' are directed, and who are expected to translate this pretentious verbiage into something practical and meaningful. Teachers surely have a hard enough task in trying to 'deliver' (merely to 'teach' seems to be no longer sufficient) the many components of the National Curriculum, without having to agonize over how they will manage to develop Form 4 H's psychic self-identity next period.

The main problem with such 'definitions' is that they resort to terminology which is itself as difficult to define as the original concept, and which begs a host of further questions. What, for example, are we to understand by 'ultimate reality', 'full humanness', 'the real self', 'one's inner core and specieshood' and 'something fundamental in the human condition'? These notions all require a particular set of moral and metaphysical values to give them any substance, but such values can readily give rise to profound disagreement. Can 'ultimate reality', for instance, be apprehended without some kind of religious awareness? What are the criteria for 'full humanness'? How do we decide what is 'fundamental in the human condition'? A Catholic, a Buddhist, a Marxist, a Darwinian biologist and a Freudian psychoanalyst would find very little common ground for agreement here because of their conflicting beliefs and values. Defining spiritual development and education in such opaque and ambiguous terms, therefore, serves merely to paper over the cracks and to pretend that these fundamental clashes of value do not exist.

These are not the only definitional pitfalls, however. Some definitions are so broad that they could be used to encompass virtually anything and everything, and so become meaningless. The British Humanist Association (1993: 165), for example, describes the spiritual dimension as: 'coming from our deepest humanity' and finding expression in 'aspirations, moral sensibility, creativity, love and friendship, response to natural and human beauty, scientific and artistic endeavour, appreciation and wonder at the natural world, intellectual achievement and physical activity, surmounting suffering and persecution, selfless love, the quest for meaning and for values by which to live' (cited in Thatcher, 1999: 165). So much is included here (with the predictable exception of any religious component) that we are left wondering what distinctive function the term 'spiritual' can possibly perform. We use concepts to classify, identify and distinguish; an all-inclusive concept is a contradiction in terms.

Further examples of amorphous definitions are to be found in OFSTED documents. The first version of the *Handbook for the Inspection of Schools* (1992) drew no distinction between the evaluation criteria for spiritual and moral development, while the 1994 version required spiritual development 'to be judged by how well the school promotes opportunities for pupils to reflect on aspects of their lives and the human condition through, for example, Literature, Music, Art, Science, Religious Education and collective worship and how well the pupils respond'. OFSTED inspection reports also refer to spiritual development being promoted by 'caring and supportive communities' and by daily acts of worship 'where pupils are given opportunities for reflection and prayer', with further opportunities being provided 'across the curriculum, especially in Religious Education, story time and Music lessons' (Ramsey, 1999).

Again we are in danger of sinking into the mire here, for as Beck (1999: 164–5) argues, '. . . to suggest that in some global and inclusive way 'the spiritual' should permeate the teaching of Art, Music, Literature, History, Science, as well as being centrally represented by RE, seems a recipe for confusion and miscommunication'. The relationship between spiritual education and development and other areas of the curriculum needs to be made much more precise and explicit if 'the spiritual' is to be taught, promoted, inspected and assessed, but this is impossible without a clearer understanding of its parameters.

Spiritual education and the curriculum

Is it helpful or necessary to think in terms of a distinctive curriculum area labelled 'spiritual'? Paul Hirst's well-known analysis (1974) of the fundamental 'forms of knowledge' upon which the HMI's 'areas of experience' were loosely based in their document Curriculum 11–16 (DES, 1977), identified the scientific, the mathematical, the aesthetic, the religious, the moral, the interpersonal and the philosophical. These categories could be said to cover quite adequately everything that is usually referred to as the spiritual (at least when it is possible to understand what is being referred to). Hirst never claimed that his 'forms of knowledge' would or should translate directly into curriculum subjects, but if a curriculum contains Religious Education, moral, personal and social education, Science and the Arts, it is difficult to see what additional content could be supplied by 'spiritual education'.

Much will depend of course on how such areas of the curriculum are conceived of and presented. The aims, objectives and methods of religious, moral, personal and social education, for example, are far from being self-evident (Straughan, 1988), and have generated heated debate and a substantial literature. Similarly the teaching of Science, Literature and the Arts may be done in such a way as to encourage or discourage questions and discussions about deeper philosophical issues and pupils' personal responses to them. These existing curriculum areas, then, certainly have the potential to deal with those 'aspects of spiritual development' listed in the NCC discussion paper on Spiritual and Moral Development (1993): beliefs, a sense of awe, wonder and mystery, experiencing feelings of transcendence, search for meaning and purpose, self-knowledge, relationships, creativity and feelings and emotions (though this list is again so broad and vague that it is of very limited value). Whether any of these 'aspects', with the exception of beliefs (which beliefs?) could be directly *taught* within a curriculum is also open to question.

Spiritual education, therefore, in addition to being virtually impossible to define satisfactorily, may also be an unnecessary and unhelpful concept if seen as an *addition* to other more substantive curriculum areas. More thought needs to be given, not to how spiritual education might be 'introduced' into the school curriculum, but to what constitutes a proper education in Science, Religion, morality, the Arts and so on, and to what opportunities pupils are being offered to go beyond the 'key skills' and pursue deeper questions of personal significance to them.

An alternative interpretation

So far this chapter has been somewhat critical and sceptical about the concept of spiritual education. To conclude on a more positive and constructive note, therefore, one possible interpretation of the spiritual will now be briefly explored which has been almost wholly ignored in the current debate, yet which could carry with it considerable educational potential. In view of the reservations and criticisms already expressed about some of the attempts at definition, it would be arrogant to suggest that this interpretation is what spiritual education 'really means' or that it is 'better' than any of the other offerings we have surveyed. All that will be claimed is that this interpretation at least reflects normal usage in picking out one fairly obvious aspect of the spiritual, and that this aspect is of educational interest; it also suggests some specific content, objectives and teaching methods, unlike the more amorphous interpretations discussed earlier.

The Concise Oxford Dictionary defines spirit as 'animating or vital principle of person or animal; intelligent or immaterial part of person, soul; incorporeal being', and spiritual as: 'of spirit as opposed to matter; of the soul'. Certainly in everyday language we often contrast 'spiritual' with 'material' or 'physical', and equate a person's spirit with non-physical aspects of their personality – or, for religious believers, with their soul.

This basic sense of 'spiritual' is paid scant attention in the literature and debate on spiritual education, though it is not totally ignored. In the Best collection of papers (1996), for example, Rebecca Nye speaks of 'the more general, universal sense' of the term, as referring to 'things of the spirit as opposed to material or worldly interests' (1996: 111); while Gavin Baldwin takes 'spiritual' to refer to ' the realm of meaning and experience arising from the abstract, non-corporeal, immaterial identity of people' (1996: 207).

Such definitions at least do justice to common usage, but they of course raise some big questions – indeed, many would say the big questions. Does this 'realm of meaning and experience' actually exist? Do we really have an 'abstract, non-corporeal, immaterial identity'? Is there some kind of non-material, spiritual component to human beings (and perhaps to animals), or are we as the materialist claims no more than merely 'four buckets of water and a bagful of salts'? To what extent is this spiritual component, if it exists, able to operate independently of our physical bodies? Might it be able to survive physical death?

Such questions concerning a possible non-material, spiritual component (to be referred to from now on for convenience as NMSC questions) can be crucial in shaping our view of the world and our place within it; our responses to them help to formulate our personalities and some of our values. Whether or not we believe that we are purely a biochemical cocktail can deeply affect what sort of people we are.

Given the fundamental importance of NMSC questions for our overall attitude towards life (and death), it would seem inexcusable for them to be ignored in any system of education, for a major function of education must always be to enable pupils to tackle significant questions of all kinds and to start to reach their own conclusions about them. But where are NMSC questions raised and explored with pupils in schools today? Religious Education might be expected to take the lead here, but in practice such questions are rarely, if ever, dealt with. A typical secondary school Religious Education syllabus seems to consist largely of a tour of 'world religions' and their festivals and rituals, plus a review of various 'contemporary moral issues' such as sex, drugs, racism and war, leaving little or no time to consider NMSC questions.

Religious Education is not, however, necessarily the most appropriate context in which to raise these questions. Obviously the issue of whether human beings (and animals) have a non-physical spirit or soul has religious implications, and all institutional religions will offer their own view on this. However, there are educational dangers in treating the issue as a purely religious one; for example:

1. Pupils who do not come from a background of institutional religion and who do not consider themselves 'religious', will be unlikely to see NMSC questions as relevant to themselves, despite their fundamental importance, if those questions are portrayed as essentially religious ones.
2. The issue will probably be presented as a matter of faith, with Religious Education teachers in their eagerness to avoid the charge of indoctrination promoting a neutral and tolerant attitude towards conflicting 'faiths', and implying that NMSC questions can only be considered within the framework of religious faith and are thus beyond the bounds of critical investigation and discussion.

Moreover, the arguments against labelling NMSC questions as purely religious matters are not only educational ones. The question of whether we possess some kind of spiritual, non-material component which is not governed by the same laws and constraints as our physical bodies has generated detailed scientific and philosophical inquiry for at least a century and a half. A vast literature has been built up over that period, and the subject has attracted the attention of many eminent thinkers and researchers. The focus of this research has continued to shift from one topic to another during this period, and some of the main topics for investigation and debate have included the possibility of:

*   apparitions and hauntings;
*   communication with the spirits of those who have died;
*   telepathy;
*   reincarnation;
*   'out-of-body' experiences, including those claimed by people very near to physical death.

This whole area is as complex as it is controversial, and no attempt can be made here to summarize or evaluate it. One indisputable fact, however, is the high level of current popular interest in such matters, if one is to judge by the number of television programmes devoted to the so-called 'paranormal' and 'supernatural', and the ever-increasing range of books to be found in any bookshop or library in sections variously labelled 'mind and spirit', 'occult', 'New Age', etc. The bewildering spectrum of topics covered by such labels and categories (including, for example, UFOs and alien abductions) may tempt us to dismiss the whole package simply as an interesting social phenomenon, stemming from the sharp decline in conventional religious belief and practice.

Yet this response does not help us to develop a rational approach to NMSC questions (which have been labelled as such to avoid the unhelpful connotations of ill-defined terms such as 'paranormal', 'occult', 'psychic', etc), nor does it do justice to the established framework of serious research and debate which cannot be dismissed merely as a temporary popular obsession. It is as irrational to dismiss as self-evident nonsense all the topics covered in the 'paranormal' section of the bookshop as it is blindly to accept them all: a rational judgement about them can be made only on the basis of an open-minded consideration of the evidence and the arguments.

This brings us back again to the role of education. To judge from my daughter's ever-growing stockpile of teenage magazines, articles and features on many aspects of the 'paranormal' and 'supernatural' are as plentiful as those on pop groups, boy friends and make-up, and presumably such publications survive only by reflecting the major interests and preoccupations of their readers. The topics covered include apparitions, communication with the dead and near-death experiences, all of which directly raise NMSC questions.

Education surely has a responsibility here not to leave young people's interest in these questions at the level of sensational, anecdotal magazine articles. A substantial body of serious literature exists on the subject which could and should be used as the basis for a balanced and systematic educational approach. The aim would not of course be to produce expert 'psychic researchers', any more than a Religious Education course in school is intended to produce expert theologians, but rather to encourage informed awareness and critical appraisal of a wide range of evidence and debate which is crucial for the consideration of NMSC questions.

Course content and teaching methods

There is an embarrassment of riches in terms of possible material which could be used with pupils, but some of the questions for consideration could include the following:

---

1. **How has this area of research developed, and who have been the leading figures associated with it?**
   This would demonstrate that interest in NMSC questions is not just a current craze, and that the subject has attracted the attention of famous scientists, philosophers, writers and other public figures, many of whom have found at least some of the evidence convincing.
2. **What are the latest trends and emphasis in current research?**
   This could include, for example, a study of the extensive data on reincarnation and of evidence concerning 'near-death experiences', where a recent review of the literature concludes: 'Scientific examination of the NDE phenomenon,

---

conducted by medical professionals since the late 1970s, presents very persuasive evidence that mind and body are separate entities, and that as a result mind can survive the demise of the physical self' (Randles and Hough, 1998: 1).

3. **What can this area of research tell us about scientific methods, attitudes and assumptions?**

   Pupils could be encouraged to consider whether scientific data could ever conclusively prove or disprove that a non-material, spiritual component exists, and what possible alternative explanations of the data might be offered. It could also be instructive to examine the reasons for many scientists' negative attitudes towards NMSC questions, highlighted in a detailed review of the evidence by the American philosopher of science, Stephen Braude (1986: ix) who claimed: 'Since dipping into the data of parapsychology, I have encountered more examples of intellectual cowardice and dishonesty than I had previously thought possible. I have seen how prominent scholars marshal their considerable intellectual gifts and skills to avoid honest inquiry'.

4. **What are the religious implications of this data, and which religious beliefs does it support or challenge?**

   The attitudes of many religious authorities towards this area of research raise as many interesting questions as those of their scientific counterparts. Why, for example, in the words of the Archdeacon of Durham, who has studied the subject in far greater depth than most of his religious colleagues, has the Christian Church only 'occasionally looked at the psychic dimension, (and) seems remarkably disinclined to take it seriously and to give it prolonged theological consideration' (Perry, 1984: 12), when one would expect it to be a subject of considerable religious significance?

NMSC questions can generate heated debate, as some of the above quotations demonstrate, and the educational point of raising such questions with pupils cannot be to provide them with conclusive answers. It is indoctrination, not education, which seeks to inculcate fixed views on essentially controversial issues. Any educational approach to a controversial area must focus on the controversy itself, the reasons for it and the arguments that can be produced on both sides; helping pupils to make their own informed judgements is always a prime educational aim, whatever the context.

One interesting attempt to tackle NMSC questions in this way has been made by Randles and Hough (1998), who present the evidence for and against on a number of NMSC-related issues, and conclude by inviting the reader to reach his or her own verdict by a method of systematic self-assessment. This kind of approach and material could quite easily be adapted by teachers for use with pupils. The posing of 'What if. . .'? questions could also have educational value in challenging assumptions and encouraging creative thinking about implications, for example:

- What if ghosts exist?
- What sort of consciousness might they possess?
- Why do they appear to behave in the ways that they do?
- What if ghosts do not exist?
- How could we explain the numerous accounts of apparitions throughout history?
- How might the existence or non-existence of ghosts fit in with a particular set of religious beliefs?

Conclusion

It is beyond the scope of this chapter to consider detailed curricular arrangements, but some form of team-teaching approach might well be appropriate here, with contributions from a range of subject areas including Science, Religious Education, Literature and History. The main requirement, as with the teaching of any controversial issues, is for teachers who are well-informed and open-minded and whose priority is not to transmit their personal views and beliefs, but to provide a reflective, rational basis upon which pupils can develop their own.

We have seen that spiritual education is an extremely murky area, where it is very difficult to determine precisely what is being attempted, how it might be achieved and how it might be assessed. Many of the problems evident here are conceptual ones, and to resolve some of these one specific sense of 'spiritual' has been identified, which is central to our normal understanding of the term. This sense raises questions about the possibility of a non-material, non-physical component and about the implications of that possibility. It also offers challenging educational opportunities to develop knowledge, understanding and critical awareness of issues which are of intrinsic interest to young people, and of fundamental importance in helping them to formulate their beliefs about themselves and the world in which they live.

13 Values education, citizenship, and the challenge of cultural diversity

George Skinner and Ann McCollum

Introduction

This chapter explores the nature of the challenges facing education systems as they try to engage with current issues and dilemmas in relation to citizenship and cultural diversity. It describes and analyses the Government's response to these issues, as contained in the Advisory Group Report on citizenship education, the 'Crick Report' (QCA/DfEE, 1998), and it argues that this report is flawed because it fails to address three core issues:

- It overlooks the ways in which society is characterized by institutional racism and social and economic inequality and the ways in which our education system is characterized by distinctive exclusionary and discriminatory practices.
- It fails to recognize the controversial nature of citizenship, and the tensions posed, for example in seeking a balance between individual and community rights, in defining the common values which underscore democratic and diverse societies, and in ensuring that all British citizens have a genuine sense of belonging to British society.
- It fails to engage with the contested and often elusive nature of core concepts such as diversity and equality.

The chapter then highlights the ways in which education for citizenship poses profound and complex challenges which are core to contemporary debates in education, it explores key concepts which lie at the centre of these debates, and identifies practical and theoretical implications for education programmes which are relevant to the conditions of modern society. Finally, it makes some practical suggestions for appropriate school responses.

Cultural pluralism and education in Britain

The United Kingdom has always been to some degree plural with a variety of national and regional cultures and languages. In terms of religion, there has been a Jewish presence since Norman times and even within Christianity there has been a much more complex pattern of denominational diversity than in most other European countries. A pluralist response to such religious diversity in education can be identified in the Government's decision at the end of the last century to provide funding for religious foundation schools and the development of the dual system of provision enshrined in the 1944 Education Act (Skinner, 1990).

There have been small numbers of Black people resident in Britain for centuries (Visram, 1986). Black people were often admired but frequently patronized and as long ago as 1601 Queen Elizabeth I was expressing concern about the impact of Black migrants on the economy and culture, devising means of expelling them from the country.

Post-war migration from commonwealth countries to meet labour shortages in Britain or to escape persecution in some East African states resulted in a significant change in the cultural and religious nature of British society. Changing economic circumstances and restrictive legislation soon reduced migration so that today, cultural and religious pluralism needs to be understood in terms of British ethnic and religious minority communities rather than 'immigrants' or 'guest workers'. Indeed, the fact that the majority of migrants came as British citizens in the first place means that most immigrant families had rights of residence and full political participation from the outset. Census figures (OPCS, 1994) indicate that in Britain today, people from minority ethnic communities make up about 6.5 per cent of the total population, although settlement patterns mean that some towns or districts of towns have a much higher proportion of minority families to the extent that some primary schools may draw their total cohort from one minority group (Skinner, 1995).

The educational response to this changing pattern has often been described as a process from assimilation to pluralism. In fact, initial responses to the presence of minority pupils is best described as 'laissez-faire' based on a political response summed up in Kirp's (1979) phrase, 'doing good by doing little'. Although educational theorists and the writers of the Swann Report (DES, 1985) may have seen a gradual progression towards a pluralist philosophy, there is little evidence that all but a few schools ever embraced such an ideal. While OFSTED inspection reports indicate that some schools continue to respond creatively to cultural pluralism, research evidence suggests that those schools without a significant number of minority ethnic pupils rarely do so. When Chris Gaine conducted his study of all white schools in the 1980s, he called his report *No Problem Here* (1987) because when he asked headteachers what they were doing to promote multicultural education he was so frequently told that 'this isn't a problem here'. Those concerned about promoting interculturalism can find little comfort in the fact that when he conducted his follow up study ten years on he felt compelled to call it *'Still No Problem Here'* (Gaine, 1998).

Even where cultural pluralism is acknowledged, school responses may slip into stereo-typical patterns, echoing the saris, samosa and steel bands syndrome noted by several authors in the 1980s. Simplistic views of culture and static concepts of ethnicity may fail to address culture in anything other than romanticized or ossified forms and perpetuate, rather than challenge, prejudice.

It is hardly surprising that the widespread failure of multicultural education in the 1970s and 1980s resulted in a more philosophically critical and morally challenging anti-racist critique of schools. The recognition of hidden forms of prejudice and of institutionalized racism, coupled with the continuing disadvantage experienced by pupils from some sections of minority ethnic communities, created a groundswell lobby among education-alist and minority communities for a model of education which, while not denying the value of intercultural study, needed to focus on inequality and disadvantage. As long ago as the early 1980s, the black sociologist Maureen Stone (1981), was arguing that multicultur-alism which does not take account of the pernicious power of racism at a personal, social and institutional level may simply become a means of satisfying the consciences of liberal educators.

The failure of this movement to have significant political impact is demonstrated by the reluctance of the Government to implement the recommendations of the Swann Report, or to integrate a pluralist model into the structure and curriculum requirements of the 1988 Education Reform Act. The quasi-market driven educational policy-making which has dominated the last ten years has done little to promote either cultural pluralism or racial equality in schools. Underachievement is still evidenced among some Black and Asian communities. Black pupils are six times more likely than white to get excluded from school (SCAA, 1996a) and, as the current DfEE (1998) guidelines on teaching standards demon-strate, student teachers are required to achieve little more than having some understanding of the 1976 Race Relations Act and an awareness that other cultures have contributed to subject knowledge during their initial training. Recent Government inclusive education initiatives do provide some support for providing a more appropriate educational expe-rience for minority pupils, though these rely largely on a deficit model of need rather than a radical reform of educational institutions.

At a wider level, the debate about models of pluralism, which has been stimulated by the request of some Muslim groups to have state funding for Muslim day schools, and the proliferation of supplementary schools and classes, raises major questions about the possi-bility of state schools creating an environment and curriculum which are genuinely inclusive. In Britain, thousands of supplementary schools provide an alternative linguistic, cultural or religious identity for young people. Children who attend them not only learn about their own minority religion, culture and history but, if only indirectly, develop views about the values and history of the state in which they live (Jones, 1999). The development of national identity and citizenship may be frustrated by such experiences unless the state is prepared to include a genuine exploration of such alternative histories within the formal curriculum. As Jones observes, the instability of modern plural and multinational states is better countered through a genuine exploration of the values and perceptions that are held by constituent groups than by seeking to maintain some fictional state unity or 'nation state' mythology.

The past 30 years has done much to extend the debate about pluralism and education from a deficit model of minority pupil needs or simplistic and stereotypical curriculum development of the saris, samosa and steel bands type. We understand more now about the dynamic nature of culture, the complex patterns of ethnic identity and the power of hidden and institutional forms of racism. As Gillborn (1995) rightly implies, the way forward in schools has probably less to do with identifying a universally applicable model of multicul-tural or anti-racist education and more to do with a genuine informed commitment on the part of all teachers to work against cultural myopia, racism and disadvantage in all areas of school life. Clearly this implies the permeation of school practice and policy with values which promote understanding and justice. How far do proposals for citizenship education do this?

One of the stated aims of the revised National Curriculum is to support the development of citizens capable of contributing to a just society, to develop their knowledge and understanding of different beliefs and cultures, and to appreciate and understand the diverse nature of society (QCA, 1999a: 5). However, at no point do the curriculum documents explicitly engage with issues of social justice, national identity and cultural diversity, or adequately explore their implications for educational policy and practice.

The proposals for citizenship education, for example, draw largely from the recommendations of the Citizenship Advisory Group, which sets out a statement of the aims and purposes and a broad framework for implementing citizenship education in schools (QCA/DfEE, 1998: 4). The report, however, has fundamental weaknesses which render the proposed framework inadequate for the development of citizenship education which addresses 'the opportunities and challenges of the rapidly changing world in which we live and work' (DfEE/QCA, 1999a: 3). The fundamental weaknesses of the report are that its problem formulation is narrow and simplistic, and, of central significance, it fails to recognize the controversial and complex nature of citizenship and the underlying tensions it embraces, particularly in relation to cultural diversity and value pluralism.

The two key issues that pose fundamental challenges for contemporary programmes of education for citizenship are, firstly, the inadequate accommodation of social and economic equity with cultural diversity and, secondly, new understandings about the constructed nature of identity and culture and the complex cross-cutting interactions which take place within culturally diverse societies. The Crick Report establishes a frame of reference which precludes any real engagement with these issues, and thereby proposes a framework for citizenship education which, at best, merely tinkers with these fundamental issues.

The need for citizenship education: the Advisory Group views

Whilst passing reference is made to the new political context of Britain, and rapid social, economic, and technological change, the issue of young peoples' negative attitudes to government and politics is pre-eminent in the report's diagnosis of the need for citizenship education. The Advisory Group presents political apathy as the central problem *per se*, which necessitates a programme of political and civic education to redress the problem: 'they (young people) feel left up in the air without the teaching of political literacy that could empower them in adult life to have some effect on these problems (drugs, health education, housing and homelessness)' (QCA/DfEE, 1998: 20).

Many commentators believe that the political attitudes and behaviour of young people in Britain today are representative of deeper problems in our democratic society in relation to major structural changes and cultural changes which have produced new patterns of social and economic exclusion and which have profound implications for how we conceptualize identity and culture. These changes also undermine traditional forms of citizenship, and alter our understandings of what it means to live in democratic culturally diverse societies. They therefore require a fundamental reappraisal of the theoretical and pedagogical assumptions that underlie our educational practices.

The Advisory Group report 'reverses causality' (Young, 1999: 130), and implies that young peoples' apathy represents the most serious threat to democracy; the simple solution being that young people must, therefore, be taught how to be effective citizens: 'We. . . dare not be complacent about the health and future of British democracy. Unless we become a nation of engaged citizens, our democracy is not secure' (Lord Chancellor, in QCA/DfEE, 1998: 8). 'We believe that the most important issue facing young people as citizens is their lack of knowledge about society, its democratic process and their actual rights and responsibilities as citizens' (British Youth Council, in QCA/DfEE, 1998: 20).

The validity of the Advisory Group's report and framework for citizenship education rests on a set of presuppositions which they apparently forgot to state in relation to the nature of citizenship, democracy and diversity and the relationship between education and society. In the absence of these presuppositions, it is helpful to note that 'a conceptual structure can be identified both by the questions that it raises and the questions that it is incapable of raising.' (Giroux, 1980: 332).

The Advisory Group's response

The Macpherson Report (1999) on Stephen Lawrence's death makes clear recommendations in relation to education. For example, it states that anti-racist policies, even where they exist, are ineffective and that there must, therefore, be specific and coordinated action, particularly through the educational system, from pre-primary school upwards and onwards, and makes a series of recommendations specifically in relation to education:

- that consideration be given to amendment of the National Curriculum aimed at valuing cultural diversity and preventing racism, in order to better reflect the needs of a diverse society;
- that local education authorities and school governors have the duty to create and implement strategies in their schools to prevent and address racism;
- that OFSTED inspections include examination of the implementation of such strategies.

(MacPherson, 1999: 334)

The current curriculum review refers briefly to the Macpherson Report and implies that these issues will be addressed through their proposals for citizenship education by playing a 'vital role in promoting a greater understanding of the rights and responsibilities that underpin a democratic society' (QCA, 1999a). The response is characterized by 'racial inexplicitness' and a side-stepping of the critical issues raised in the Macpherson Report, for example; it effectively dismisses the report's assertion that there is a need to amend the curriculum.

> The Macpherson report has placed a particular emphasis on the role of the curriculum in encouraging children to value cultural diversity and in combating the development of racism. Our proposals for education for citizenship, which reflect the best work done by schools, will play a vital role in promoting a greater understanding of the rights and responsibilities that underpin a democratic society.
>
> (David Blunkett, in QCA ,1999b: 5)

The report also recognizes 'wider social questions' such as the increasingly complex nature of our society, the greater cultural diversity and the apparent loss of a value consensus. The group's response to this issue is, again, platitudinous and inadequate. Furthermore it appears to echo and reinforce a very narrow view of citizenship. Mason (1995), for example, argues that in the 1980s, the Government sought a reinvigoration of British nationalism, and he states that a key feature of the conceptions of Britishness deployed on these occasions was an emphasis on the antiquity of British national culture, traditions and institutions, which were portrayed as being under threat. He also refers to a renewed emphasis on a unified and unitary British national culture which defined as un-British any but the most minimal manifestations of cultural difference (1995: 115).

> Responding to these worries, a main aim for the whole community should be to find or restore a sense of common citizenship, including a national identity that is secure enough to find a place for the plurality of nations, cultures, ethnic identities and religions long found in the United Kingdom. Citizenship education creates common ground between different ethnic and religious identities.
>
> (QCA/DfEE, 1998: 17)

The report also refers to a submission made by the Policy Studies Institute that there was a need to formulate an explicit idea of multicultural citizenship, arguing that a plural approach to racial disadvantage requires forms of citizenship which are sensitive to ethnic diversity. The response in the Advisory Group report states:

> Majorities must respect, understand and tolerate minorities and minorities must learn and respect the laws, codes and conventions as much as the majority – not merely because it is useful to do so, but because this process helps foster common citizenship.
>
> (QCA/DfEE, 1998: 17–18)

Citizenship is conceptualized here in terms of conformity to the core values of the 'majority'. A self-evident 'us and them' is assumed, common ground is based on the rules of the 'majority' and there is an implicit view that 'minorities' potentially threaten the rules and security of the 'majority'. The minority groups are thus defined as outsiders, as 'not really belonging, or as marginal to the mainstream of social life' (Mason, 1995: 115). A multicultural conception of citizenship should be based on an understanding of the dynamic and constructed nature both of identity and of culture. However, there is an implicit racism in the essentialist tones adopted in the report.

Citizenship: a contested concept

A key reference point in the citizenship discourse has been Marshall's (1952) conceptualisation of citizenship as being comprised of civil rights, political rights and social rights. The Advisory Group, for example, bases its education framework on these three dimensions, and a number of feminist writers have offered critical analyses of his work. Marshall views the extension of citizenship rights as a process of gradual incorporation of previously excluded groups (working classes, women, immigrant groups) in which citizenship expresses full membership in the national political community (Mason, 1995: 108).

This conception of the citizenship narrative with its emphasis on the progressive rise of democratic institutions, and a seemingly unproblematic extension of rights underpins the work of the Advisory Group, and as Gilbert argues, this perspective has been identified in many studies of educational policy and curriculum (1992: 57). However, elsewhere it is argued that the civil, social and political elements in citizenship have created logical tensions and social conflicts in the concept's application, and that citizenship is in a contradictory relationship with its capitalist context (Barbalet and Turner, in Gilbert, 1992: 56). From these perspectives, the citizenship narrative is, therefore, primarily a story of systematic exclusion, and a 'disconnected series of struggles for rights' contingent upon changing power relations at different times. (Gilbert, 1992: 61; Torres, 1998). Furthermore, it is argued that ethnic minorities and women are still denied full citizenship rights. Thus whilst the concept of citizenship embodies the principle of equality, in practice it entails inclusion and exclusion, and its central motif is not that of universal equality but that of social conflict, and the struggles of marginalized groups for equal rights and recognition.

Mason argues, for example, that the clearly consistent theme in immigration and citizenship legislation in Britain has been a distinction between those who were thought of as 'white' and those who were not, (Mason, 1995) and that in the context of a 'national origin myth' ethnic minorities are marginalized because their difference is defined as a problem, and they are defined as outsiders. The parallel in education is identified by Gillborn who argues in relation to schooling in the UK:

> Through the operation of the hidden curriculum, schools already teach a great deal about the realities of citizenship for black people. . . (such experiences) fundamentally challenge the ideology of a liberal, pluralist democracy which is presented in official guidance about Citizenship education in the UK.
>
> (Gillborn, 1992: 17)

In relation to earlier National Curriculum documentation, for example, Gillborn argues that it ignores the important day-to-day messages that schools transmit concerning the citizenship of their students, that is the degree to which students truly belong and may expect full participation and equal access within education and society. Giroux states that pluralism as a philosophy of equality and justice is a noble political ideal, but warns us that 'when the ideal is not measured against a society that rests on fundamental inequalities it tilts over into empty formalism' (Giroux, 1980: 345).

Giroux's observation neatly highlights the need for debates around education for citizenship to explicitly articulate and engage with the realities of existing inequalities that operate through race, gender, class and disability codes, and to attend to the ways in which education currently addresses and formulates citizenship and cultural diversity in its practice. For whilst schools may not explicitly have educational policies relating to questions of citizenship and diversity, it has been observed that the curriculum of modern mass education has always addressed the issue of citizenship and cultural diversity, and furthermore that 'one of the central functions of institutionalized schooling in the rise of the modern nation state was to erase diversity ... To establish standard forms of official state languages and a homogeneous sense of identity and to inculcate loyalty to the state' (Gellner, in Kalantzis and Cope, 1998: 248).

Citizenship and cultural diversity: some practical implications

Torres (1998) states that questions of citizenship, democracy and multiculturalism are at the heart of discussions world wide on educational reform, and affect most of the decisions we face in dealing with the challenges of contemporary education. Educational researchers and practitioners from diverse backgrounds are converging around the shared belief that 'A rethinking of educational intervention is required to address issues of race, culture and ethnic difference' (Rattansi, 1992: 12).

The questions at the heart of these discussions have far-reaching implications for we know we conceptualize educational responses to the needs of culturally diverse democratic societies:

● Should schools participate in the struggle for cultural justice and civil rights?
● How can education support in children the development of an open sense of identity, in which they embrace rather than suppress difference?
● How can education promote a British sense of identity so that people from different backgrounds can identify with it, contribute to it and be enhanced by it?
● What are the historically concrete and sociological ways that white discourses (and educational practices) are guided by Western philosophies of citizenship, identity, difference and justice? (McLaren, 1997)
● How can white people be made aware of their own cultural identities and values?
● Whose cultural practices, values and beliefs should constitute the official curriculum?

The Advisory Group report claims that the benefit of citizenship education for pupils is an entitlement in schools that will empower them to participate in society effectively as active, informed, critical and responsible citizens (QCA/DfEE, 1998: 9). However, by failing to engage with the type of questions identified above, the group proposes forms of citizenship education which are at best ineffectual in relation to the report's stated aims, and perhaps even counter to the provision of educational entitlements to all pupils. We conclude by highlighting three broad areas in which school responses to citizenship education may be enhanced by taking cultural diversity seriously.

The curriculum

Earlier chapters have discussed in some detail the implications for citizenship education for key areas of the curriculum. At this point we wish simply to reiterate the points made earlier in this chapter concerning genuine curriculum responses to cultural diversity, racism and social injustice.

Introducing cultural diversity to the curriculum will not in itself ensure that pupils develop an understanding of the values that underpin cultural forms or the skills needed to handle the challenge of conflicting values, not only between cultures but also within them. Much of this can occur quite naturally within the day-to-day teaching of the normal curriculum. But the impact of racism, particularly in its hidden and institutional forms, will need to be addressed explicitly at appropriate points. As the research of Gillborn (1995) and Gaine (1998) has shown, while such an approach requires a willingness to rethink some aspects of the curriculum, it can be highly effective. Although produced before the present debate about citizenship education, the Runnymede Trust's (1993) simple checklist of indicators for ensuring good practice in equality assurance across the curriculum provides an appropriate starting point for all heads of departments and subject coordinators. It includes:

- use of all pupils' experiences and heritages;
- exploration of cultural diversity;
- exploration of the global context of the subject;
- recognition of inter-cultural influences;
- recognition of common elements in human experiences;
- challenging bias and stereotypes;
- promotion of democratic and anti-racist skills and attitudes;
- concern for justice and human rights;
- awareness of power relationships and conflicts of interest.

School policy

One of the criticisms directed at early attempts to develop multicultural education in schools was that in focusing on the curriculum it failed to take account of the impact of the values which underpinned the schools response to diversity. Pupils were hearing about the importance of understanding the role of food prohibitions in Religious Education, but little account of such requirements was taken in the provision of school meals. Even where pupils were going beyond this to discuss implications of slavery and racism they did so in a school environment which failed to take seriously the impact of racism and prejudice in its own examination systems or staff appointments. If pupils are to develop skills in understanding models of citizenship which go beyond simply conforming to the ideas of the majority and which take seriously pluralism and the need to identify genuinely shared values, they need to experience this in the policies and the policy making processes of their schools.

The need for participation in policy development, if there is to be ownership by all those affected by the policies, is well documented. Evidence from our study of race relations in secondary schools (Verma, Zec and Skinner, 1992) suggests that school responses to cultural diversity which fail to take account of pupil perspectives easily lead to tension and alienation. One northern school in our study drew half of its pupils from the local Muslim community. Seeking to respond to the Islamic requirement of modesty in dress the school had modified its dress code to allow Muslim girls to wear trousers. But our interviews with non-Muslim girls revealed that this apparently reasonable cultural response had led to widespread resentment of Muslim girls by non-Muslim girls because in the cold northern winter, non-Muslim girls were required to wear skirts while Muslim girls could take full advantage of warm trousers. The problem had arisen in part because the pupils had not been involved in the process of making the policy decision. The school set up a working party of staff, pupils and parents which developed a new dress code that took account of all views.

Oscarsson (1995), speaking of the Swedish situation, concludes that 'if pupils are given the opportunity to practice democracy in school. . . the chance of increasing their positive view of the future is enhanced as is the possibility of their being able to influence future societal development by taking an active part in its democratic processes.' Such involvement can help both pupils and staff to understand more about the problems and possibilities of developing rules and regulations in plural environments. A recent DfEE (1999b) study of multi-ethnic schools concluded that 'an important feature of successful race relations work is a school ethos which is open and vigilant, in which pupils can talk about their concerns and share in the development of strategies for their resolution' but that 'very few schools review their curricular and pastoral strategies to ensure that they are sensitive to the ethnic groups in the student population'.

International links

The concept of citizenship, like that of pluralism, finds no universally accepted definition. If education about citizenship is to be a liberal force for democracy rather than nationalism or even xenophobia, it will need to help pupils to engage with the international debate about what it means to be a citizen. This, as earlier chapters have shown, can be done effectively through the curriculum. It can also be done through whole-school responses. Schools which take seriously the requirement to provide an environment for the social, spiritual and cultural development of children find that links with international programmes provide one such opportunity.

In Britain, The Central Bureau for Educational Visits and Exchanges coordinates several programmes designed to promote international activity and understanding (see http://www.britcoun.org/cbeve/ for more information). The EU Comenius 1 project which seeks to link schools in three or more European countries round a shared project or interest is proving to be an effective way of helping children to engage with internationalism and national identity. A primary school in Bolton embarked on one such project as a result of a visit by a group of Finnish teachers to the school. A long-standing town-twinning link was used to draw in a French school. Through the Comenius programme a project on transport was established in which pupils developed and exchanged materials on aspects of transport in their own district. The learning experience went well beyond increasing knowledge of transport because the commitment of the staff and enthusiasm of the pupils led to a wide ranging discussion and exploration of language, culture and life in the three countries. A classic case of learning more about someone else through working with them rather than looking at them. The Bolton school is now working towards drawing in a fourth school in Kenya, thus introducing a non-European dimension to pupils' experiences.

Such partnerships with schools in developing countries are supported by Education Partners Overseas and the North-South Reciprocal Visits scheme. A link between schools in Mirpur in Pakistan and Oldham (which has strong family links with Mirpur) has not only raised awareness of global issues and developed international curriculum resources, but has also led to the discussions of important values questions such as the education of children who spend time in both countries, a very practical citizenship issue (Central Bureau, 1999a).

The Socrates language programme, Lingua E, is also designed to promote international learning focusing primarily, but not exclusively, on language issues. The evidence from Sunderland schools is that the recent re-introduction of language assistants through the programme has had an important impact on pupils' cultural, social and personal dimensions, as well as the more predictable linguistic ones (Central Bureau, 1999b).

Programmes of school links do not necessarily guarantee meaningful learning. Much can go wrong, not least because of the different educational systems and individuals involved. However, learning what it might mean to be a citizen in such an international context can provide the kind of reflective response most teachers would want from their pupils.

Conclusion

The debate concerning the nature of citizenship in plural societies has only just begun. Education for citizenship cannot ignore this debate. We need to help pupils to engage with it and to explore the creative possibilities which pluralism brings. We also need to recognize the challenges which multiple identities and loyalties bring to simplistic models of citizenship. Not least, pupils need to be aware that any effective and inclusive concept of citizenship must take seriously the impact of inequality, racism and discrimination, not only on the lives of those discriminated against but for all members of society.

14 Beyond the work-related curriculum: citizenship and learning after sixteen

Karen Evans

Introduction

> I believe that citizenship, like anything else, has to be learned. Young people do not become good citizens by accident any more than they become good nurses or good engineers or good bus drivers or computer scientists. My concern is whether we offer enough encouragement to our young people to learn how to be good citizens.
>
> (Rt Hon Bernard Weatherill, Commission on Citizenship, 1990)

Becoming a citizen can be seen as more than a simple matter of acquiring civil status with accompanying rights and obligations. In learning to be citizens, young people need to exercise responsibility and social contribution while having entitlements to support and provisions which enable them to manage their own transitions to adulthood and pursue their own projects. However, learning for citizenship is almost invisible in post-16 education. Why does education for citizenship disappear from the curriculum at the very stage at which young people are becoming able to exercise full citizenship rights? These issues are now beginning to be addressed through the recommendations of the Crick Report (QCA/DfEE, 1998). Now is a very significant time for post-16 educators to engage with these questions and influence the debate.

The discussion of citizenship in post-16 education which follows is in three parts. The first section outlines 'minimal' and 'maximal' versions of citizenship and citizenship education. Are they appropriate to the changing social context and situation of young adults? The second section explores further the social dynamics and social conditions of the time and argues that the workplace as the dominant source of values, standards and the curriculum cannot continue to drive developments in the post-compulsory curriculum. The goals of learning must derive from broader frameworks providing learners with the means and capacities for interpreting and acting in the world as a social whole. The approach that places work at the centre with citizenship as an adjunct is reversed. The final section considers how we can educate people as citizens, with the capacities necessary for work and independent economic contribution to society as a significant component of that process. Salient features of approaches to post-compulsory education and training that would foster maximal versions of citizenship are outlined.

Education for citizenship

I have discussed in previous work (Evans, 1995, 1998) some relationships between the contested concepts of citizenship and competence, and have argued that both have 'minimal' and 'maximal' versions. Education for citizenship in minimal interpretations requires only induction into basic knowledge of institutionalized rules concerning rights and obligations. Maximal interpretations require education that develops critical and reflective abilities, independence of thought on social issues and capacities for active participation in social and political processes. As educators we need to be clear about which version we wish to adopt and that the version chosen is consistent with our wider educational values and vision of what is required for the ethical advancement of society and the state.

The policies of the last two decades in the fields of upper-secondary and higher education have increased steadily the emphasis on the work-related curriculum, with values and standards derived from the Government's interpretation of the needs and practices of employers. In further education too, the Work-Related Non-Advanced Further Education initiatives of the 1980s were carried through into the 1990s in the vocational education and training 'tracks' which the Dearing 1996 Report has sought to strengthen.

Education for citizenship was receiving little serious attention in Britain at the time the Commission on Citizenship was established, with the Rt. Hon. Bernard Weatherill MP, Speaker of the House of Commons as patron in 1988. The Commission (1990) identified a threat to democracy in an increasingly commercial society, where insecurity and sense of isolation and powerlessness become the everyday experience of growing numbers of individuals, and asked whether we are, as a society, creating conditions of the 'mass society of mutually antagonistic individuals, easy prey to despotism'.

The Commission produced what Morrell termed a traditional British analysis of citizenship, following the classic approach of Marshall (1952) based on civil, political and social elements, and emphasizing individual freedom, rights to participate in the exercise of political power and the right to share 'to the full' in the social heritage. Rights and responsibilities were seen as standing 'in their own right' as Morrell puts it, and not necessarily as a quid pro quo arrangement, a deal between the individual and society.

The Commission's work had some influence on the re-emergence of education for citizenship as a cross-curriculum theme in the framing of the National Curriculum. Citizenship was one of five non-mandatory cross-curricular themes identified by the National Curriculum Council, the others being careers education and guidance, economic awareness health education and environmental education. Schools were guided to teach these themes largely through the mandatory core and other foundation subjects. The National Curriculum Council Report (1990) which elaborated this theme emphasized 'increasing diversity, Europeanization, multiculturalism' and put forward a wide range of approaches through which, it states, the foundation can be laid for 'positive, participative citizenship'. As McLaughlin (1992) shows, there are some aspects of the Report that can be read in maximal ways as well as many which lend themselves to minimalist readings. For example, maximal interpretations are suggested by the references to awareness of political structures and processes and 'independence of thought on social and moral issues', based on consideration of questions of diversity, justice and inequality in society.

While no explicit statement is made of underlying values, a clear value position is discernible in the emphasis on duties and responsibilities and on the pluralist conception of society. The latter is reflected in the emphasis on diversity as a source of tensions and the implicit assumption that these tensions can be resolved by consensus around a set of shared values. There is little acknowledgement, for example, of the position that power is contested and that society is made up of competing interest groups with differentials of power and influence operating at all levels. The emphasis is on normative concepts of the 'good citizen' rather than on critical participation in social and political processes. This represents a packaging of social and political values as though they were part of an agreed syllabus for an uncontested subject, despite its apparent breadth and scope.

The Report of the independent National Commission on Education, *'Learning to Succeed'* (1993) adopted a pluralistic model of society combined with treatments of citizenship which are more open to maximal readings, but also failed to acknowledge the contested conceptual frameworks within which notions of citizenship are discussed and operationalized. Crick's 1998 Report of the Advisory Committee on Citizenship places more emphasis on 'dispositions' than its predecessors. Courage to speak out and defend a view, determination to act justly, commitment to equality as well as service, all appear as essential elements to be reached by the end of compulsory schooling. They are linked with critical skills which include the ability to 'recognize manipulation and persuasion' and the ability to '. . . influence social, moral and political challenges and situations' as well as knowledge elements which emphasize concepts of equality alongside diversity, conflict alongside co-operation, fairness and justice alongside freedom and order,' (1998: 44). These all signal a further shift towards maximal approaches.

Morrell, a member of the Speaker's Commission on Citizenship, highlighted the contrast between the way academics philosophize about meanings of citizenship with the apparent unity of views of young people surveyed in an associated study, carried out by Richardson:

> It is unusual to find wide consensus on any issue. Yet in this study, there was one issue which united virtually everyone across the social spectrum. From those who had left school with few qualifications to those in University or beyond, there was a strong call for more teaching of the issues surrounding citizenship in schools. . .
>
> (Morrell 1990: 35)

The Speaker's Commission emphasized that the skills of citizenship need to be learned and that considerations of citizenship should be incorporated in education at all levels, from the earliest years, through further and adult education, and also in professional education and training. The theme of continuity of learning has also been picked up in the 1998 Crick Report, although there is little of substance said about how this is to be achieved.

In practice, citizenship education is little in evidence at any level. While nominally present in the form of a cross-curricular theme associated with the National Curriculum, evidence has shown that, in practice, these themes are 'submerged' within the strongly framed National Curriculum subjects, with very limited opportunities for pupils to relate the themes to their everyday lives:

> Very few pupils had heard of the term 'economic and industrial understanding' or thought they were being taught any. The findings were similar for education for citizenship except in one school which had a specific citizenship module as part of a PSE (Personal and Social Education) module.
>
> (Whitty, Aggleton and Row, 1996: 62)

Even where identifiable forms of citizenship education exist, schooling may, in the assumptions implicit in its structures, be promulgating 'passive knower' models in 'civics education' on the rights and duties of citizenship in a democracy. It may in political and debating societies simply be giving openings for the 'movers and shakers' of academic or social elites to practise their skills in a safe institutional environment. Or it may through Community Service or voluntary activity, be promulgating versions of citizenship which emphasize citizen duties or voluntarism and private contribution, without the concomitant understanding of wider citizen rights, obligations and roles. Education for citizenship may become ineffectively minimalist, or seriously controversial when maximal in approach. The institutional educator committed to maximal versions of citizenship is thus potentially caught in contradictions of a fundamental kind.

For some of those who subscribe to maximal versions of citizenship, education for citizenship is better tackled outside the formal structures of schooling, in non-formal youth or community organisations in which aims, values and structures are more congruent with the processes being learnt? However, does that marginalize citizenship education, open its proponents to accusations of 'indoctrination', and limit exposure to these forms of education to the voluntary users of the organisations in question?

Despite increasing interventions and constraints from Government on its resources and scope of action, in 1990, the Youth Service and its agencies at national level restated its maximal position on citizenship through local and political education in the following 'mission statement' for the Youth Service:

> The intent of the Youth Service is to assist young people to make sense of the personal, social and political issues which affect their lives; to promote young people's self-awareness, self-confidence and competence in relationships; to encourage the making of decisions and choices (for example, education and training); to support the development of independent judgement by young people and their ability to express their opinions and values; and to advocate with and for young people the defence and extension of opportunities and choices available to them.
>
> (National Youth Bureau, 1990: 35)

Citizenship education in this approach must enable young people both to understand the social processes which produce diversity and reproduce inequalities and to see how they can act from the social positions they hold. However, many young people cease their participation in youth organizations by 16 and do not experience the service in the way envisaged (Evans, 1994). For the majority of young people, their understanding of social processes comes through their day-to-day experiences inside, outside, and beyond schooling.

In post-16 education and training, citizenship education *per se* has all but disappeared, since the virtual demise of 'liberal studies' as a self-contained and much criticized curriculum component. The subsequent encouragement of 'balancing studies' of various kinds for those following primarily academic routes may be seen as an attempt to develop learners' ability to inquire within and through a broader set of frameworks and perspectives than previously narrowly specialized programmes allowed or encouraged. Such approaches have been beset with problems of not being taken seriously, often being seen as timetable-fillers by students and some teachers. Through what Dale (1985) terms 'ideological characteristics' of vocationalism, values and priorities of egalitarianism in education in the 1960s and early 1970s have gradually been replaced by the needs of industry, the economy and workforce, encouraging not only increased skills training but attitude changes and status adjustment. These ideological characteristics have been contested and a tendency for gender, race and class-based inequalities to be reinforced by the work-related curriculum has been countered to some degree by other ideological forces and interests which have 'continually reasserted the values of education' (Dale, 1985: 7). Pring (1991) has suggested a return to the industrial spirit of the Victorian era was envisaged, in the 'new vocationalism' initiated in the late 1970s, with increased emphasis on qualities such as 'a sense of individual responsibility' permeating the curriculum. In 1996 proposals for reform of post-16 education have incorporated versions of moral education and citizenship, but only as adjuncts to the main business of educating for work (Dearing, 1996). The Further Education Funding Council (1996) report *Enrichment of the Curriculum* noted that aims and activities loosely associated with 'citizenship' were not well-defined.

New impetus has been given to the promotion of citizenship in the post-16 curriculum through the Advisory Group, in its Final Report (QCA/DfEE, 1998), which states its 'strong support for the continuation of citizenship education as an entitlement for all students involved in post-16 education. (1998: 74). The impetus comes not only from the statement but also from its brevity and form. This is effectively a blank sheet, on which the considerable implications that this statement carries have yet to be written.

The 1999 Report of the National Advisory Group on Personal, Social and Health Education makes a similar statement. It stresses the need to build upon pre-16 school experience, taking into account 'the increasing complexity and flexibility of the world of work and of community activity, and of the range and comprehensiveness of post-16 courses. (DfEE, 1999a: 28). The contradictions in ending citizenship education at 16 when the rights and responsibilities of adult citizenship develop from the age of 18 onwards are also recognized:

> Preparation for citizenship clearly cannot end at age sixteen just as young people begin to have more access to the opportunities, rights and responsibilities of adult citizenship and the world of work. The need for an exploration of the ideas and practices of citizenship is evident whether young people are in education or in work-based training.
>
> (DfEE, 1999a: 27)

Social dynamics, experience and participation

Turning to accounts of the changing nature of work and the effects of social change on participation in the structures of society, what are conditions under which learning for adult life takes place? Which versions of citizenship are required? How can they best be achieved?

In all European countries, young adults are experiencing uncertain status and are dependent upon state and parental support for longer periods than would have been the case a generation ago (Chisholm and Bergeret, 1991). Faced with changing opportunity structures, people have to find their own ways of reconciling personal aspirations with available opportunities and their own values in the domains of education, consumption, politics, work and family life. Achievement and recognition of adult status comes at different times to different spheres of life. They may, for example, be supporting a family while on a grant, or still in training. They may hold responsible positions in work while remaining in their family of origin, still the child in the household but supporting other members financially. In this way individual roles and status become differentiated across the different domains of life and experience, and defining an individual as an adult and citizen may hinge on multiple roles performed. Young adults may be caught in disjunctions and contradictions of policies which do not recognize the interplay of the private and public domains and are based on invalid assumptions about common characteristics and needs of age ranges. To understand transitions to adult, worker and citizen status, we also have to understand the 'private world of family life' (Chisholm and Bergeret, 1991: 69).

Social changes in the inter-related domains of work, education, family and community all affect transition behaviours, which themselves reflect personal identities and aspirations as well as the opportunity structures with which young adults are faced. The social dynamics against which policies and programmes should now be assessed are those of growing individualization of the life course.

In the work arena, transitions to worker status are defined by institutionalized rules concerning recognized qualifications and credentials. These credentials testify to the knowledge, competence and experience of the holder and their acquisition and application depend on the way in which the various credentials and selection systems are negotiated (Ainley, 1994; Raffe, 1991). This in turn is heavily influenced by cultural capital, particularly in respect of access to information, advice, social support and personal networks. Young adults bring different transition behaviours to these situations, and success in negotiating these structures and networks can bring stability or instability to the life course. For those who are unsuccessful in gaining entry to jobs, long term unemployment cuts young adults off from the opportunities of the market, from access to work-based credentialling systems and from the exercise of citizenship in any significant sense (Evans and Heinz, 1994). Even successful entry to the labour market can bring another set of limitations and instabilities. Early work entry can create premature foreclosure of options and stereotyped work identities. In the 1950s workplaces were described in the Crowther Report (Ministry of Education, 1959) as deadening to the minds of young school leavers. Post-Fordist discourses now talk of learning organizations, providing new opportunities for democratic access to knowledge, but for those in the increasing ranks of casualized labour, narrow competences are unlikely to be of any use over time and membership of a casualized pool of labour kept

in on-going insecurity and instability is also unlikely to be able to engage in full participation in society in the sense implied in the maximal definitions of citizenship discussed
earlier.

How have the changing employment situation of the 1980s and 1990s affected young
people's attitudes to work? For some time, there was a version of the 'moral panic' over the
effects of unemployment of young people's motivations to work. The traditional incentives
of 'get good qualifications and get a good job' for the majority of school leavers could not be
invoked by teachers, and fears that a generation would be raised lacking the 'work-ethic'
were pronounced in the early 1980s. In fact, the decline of employment opportunities for
young people 'tightened the bonds' between education and employment in a host of ways.
High levels of work motivation and beliefs in personal responsibility for employment
success were sustained. While motivations can be sustained in education, preparation for
what may be the harsh realities of the labour market requires development of strong learner
identities with an orientation towards lifelong learning and continuous development of
knowledge-based skill.

The expansion of post-compulsory education has produced a new set of structures and
experiences between the end of the compulsory phase of schooling at 16 and first entry to
the labour market, at ages up to the mid-twenties. In England, the approach of 'vocationalism' has been to surround young people with a range of work-related opportunities for
learning relatively early in their educational careers, but the opportunities for progressing
from learning into work are haphazard and risky. There is also a prolonged dependency
associated with extended post-compulsory education, which runs counter to the deeply
embedded cultural values and expectations of a significant proportion of the working class
population, particularly among males. While access to education is a right of social citizenship, in the post-compulsory phase this has become associated with decreased social
citizenship rights in other areas, associated with increased dependency and expectations of
family support.

Families can impede or support the transitions of early adulthood. For many young
adults the experience of physical separation from the family for extended periods may
result in improved understanding and appreciation and is part of the process of negotiating
independence, as Banks *et al* (1992) have shown. For others, escape from the parental home
is seen as the only way to achieve a sense of self and to exercise choices, however restricted
these may in reality be. For some young adults thrown back into involuntary dependence
on family through welfare policies, prospects for achievement of independence and citizenship may be impaired. It can be argued further that it should be a basic social right not to
'have to rely' on their family because alternatives do not exist (Finch, 1995).

In the context of social changes and individualized transitions, the parental role becomes
even more one of support rather than guidance. Few parents have experience of the options
facing their children because of the pace of change in all aspects of work and education. A
'double-bind' occurs because young adults are expected to become emancipated and independent, and one of the roles of the family is to assist in this process. The economic
dimension is important here. When young people have a degree of financial independence,
through an independent source of income, their progress towards emancipation is
enhanced. They become less subject to parental control and more able to exercise rights
both inside and outside the home. Policies have progressively increased financial

dependence of young people on their parents in the 16–18 age range and beyond as access to unemployment benefit has been removed and training rates have assumed parental support. Coles (1996) has argued that the inter-connections between the three main transitions (or 'careers') of the youth phase become significant here, and are:

- education, training and labour market careers (from schooling into post-school education and training and jobs;
- domestic careers (from families of origin to families of destination);
- housing careers (from living dependent on families to living independently of them).

In many of our European counterparts, different cultural norms apply concerning dependency and age of accession to adult status. Young people are not expected to be earning until their twenties, there is not the same pull of the labour market and strong institutional structures allow for a degree of experimentation, false starts, and provide 'safety net' financial support for those for whom family support is not available. The wage packet as a symbol of growing up in Britain does not hold to the same degree in other advanced economies. In the less institutionalized, less supportive British context, young people need help to break out of the vicious circles operating, but the circles themselves need to be tackled.

While participation in work has been a preoccupation for policy makers, learning for citizenship must also relate to the ways in which younger people participate in their communities. As well as being producers at work, they are also consumers and they have a right to participate in the life of their local communities as citizens and voters. Fragmentation and diversification of the opportunity structure are combined with the effects of globalization in which people increasingly become disassociated from their traditional contexts. This means that the search for identity or sense of wholeness and continuity as a person, gains a new intensity (Baethge, 1989). Intergenerational transmission of 'virtues' is reduced, and the channels to participation in political and social structures may become obscured. Engagement in citizenship in its maximal sense is thus made more difficult, and the pursuit of 'ego-driven' projects may become paramount, as young adults act to maximize personal opportunity and reduce risk.

Many of these 'choices' are rooted in partly formed social identities, the sense young people have of who they are and what their capabilities are. Self-definition involves internalizing the definitions and attributes ascribed by others. These subjective identities are associated with social class, gender and ethnicity. They also reflect educational credentials and other mediating factors association with experiences in the labour market and wider social context, with narrowing career options playing a part in shaping identities over time. While the latter are increasing in relative significance as traditional transition patterns become 'fractured' and extended, disadvantage continues to be concentrated in groups defined by class, gender and ethnicity in particular localities, as the 16–19 Initiative demonstrated (Banks *et al,* 1992). Social identities are reflected in social attitudes.

Changes in political involvements between 16 and 20 were incremental, with 'only a tiny minority (developing) any serious involvement in politics of the conventional kind' (Banks *et al,* 1992: 176). Their attitudes were not organized around political positions but around the politics of the personal. Changes in early adult life involved gradual increases in interest in political issues.

The structures for democratic experience exist in many community groups yet youth participation in these, in so far as it is quantified, appears small (Evans, 1987; Evans and Heinz, 1994). Local organizations provide a means by which people engage with public life. Engagement in associations, clubs, councils and other aspects of neighbourhood life featured in the proposals for the Active Society (YSDC, 1969) that aimed to encourage young people's active and critical participation in their communities through the vehicles of Youth and Community education. The approaches of the 'Learning by Participation' projects of the 1980s also aimed to harness both work and wider community experience in helping young people to learn responsibility by experiencing it in authentic settings (Dalin, 1994: 172).

As employment status and consumer power increasingly determines citizen status and rights, there is a fundamental problem of motivation to be addressed in communitarian activities and approaches, if those disadvantaged in and by the operation of labour and consumer markets are to be actively engaged. Many factors can combine to marginalize and exclude young people. As citizenship has become increasingly equated with consumer power, what is the position of young people unable to gain a foothold in work? Unemployment cuts young people off not only from work, but also from exercising consumer power in their leisure time. Adults' monopolies on local politics and democratic structures may also make it difficult for young people to participate and the 16–19 Initiative and the author's Anglo-German Studies found widespread apathy among British youth, with the most politically alienated also likely to be the most politically impotent. However, these studies have also shown keen interest in issues such as equality of opportunity and the environment and particular receptivity to changes in lifestyles and values.

Minimal versions of citizenship and competence are inadequate to deal with the social dynamics of the time, and young people's responses to them, since they neither equip them with the critical skills necessary to engage with an uncertain world nor cultivate the sense of shared autonomy and social being, in the broader context within which individual projects and tasks are pursued. Maximal approaches to the development of citizenship and competence have these processes at their centre. Interventions through education and social support must begin with respect for individual autonomy. Young people's subjective emotional experiences of support and satisfaction, their future perspectives of optimism or pessimism and their feelings of control in relation to norms and external expectations are all significant variables. In maximal approaches, the educator may exercise *influence* through providing information, discussion of courses of action and their possible consequences, and creating conditions for exposure to, and engagement with, different points of view. Through all of these, the educator can create conditions for attitude change, personality development and unfolding of competences. The potential for personal competences to 'unfold' is also affected by particular societal conditions. The interactions which are necessary to develop capacities for social action are thus enhanced or impeded by social structures and the removal or reduction of structural barriers are as important as the facilitation of personal growth.

Thus, person-centred approaches must be combined with altering the material and social environment so that demands do not become so great that young people cannot cope unaided. When demands exceed capacity to cope, social citizenship is eroded and social exclusion results for many. While much emphasis is placed on the obligations and responsibilities of the young, the social rights which provide the material and cultural conditions for social inclusion and participation, must not be lost sight of. These enable the 'social self' to develop.

Each individual needs to be able to balance and manage 'internal and external' realities, that is their felt needs in relation to the environment in which they operate. Where there is a mismatch between felt needs and the opportunities the environment can provide, dissatisfaction results. Expectations may be 'unrealistic' because they stem from self concept and identity formation which is at odds with the environment or they may be unrealistic because the environment is overly constrained or hostile and the expectations could be better met through changes to the environment. Individuals may accommodate or resist aspects of the social world, the structural influences around them. They may do so individually or collectively. Individuals need to be able to regulate their behaviour and expectations in relation to the environment, while maintaining and developing a values base, which gives meaning to goals and actions. They need to become 'productive processors of reality' in Hurrelmann (1988) terms, goal directed in their behaviour, with the capacities to regulate and adjust their actions, achieve and redefine goals and boundaries and to participate in change.

In this sense, they are engaged in the transformation of experience into knowledge and action, the foundations of experiential learning, which emphasizes the process of adaptation and learning rather than content or outcomes. These processes lie at the heart of maximal approaches to learning for competence and citizenship, when set in a modernized framework of material and social support.

Embedding maximal approaches in a wider framework of provision

In Britain, transition structures are weakly institutionalized, and post-compulsory education and training arrangements reflect historically embedded narrowness and divisions, with the 'elite' Advanced level and the narrowly based National Vocational Qualifications exemplifying the academic/vocational divide. The curriculum has been progressively shaped by instrumental values and the presumed needs of employers. In particular, the NVQ system is predicated on minimalist notions of competence based performance, which are of questionable relevance to future skill needs and are outdated quickly. Not only do they fail to develop the broad-based underlying capabilities appropriate to the social dynamics of the time (Skilbeck *et al*, 1986) but they are also highly individualistic, reinforce structural inequalities and run counter to the development of interdependence (Blackman and Evans, 1994). Criticisms of narrowness are offset by posthoc attempts to broaden the curriculum by 'entitlements' and 'transferable skills' which occupy an ambiguous and weak place in the curriculum, and are not comparable in breadth or depth to the 'general education' provided at this stage of education in many European countries.

In England the preferred response to all difficult financial and family situations is to terminate education and seek a job. Young adults are much closer to the labour market than many of their European counterparts, and enter it at least two years earlier, so in many respects the range of work attributes they have acquired in their early careers is wider than in other Northern European countries. While the narrowness of curriculum content for many users of Further Education colleges is a weakness, the *processes* and *climate* of learning in the colleges contribute to the status passage to adulthood, helped by the extended age range involved, 16–25 and beyond. Young people report very positively that they are 'treated as adults'. In allowing and encouraging young people to exercise a reasonable degree of responsibility and self-determination, there is some evidence that the colleges are significantly contributing to the *process* of becoming adult citizens, if failing to provide broad perspectives via the content of the curriculum. (Rudd, 1997).

Some argue that by broadening vocational education, redefining it to incorporate some aspect of 'liberal' education, it becomes preparation for life. This is one way in which instrumental orientations of the work-related curriculum are brought into the wider domains of education for adult life and citizenship. But can the multiple purposes of education be resolved in a simple 'broadening' of work-related studies in this way? The same analysis could be applied to further education in the 1990s, where generic skills and key skills are emphasized and seen as central to this process of 'broadening' work-related education. They are represented as being in the general interest of society yet they are derived from and defined in terms of the needs of employers. In some contexts, generic skills are construed as being superior to knowledge since the skills are as being somehow timeless and independent, while knowledge is seen as provisional and context bound.

Whether context-free transferability is possible, in the way suggested by the proponents of 'key skills', is debatable since the 'freeing' of skills from their contexts can lead to superficiality and detaches 'flexibility' from deeper capability (Barnett, 1994). As propounded, key skills also reflect a restricted set of social values, derived from the needs of employers. Education, as distinct from training, must maintain a degree of independence from any particular dominant set of social values although the prevailing economic conditions will influence those qualities and skills which are emphasized. For this degree of independence, critical skills, and research-mindedness have to be preserved alongside the development of capabilities and competence.

In the approaches based on experiential learning set out above, education is distinct from the experience on which it draws. Multiple purposes are embodied within it without collapsing it into the values of the work or community service experience which it seeks to use as a learning resource. If education is to be tranformative, not reproductive, the role of education at all levels is to develop *educated attributes*. These incorporate core skills, key skills and transferable skills in their various manifestations, but go far beyond these. Key skills may enable us to survive, to stay afloat in the rapids; they do not encourage us to think about the influences we have on our context, individually and collectively. Are we in danger of a new generation engaged in ego-driven projects with no sense of mutual responsibility? Thatcher's children, perhaps, to whom there is no such thing as society. The Speaker's Commission on Citizenship in 1990 concluded that the skills of citizenship need to be learned. The greatest challenge facing us is how to create a society in which all can actively participate, can understand, can influence, can whistle blow, and can work together in pursuit of the common good. What are the real educated attributes in this context? I have argued elsewhere (Evans, 1998) that they are the intellectual and critical skills that go hand in hand with the knowledge society, the information society. They need to be cultivated at all levels, with Higher Education there to secure and promote the highest forms of learning with understanding, critical skills, creativity and, above all, lifelong learning and inquiry centre stage. 'Knowing how' is not the same as 'knowing why' and the social dynamics of the time demand that we know 'why' as well as 'how' , and that we have the values base and dispositions which enable us to act in defence of what we believe to be right. This links with the 'Rubik's Cube' of the Crick Report (QCA/DfEE, 1998).

To develop maximal versions of citizenship and competence in ways which are complementary *does* require at the very least an enlargement of the curriculum, irrespective of the post-16 'track' followed, whether this is academic, applied/vocational or work-based. Silver and Brennan (1988) have argued that the enlarged post-16 curriculum should feature:

- studies selected from several disciplines;
- problem-solving related to real world problems;
- breadth of courses and of outcomes;
- concern with long-term employment needs;
- concern to produce questioning and critical adults;
- an openness to external influences.

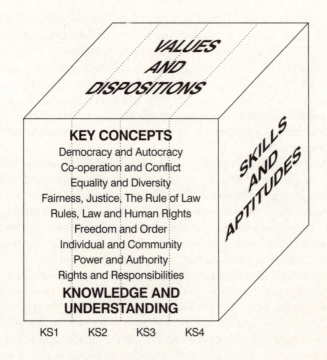

Figure 14.1 'Rubik's Cube' of the Crick Report

Developing competence and citizenship in maximal terms goes beyond this. It means bringing together some of the successful teaching and learning processes developed in English Further Education, coupled with the breadth of curriculum which is the norm in the wider European context. The effective worker with a 'beruf' in Germany, for example, has also to be an educated citizen.

However, achievement of maximal versions of citizenship and competence requires still more than this. It requires approaches to teaching and learning which promote a sense of social being and shared autonomy in decision-making and arriving at judgements. There is also a need to move beyond enlargement of the curriculum to strategies for inclusion of groups at risk of social exclusion. Support services are required which encourage pro-active rather than passive transition behaviours and are made available in ways which are less dependent on the cultural capital of users. A redistributive approach to social and financial support provides targeted support where it is needed, to optimize individual or group life chances to negotiate transition structures successfully.

Interventions should draw on support both inside and beyond the walls of educational institutions, involving a range of providers in concerted strategies which can extend individual capacities while adapting the more hostile features of the environment which can defeat and ultimately exclude. Thus, measures must aim to:

- *encourage active transition behaviours* by developing problem-solving behaviours, 'action competences' and encourage self-managed learning;
- *make the social/material environment less hostile to those most at risk of exclusion through*:
  - social support;
  - targeted help and guidance;
  - financial support and entitlements for study;
  - access to affordable housing.

In the move from *enlargement* to *inclusion,* and from *key skills* to *educated attributes* the workplace cannot be the 'ultimate curriculum authority' and neither can the 'academy'.

The curriculum must relate, at any age or stage, to a framework for interpreting the world as a 'social whole', to use Sedunary's (1996) expression, while understanding the sources of diversity and differentiation within it. In conjunction with this, inclusive policies, strategies and forms of educational support are needed which value and recognize the capabilities of all, policies which recognize diversity and move away from assumptions about the condition of the age group as a whole. The idea that a curriculum based on bundles of core and technical skills combined with action planning will equip young people to be the active and effective citizens of the future is wholly inadequate. The current debates provide post-16 educators to exercise active citizenship in influencing the direction of thinking and planning. Policies need to be based on more holistic analyses of social dynamics and an understanding of ways in which experiences in early adulthood can give stability or instability to the life course. Effective education for the future depends on the extent of free and equal access and the 'redistributive' mechanisms for resources and social support; the ways in which provision is linked structurally and methodologically, and relates to the life course; the ways in which education links and draws upon different

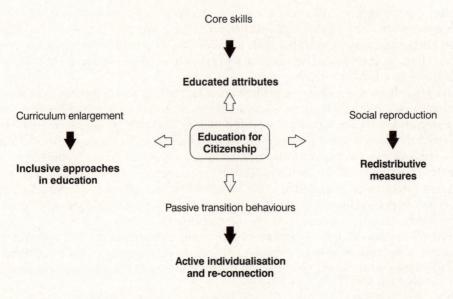

Figure 14.2

domains of experience in work, community and family. Moreover, future oriented, maximal versions of education for citizenship derive their values from what is required for the ethical advancement of society and the state, and it is these, beyond and above the values of the workplace and the immediate requirement for material economic progress, which shape effective learning for citizenship at all levels.

References

Abbs, P (1982) *English within the Arts: A radical alternative for English and the Arts in the curriculum,* Hodder & Stoughton, London

Ainley, P (1994) *Class and Skill,* Cassell, London

Allen, F (1988) *Language and the Learning of Mathematics,* speech to NCTM Annual Meeting.

Almond, L (2000) Physical Education and Primary Schools, in *Teaching Physical Education 5–11,* ed R P Bailey and T M Macfadyen, Cassell, London

Arnheim, R (1966) *Towards a Psychology of Art,* Faber and Faber, London

Arnheim, R (1970) *Visual Thinking,* Faber and Faber, London

Arnold, P J (1984) *Meaning in Movement, Sport and Physical Education,* Heinemann, London

Arnot, M (1997) Gendered citizenry: new feminist perspectives on education and citizenship, *British Educational Research Journal* **23**, pp 275–295

Arthur, J and Bailey, R P (1999) *Schools and Community: The communitarian agenda in education,* Falmer Press, London

Arthur, J and Bailey, R P (2000) *Schools and Community: The communitarian agenda in education,* Falmer Press, London

Aspin, D (1975) Games, winning and education – some further comments, *Cambridge Journal of Education,* **5** (1), pp 51–61

Augustine, (1982) De Genesi ad Litteram, *Ancient Christian Writers,* **41,** ed and tr J H Taylor, Newman, London

Augustine, (1998) *De Civitate Dei,* ed and tr R W Dyson, Cambridge University Press, Cambridge

Babila-Njingum, J (1995) *Perceptions of First Cycle Secondary School Mathematics in Anglophone – Cameroon and the Potential for Change,* Unpublished PhD Thesis, The University of Reading

Baethge, M (1989) Individualisation as hope or disaster, in *The Social World of Adolescents,* ed K Hurrelmann and U Engel, de Gruyter, Berlin

Baldwin, G (1996) Modern spirituality, moral education and the history curriculum, in *Education, Spirituality and the Whole Child,* ed R Best, Cassell, London

Banks, M, Bates, I, Breakwell, G, Bynner, J, Emler, N, Jamieson, L and Roberts, K (1992) *Careers and Identities,* Open University Press, Milton Keynes

Barbalet, J M (1988) *Citizenship,* Open University Press, Milton Keynes

Barnett, R (1994) *The Limits of Competence,* Open University Press/Society for Research in Higher Education, Milton Keynes

Barr, D and McGhie, M (1995) Values in education: the importance of the preposition *Curriculum,* **16** (2), pp 102–08

Batho, G (1990) The History of the teaching of citizenship in English schools, *The Curriculum Journal,* **1** (1), pp 91–100

Beattie, A (1987) *History in Peril: May Parents Preserve It*, Centre for Policy Studies, London

Beck, J (1996) Citizenship education: problems and possibilities, *Curriculum Studies* **4** (3), pp 349–66

Beck, J (1999) Spiritual and moral development and religious education, in *Spirituality and the Curriculum*, ed A Thatcher, Cassell, London

BECTa (1999) *Superhighways Safety: Children's Safe Use of the Internet*, Department for Education and Employment, Sudbury

Beiner, R (1983) *Political Judgement*, Methuen, London

Bentley, T (1998) *Learning Beyond the Classroom: Education for a Changing World*, Routledge, London

Best, D (1992) *The Rationality of Feeling: Understanding the Arts in Education*, Falmer Press, London

Best, R (1996) *Education, Spirituality and the Whole Child*, Cassell, London.

Binch, N (1994) The implication of the National Curriculum orders for Art for GCSE and beyond, *Journal of Art and Design Education* **13** (2), pp 117–32

Blackman, S J and Evans, K (1994) Comparative skill acquisition in Germany and England, *Youth and Policy*, **43**, pp 1–23

Blunkett, D (1998) Foreword to *The Learning Age:* http://lifelong.co.uk.greenpaper./index.html.

Board of Education (1905) *Handbook of Suggestions for the Consideration of Teachers and Others Concerned in the Work of Public Elementary Schools*

Bottery, M (1988) Education, objectivity, and tolerance, *Westminster Studies in Education*, **11**, pp 69–80

Bottery, M (1990) *The Morality of the School,* Cassell, London

Bottoms, J (1999) Familiar Shakespeare, in *Where Texts and Children Meet,* ed E Bearne and V Watson, Routledge, London

Bowles, S and Gintis H (1998) The correspondence principle, in *Bowles and Gintis Revisited: Correspondence and Contradiction in Educational Theory,* ed M Cole, Falmer Press, London

Braude, S E (1986) *The Limits of Influence: Psychokinesis and the Philosophy of Science,* Routledge and Kegan Paul, New York

Brighouse, T (1996) The need to go beyond the National Curriculum, *Royal Society of Arts Journal,* CXLIV, June

Brindley, S (1994) *Teaching English,* Routledge/The Open University Press, London

British Humanist Association (1993) *The Human Spirit,* British Humanist Association, London

Broudy, H S (1987) *The Role of Imagery in Learning,* Getty Centre for Education in the Arts, Los Angeles CA

Browne, N (1999) *Young Children's Literacy Development and the Role of Televisual Texts,* Falmer Press, London

Bullock, A (Chair) (1975) *A Language for Life,* HMSO, London

Calouste Gulbenkian Foundation (1982) *The Arts in Schools: Principles, Practice and Provision,* Calouste Gulbenkian Foundation, London

Carr, E H (1963) *What is History?* Penguin, Harmondsworth

Catling, S (1992) The Future of Primary Geography, in *Geography and Education: National and International Perspectives* ed M Naish, Institute of Education, London

Central Bureau (1999a) Case Study: Oldham/Mirpur LEA Link, *Education Partners Overseas Bulletin* (British Council) May

Central Bureau (1999b) Language Assistants, *Central Bureau News* (British Council), Summer

Chisholm, L and Bergeret, J M (1991) *Young People in the European Community: Towards an Agenda for Research and Policy*, EC Commission on Citizenship, Task Force Human Resources, Youth, Training and Education, Brussels

Claire, H (1996) *Reclaiming Our Pasts: Equality and Diversity in the Primary Curriculum*, Trentham, Stoke

Clark, J (1996) Curriculum, Culture and Society in SCAA, Conference Report

Clarke, J and Newman J (1996) *The Managerial State,* Sage, London

Claxton, G (1999) *Wise Up: the Challenge of Lifelong Learning,* Bloomsbury, London

Clay, G, Hertrich, J, Jones, P, Mills, J and Rose, J (1998) *The Arts Inspected: Good Teaching in Art, Dance, Drama, Music,* OFSTED/Heinemann Educational, Oxford

Clay, J, Cole, M and Hill, D (1990) 'The citizen as 'individual' and 'nationalist' or 'social' and 'internationalist'? What is the role of education?' *Critical Social Policy,* **30** Winter

Coles, R (1996) *Vulnerable Groups and Social Exclusion Paper* presented at Conference on British Youth Research: A New Agenda, University of Glasgow, 26–28 January

Commission on Citizenship (1990) *Encouraging Citizenship,* HMSO, London

Cooper, M, Burman, E, Ling, L, Razdevsek-Pucko and Stephenson, J (1998) Practical strategies in values education, in *Values in Education,* ed J Stephenson, L Ling, E Burman and M Cooper, Routledge, London

Copeland, T (1998) Constructing history: all our yesterdays, in *Teaching the Primary Curriculum for Constructive Learning,* ed M Littledyke and L Huxford, Falmer Press, London

Crewe, I, Gosschalk, B and Bartle, J (1998*) Political Communications: Why Labour Won the General Election of 1997,* Frank Cass, London

Dahrendorf, R (1994) The changing quality of citizenship, in *The Condition of Citizenship,* ed B van Steenbergen, Sage, London

Dale, R (1985) *Education, Training, and Employment: Towards a new vocationalism?* Pergamon, Oxford.

Dale, R *et al* (1990) *The TVEI Story: Policy, Practice and Preparation for the Workforce,* Open University Press, Milton Keynes

Dalin, P (1994) Learning by participation, in *Learning from Work and Community Experience,* ed H Chisnall, NFER-Nelson, Slough

Dearing, R (1996) *Review of Qualifications 16–19 year olds,* HMSO, London

DES (1977) *The Curriculum 11–16,* HMSO, London

DES (1985) *Education for All: The Report of the Committee of Inquiry into the Education of Children from Ethnic Minority Groups (The Swann Report),* HMSO, London

DES (1988) *History from 5–16,* HMSO, London

DES (1991) *The National Curriculum: History,* HMSO, London

Department of Education (DfE) (1995) *Key Stages 1 and 2 of the National Curriculum,* HMSO, London

Department of Education and Employment (DfEE) (1995) *The National Curriculum,* HMSO, London

DfEE (1998) *Teaching: High Status, High Standards* (Circular 4/98), DfEE, London

DfEE (1999a) *Preparing Young People for Adult Life: A Report by the National Advisory Group on Personal, Social and Health Education,* DfEE, London

DfEE (1999b) *Raising the Attainment of Minority Pupils,* London, DfEE

DfEE/QCA (1999a) *Citizenship (National Curriculum for England),* Stationary Office, London

DfEE/QCA (1999b) *Art and Design (National Curriculum for England),* Stationary Office, London

DfEE/QCA (1999c) *Music (National Curriculum for England),* Stationary Office, London

DNH (1995) *Sport: Raising the Game,* Department for National Heritage, London

Deuchar, S (1989) *The New History: A Critique,* Campaign for Real Education,York

Dewey, J (1900) *The School and Society* (1915 edn), University of Chicago Press, Chicago

Dewey, J (1961) *Democracy and Education,* Macmillan, London

Earl, M (1999) Narrative and the development of values, in *Use of Language Across the Secondary Curriculum,* ed E Bearne, Routledge, London

Edwards, J and Fogelman, K (1991) Active Citizenship and Young People, in *Citizenship in Schools,* ed K Fogelman, Fulton, London

Eisner, E (1985) *The Educational Imagination,* Collier Macmillan, London

Eisner, E (1998) Does experience in the Arts boost academic achievement? *Journal of Art and Design Education,* **17** (1), pp 51–60

Ernest, P (1991) *The Philosophy of Mathematics Education,* Falmer Press, London

Etzioni, A (1993) *The Spirit of Community – Rights, Responsibilities and the Communitarian Agenda,* Fontana, London

Evans, C (1979) *The Mighty Micro: the Impact of the Computer Revolution,* Victor Gollancz, London

REFERENCES

Evans, J and Penney, D (1995) Physical Education, restoration and then politics of sport, *Curriculum Studies*, **3** (2), pp 183–96

Evans, K (1987) Participation of Young Adults in Youth Organisations in the United Kingdom, in *International Journal of Adolescence and Youth*, **1** (1), pp 7–37

Evans, K (1994) Patterns of leisure activity and the role of the youth service, *International Journal of Adolescence and Youth* **4** (4), pp 179–95

Evans, K (1995) Competence and Citizenship: towards a complementary model for times of critical social change, *British Journal of Education and Work*, **8** (2), pp 14–27

Evans, K (1998) *Shaping Futures: Learning for competence and citizenship*, Ashgate, Aldershot

Evans, K and Heinz, W (1994) *Becoming Adults in England and Germany*, Anglo-German Foundation, London/Bonn

Fien, J and Slater, F (1991) Four strategies for values education in Geography *Geographical Education*, **4**, pp 39–52

Finch, J (1995) Family responsibilities and rights, in *Citizenship Today: the Contemporary Relevance of T H Marshal,* ed M Bulmer, UCL Press, London

Finney, J and Hendy, L (1990) *The Development of Effective Communication Through the Performing Arts*, Syndicate Report **1**, Faculty of Education and Community Studies, University of Reading

Fogelman, K (1991) Citizenship in secondary schools: the national picture, in *Citizenship in Schools,* Fulton, London

Fountain, S (1994) *Education for Development. Resource for Global Learning,* Hodder & Stoughton, London

Fox, C, A study of children's literature of war and peace, *Reading* **33** (3)

Foxley, B (1974) *Jean-Jacques Rousseau: Emile*, Dent, London

Frazer, N and Gordon, L (1994) Civil citizenship against social citizenship? On the ideology of contract versus charity, in *The Condition of Citizenship,* ed B van Steenbergen, Sage, London

Freudenthal H (1991) *Revising Mathematics Education*, Kluwer, Dordrecht

Fukuyama, F (1992) *The End of History and the Last Man,* Penguin, London

Gaine, C (1987) *No Problem Here*, Hutchinson, London

Gaine, C (1998) *Still No Problem Here*, Trentham Books, Chester

Gamble, A (1988) *The Free Economy and the Strong State: The Politics of Thatcherism,* Macmillan, London

Gardner, H (1999) *The Disciplined Mind*, Simon & Schuster, New York

Gasking, D (1960) Mathematics and the world, in *The World of Mathematics Vol III*, ed J R. Newman, George Allen and Unwin, London

Gatto, J T (1992) *Dumbing Us Down: The Hidden Curriculum of Compulsory Schooling,* New Society Publishers, Philadelphia, PN

Giddens, A (1994) *Beyond Left and Right: The Future of Radical Politics,* Polity Press, Cambridge

Gilbert, R (1992) Citizenship, education and postmodernity, *British Journal of Society in Education* **13** (1), pp 51–68

Gillborn, D (1995) *Racism in Real Schools*, Open University Press, Milton Keynes

Giroux, H (1980) Critical Theory and Rationality in Citizenship Education, *Curriculum Inquiry* **10** (4), pp 329–66

Giroux, H (1983) *Theory and Resistance in Education: A Pedagogy for the Opposition,* Heinemann, London

Gouk, P (1988) The harmonic roots of Newtonian science, in *Let Newton Be!* ed J Fauvel, R Flood, M Shortland and R Wilson, Oxford University Press, Oxford

Gould, C (1988) *Rethinking Democracy: Freedom and Social Co-operation in Politics, Economy and Society,* Cambridge University Press, Cambridge

Graham, A and Ballin, A (1999) *Writing our Past,* Birmingham: Development Education Centre (available from the Development Education Centre, 998 Bristol Road, Selly Oak, Birmingham B29 6LE)

Green, A (1997) *Education, Globalisation and the Nation State,* Macmillan, London

Griffith, R (1998) Educational Citizenship and Independent Learning, *Jessica Kingsley, London*

Guthrie, W K C (1956) *Plato's Protagoras and Meno,* Penguin, Harmondsworth

Habermas, J (1994) Citizenship and national identity, in *The Condition of England,* ed B Steenbergen, Sage Publications Ltd

Hahn, C L (1999) Citizenship education: an empirical study of policy, practices and outcomes, *Oxford Review of Education,* **25** (1 & 2), pp 231–50

Halstead, J M (1996) Values and values education in schools, in *Values in Education and Education in Values,* J M Halstead and M J Taylor, Falmer Press, London

Hart, R (1992) *Children's Participation: From Tokenism to Citizenship*, UNICEF, Florence

Heater, D (1990) *Citizenship: The Civic Ideal in World History, Politics and Education,* Longman, London

Hellison, D R and Templin, T J (1991) *A Reflective Approach to Teaching Physical Education,* Human Kinetics, Champaign, IL

Hersh, R, Miller, J, and Fielding, G (1980) *Models of Moral Education*, Longman, New York

Hicks, D (1995) Citizenship for today and tomorrow, in *Adding Value? Schools' Responsibility for Pupils' Personal Development,* ed S Inman, & M Buck, Trentham, Stoke

Hill, D (1989) *Charge of the Light Brigade: The Radical Right's Attack on Teacher Education,* Hillcole Group, Brighton

Hillgate Group (1986) *Whose Schools? A Radical Manifesto,* Sherwood, London

Hirst P H (1974) *Knowledge and the Curriculum*, Routledge and Kegan Paul, London

Hughes, A (1997) The evisceration of Art education? *Journal of Art and Design Education* **16** (2), pp 117–26

Hurrelmann, K (1988) *Social Structure and Personality Development*, Cambridge University Press, Cambridge

Israely, Y (1985) The moral development of mentally retarded children: review of the literature, *Journal of Moral Education,* **14** (1), pp 33–42

Jackson, R (1997) *Religious Education: An Interpretive Approach,* Hodder & Stoughton, London

Jarvis, H and Midwinter C (1999) *Talking Rights; Taking Responsibility,* Manchester Development Education Project and the UK Committee for UNICEF, Manchester

Jones, C (1999) Warfare, state identity and education in europe, *European Journal of Intercultural Studies,* **10** (1)

Jones, K (1999) *English and the National Curriculum: Cox's Revolution?* Kogan Page, London

Jowell, R, Curtice, J, Park, A, Brook, L and Thomson, K (1996) *British Social Attitudes: the 13th Report,* SCPR, Aldershot

Kalantzis, M and Cope, B (1999) Multicultural education: transforming the mainstream, in *Critical Multiculturalism – Rethinking Multicultural and Anti-racist Education,* ed S May, Falmer Press, London

Kempe, A (1980*) The Cross-curricular Uses of Drama and Theatre in Education,* Report on behalf of the syndicate, Faculty of Education and Community Studies, University of Reading

Kennedy, M (1995) Issues based work at Key Stage Four: Crofton School – a case study, *Journal of Art and Design Education,* **14** (1), pp 7–20

Kerr, D (1996) *Citizenship Education in Primary Schools,* Leicester University, Leicester

Kershensteiner G (1911) *German Youth and Education for Citizenship*, 5th edn, Villaret

Kidder, R (1995) *How Good People Make Tough Choices: Resolving the Dilemma of Ethical Living,* William and Morrow, New York

Kilpatrick, W (1992*) Why Johnny Can't Tell Right from Wrong?* Simon and Schuster, York

Kirp, D (1979) *Doing Good by Doing Little – Race and Schooling in Britain*, Cambridge University Press, Cambridge

Kline, M (1991) *World Treasury of Physics, Astronomy and Mathematics,* ed T Ferris, Little, Brown and Co, Boston

Knight, P (1987) Historical values, *Journal of Moral Educatio*n, **16** (1), pp 46–53

REFERENCES

Kohlberg, L (1981) *The Philosophy of Moral Development*, Harper and Row, San Francisco

Kress, G (1995) *Writing the Future: English and the Making of a Culture of Innovation*, National Association for the Teaching of English, Sheffield

Kymlicka, W (1991) *Liberalism, Community and Culture*, Clarendon Press, Oxford

Lawton, D (1995) The Dearing Reports, *Education Today and Tomorrow*, **47** (1), pp 8–9

Lee, H D P tr (1955) *Plato – The Republic*, Penguin, Harmondsworth

Lee, P (1993) in P Lee, J Slater, P Walsh, and J White *The Aims of School History: The National Curriculum and Beyond*, Institute of Education, London

Leonard, G B (1972) *The Transformation: A Guide to the Inevitable Changes in Humankind*, Delacorte Press, New York

Lickona, T (1991) *Educating for Character*, Bantam, New York

Loukes, H (1961) *Teenage Religion*, SCM Press, London

Lynch, J (1992) *Education for Citizenship in a Multicultural Society*, Cassell, London

Macfadyen, T M (2000) Using teaching styles for effective teaching, in *Teaching Physical Education 5–11*, ed R P Bailey and T M Macfadyen, Cassell, London

MacIntosh, P (1957) Games and gymnastics for two nations in one, in *Landmarks in the History of Physical Education*, ed J Dixon, P McIntosh, A Munrow and R Willetts, Routledge and Kegan Paul, London

MacIntyre, A (1982) *After Virtue*, Duckworth, London

Macpherson, W (1999) *The Stephen Lawrence Inquiry: Report of an Inquiry by Sir William Macpherson of Cluny*, The Stationery Office, London

Mangan, J A (1981) *Athleticism in the Victorian and Edwardian Public school*, Cambridge University Press, Cambridge

Manser, S J with Wilmot, H (1995) *Artists in Residence. A Teachers' Handbook*, London Arts Board, London

Marshall, T H (1952) *Citizenship and Social Class*, Cambridge University Press, Cambridge

Marum, E (1996) *Children's Books in the Modern World*, Falmer Press, London

Marx, K (1975) On the Jewish Question, in *Early Writings*, Penguin, Harmondsworth

Mason, D (1995) *Ethnicity and Race in Modern Britain*, Oxford University Press, Oxford

Massey, D (1991) A global sense of place, *Marxism Today*, pp 24–29

Mathematically Correct (1998) *Towards a Cease-Fire in the Math War*, http://mathematically correct.com/cease.htm (as at 3/04/98)

Mathematically Correct (2000) http://mathematicallycorrect.com/lincoln.htm (as at 10/01/00)

Mathieson, M (1975) *The Preachers of Culture*, George, Allen and Unwin, London

McLaren, P (1997) Decentering whiteness: in search of a revolutionary multiculturalism, *Multicultural Education* **5** (2), pp 4–11

McPhail, P (1982) *Social and Moral Education*, Basil Blackwell, Oxford

Meakin, D (1981) Physical Education: an agency for moral education? *Journal of Philosophy of Education*, **15** (2), pp 241–54

Meakin, D (1982) Moral values and Physical Education, *Physical Education Review*, **5** (1), pp 62–82

Mercer, N, Wegerif, R and Dawes, L (1999) Children's talk and the development of reasoning in the classroom, *British Education Research Journal* **25** (1), pp 95–111

Mills, C W (1970) *The Sociological Imagination*, Penguin, Harmondsworth

Ministry of Education (1959) *15–18 (Crowther Report)*, HMSO, London

National Advisory Committee on Creative and Cultural Education (1999) *All Our Futures: Creativity, Culture and Education*, DfEE, London

National Commission on Education (1993) *Learning to Succeed*, Paul Hamlyn, London

National Curriculum Council (NCC) (1990) *Education for Citizenship, Curriculum Guidance 8*, National Curriculum Council, York

NCC (1993) *Spiritual and Moral Development – A Discussion Paper*, National Curriculum Council, York

NCC (1990a) *Curriculum Guidance 3: The Whole Curriculum,* National Curriculum Council, York

NCC (1990b) *Curriculum Guidance 8: Education for Citizenship,* National Curriculum Council, York

National Youth Bureau (1990) *Danger or Opportunity?* NYB, Leicester

Newbolt, H (Chair) (1921) *The Teaching of English in England,* HMSO, London

Newsom, J (Chair) (1963) *Half Our Future,* HMSO, London

Nucci, L (1989) *Moral Development and Character Education: A Dialogue,* McCutchan, Berkeley, CA

Nuffield Foundation (1998) *Beyond 2000: Science Education for the Future,* the report of a seminar series

Nye, R (1996) Childhood spirituality and contemporary developmental psychology, in *Education, Spirituality and the Whole Child,* ed R Best, Cassell, London

O'Brien, J (1996) *Secondary School Pupils and the Arts, Report of a MORI Research Study,* ACE Research Report **5**, Arts Council of England, London

Office for Standards in Education (OFSTED) (1992) *Handbook for the Inspection of Schools, HMSO,* London

OFSTED (1994) *Spiritual, Moral, Social and Cultural Development: An OFSTED Discussion Paper,* Office for Standards in Education, London

OPCS (1994) *Country of Birth and Ethnic Group,* HMSO, London

Ormell, C P (1980) Mathematics, in *Values and Evaluation in Education*, ed R Straughan and J Wrigley, Harper and Row, London

Oscarsson, V (1995) Pupils' views of the future, in *Teaching for Citizenship in Europe,* ed A Osler, H Rathenow and H Starkey, Trentham, Chester

Osler, A and Starkey, H (1999) Rights, identities, and inclusion: European action programmes as political education, *Oxford Review of Education, 25* (1 & 2), pp 199–216

Oxfam (1997) *A Curriculum for Global Citizenship,* Oxfam, London

Pankhania, J (1994) *Liberating the National History Curriculum*, Falmer Press, London

Perry, L (1973) Education in the Arts, in *The Study of Education and Art*, ed D Field and J Newick, Routledge and Kegan Paul, London

Perry, M (1984) *Psychic Studies: A Christian's View*, Aquarian Press, Wellingborough

Peters, R S (1966) *Ethics and Education,* George Allen and Unwin, London

Phillips, M (1998) Curriculum, culture and society, in *SCAA, Curriculum, Culture and Society Conference Report*, SCAA, London

Phillips, R (1996) *History Teaching, Nationhood and the State,* Cassell, London

Popper, K (1945) *The Open Society and its Enemies*, Routledge and Kegan Paul, London

Pring, R (1991) The curriculum and the new vocationalism, in *Education, Training and Employment Vol 2: The Educational Response,* ed G Esland, Addison-Wesley/Open University, Wokingham

Qualifications and Curriculum Authority (QCA) (1999a) *The Review of the National Curriculum in England – The Consultation Materials*, QCA, London

QCA (1999b) *The Review of the National Curriculum in England, the Secretary of State's Proposals,* QCA, London

QCA (2000) *The National Curriculum for England,* QCA, London

QCA/DfEE (1998) *Education for Citizenship and the Teaching of Democracy in Schools,* QCA, London

QCA (1997) *The Promotion of Pupils' Spiritual, Moral, Social and Cultural Development: Draft Guidance for Pilot Work,* QCA, London

Raffe, D (1991) Beyond the mixed model, in *Social Research and Social Reform,* ed C Crouch and A Heath, Oxford University Press, Oxford

Ramsey, A E (1999) Poor in spirit? The child's world, the curriculum and 'spirituality', in *Spirituality and the Curriculum,* ed A Thatcher, Cassell, London

Randles, J and Hough, P (1998) *The Afterlife,* Piatkus, London

Raths, L, Harmin, M, and Simon, S (1966) *Values and Teaching: Working with Values in the Classroom,* Charles Merrill, Columbus, OH

Rattansi, A (1992) Changing the subject? in *Race, Culture and Difference*, ed J Donald and A Rattansi, Open University Press, Milton Keynes

Read, G, Rudge, J and Howarth, R B (1986) *How do I teach RE? The Westhill Project RE 5–16,* Mary Glasgow, London

Reich, B and Adcock, C (1976) *Values, Attitudes and Behaviour Change*, Methuen, London

Richards, I A (1960) *Principles of Literary Criticism,* Routledge, London

Robinson, J (1963) *Honest to God*, SCM Press, London

Robinson, J (1964) *Christian Morals Today, SCM* Press, London

Rogers, P (1987) *History: Why, What and How?* Historical Association, London

Rogers, R (1995) *Guaranteeing an Entitlement to the Arts in Schools,* Royal Society of Arts, London

Romance, T J, Weiss, M R and Bockoven, J (1986) A program to promote moral development through elementary school physical education, *Journal of Teaching in Physical Education*, **5**, pp 126–36

Ross, M (1995) National Curriculum Art and Music, *Journal of Art and Design Education*, **14** (3), pp 271–76

Rudd, P (1987) *Structure and Agency in Youth Transitions: Student perspectives on vocational further education*, PhD thesis, University of Surrey, Guildford

Runnymede Trust (1993) *Equality Assurance in Schools*, Trentham, Stoke

Sagan, C (1996) *The Demon-haunted World: Science as a Candle in the Dark,* Headline, London

Sanger, J with Willson, J, Davies, B and Whittaker, R (1997) *Young Children, Videos and Computer Games: Issues for Teachers and Parents,* Falmer Press, London

Sarland, C (1996) The revenge of the teenage horrors, in *Voices Off: Texts, Contexts and Readers,* ed M Styles, E Bearne and V Watson, Cassell, London

Scholes, R (1985) *Textual Power: Literary Theory and the Teaching of English,* Yale University Press, New Haven

Schools' Curriculum Assessment Authority (SCAA) (1994) *Model Syllabuses for Religious Education: Model 1: Living Faiths Today,* SCAA, London

SCAA (1996a) *Recent Research on the Achievement of Ethnic Minority Pupils*, HMSO, London

SCAA (1996b) *The National Forum for Values Education and the Community: Consultation on Values in Education and the Community*, SCAA, London

Schon D (1983) *The Reflective Practitioner: How Professionals Think in Action*, Ashgate, Aldershot

Scruton, R (1986) The myth of cultural relativism in *Anti-Racism: An Assault on Education*, ed R Balmer, Sherwood Press, London

Secondary Heads Association (SHA) (1995) *Whither the Arts? The State of the Expressive Arts in Secondary Schools,* Secondary Heads Association, London

Sedunary, E (1996) Neither new nor alien to progressive thinking: interpreting the convergence of radical education and the new vocationalism in Australia, *Journal of Curriculum Studies*, **28** (4), pp 369–96

Selbourne, D (1994) *The Principle of Duty*, Sinclair-Stevenson, London

Sewell, B (1981) *The Use of Mathematics in Adults in Daily Life*, Advisory Council for Adult and Continuing Education, Leicester

Sharp, C and Dust, K (1990) *Artists in Schools: A Handbook for Artists and Teachers,* Bedford Square Press, London

Sherwood, M (1996) Sins of omission and commission: history in English schools and the struggle for change, *Multicultural Teaching,* **16** (2), pp 14–22

Shields, D L L and Bredemeier, B J L (1995) *Character Development and Physical Education,* Human Kinetics, Champaign, IL

Silver, H and Brennan, J (1988) *A Liberal Vocationalism*, Methuen, London

Skilbeck, M, Tait, K, Lowe, M (1986) *A Question of Quality*, Institute of Education, London

Skinner, G D (1990) Religion, culture and education, in *Race Relations and Urban Education*, ed P D Pumfrey and G K Verma, Falmer Press, London

Skinner, G D (1995) *Primary Schools with All Pupils from Asian Backgrounds: Research Report to the Leverhulme Trust,* Centre for Ethnic Studies in Education, University of Manchester, Manchester

Slater, F (1992) To travel with a different view, in *Geography and Education: National and International Perspectives*, ed M Naish, Institute of Education, London

Slater, F (1994) Education through Geography: knowledge, understanding, values and culture, *Geography* **79**, pp 147–63

Slater, J (1993) in P Lee, J Slater, P Walsh, and J White (1993) *The Aims of School History: The National Curriculum and Beyond*, Institute of Education, London

Smith, I F (1980) Art, in *Values and Evaluation in Education,* ed R Straughan and J Wrigley, Harper Row, London

Smith, I F (1983) Preparing for examination in Art, *Educational Analysis*, **5** (2), pp 77–87

Smith, I F (1990) *Curriculum Development in Art and Design in the context of TVEI,* Syndicate report no 8, Faculty of Education and Community Studies, University of Reading

Staines, R (1999) Transfer revisited: re-evaluating the non-musical potential of learning and listening to music. An overview of selected literature, *British Journal of Music Education* **16** (2), pp 123–38

Stevenson (1975) Socialization effects of participation in sport: a critical review of the research, *Research Quarterly*, **46** pp 287–301

Stone, M (1981) *The Education of the Black Child in Britain,* Pelican, London

Stone, M H (1957) Mathematics and the future of science, *Bulletin of the American Mathematical Society,* **63** (2), pp 61–76

Stonier, T (1983) *The Wealth of Information*, Thames Methuen, London

Straughan, R (1988) *Can We Teach Children to be Good?* Open University Press, Milton Keynes

Swanwick K (1988) *Music, Mind and Education*, Routledge, London

Tate, N (1994) The role of the school in promoting moral, social and cultural values, *Education Review* **10** (1), pp 66–70

Taylor, R (1988) *Education for Art: Critical Response and Development,* Longman, Harlow

Taylor, R (1992) *The Visual Arts in Education: Completing the circle,* Falmer Press, London

Thatcher A (1999) Theology, spirituality and the curriculum – an overview, in *Spirituality and the Curriculum*, ed A Thatcher, Cassell, London

Thatcher, M (1993) *The Downing Street Years*, Harper Collins, London

Thom, R (1973) Modern Mathematics, does it exist? in *Developments in Mathematical Education,* ed A G Howson, Cambridge University Press, Cambridge

Thomson, D (1970) *The Aims of History*, Thames and Hudson, London

Toffler, A (1970) *Future Shock*, Random House, New York

Torres, C A (1998) Democracy, education, and multiculturalism: dilemmas of citizenship in a global world, *Comparative Education Review* **24** (4), pp 421–47

Tuan, Y F (1971) Geography, phenomenology, and the study of human nature, *Canadian Geographer,* **15** (3), pp 181–92

Twine, F (1994) *Citizenship and Social Rights,* Sage, London

Verma, G K, Zec, P and Skinner, G D (1994) *The Ethnic Crucible – Harmony and Hostility in Multi-ethnic Schools,* Falmer Press, London

Visram, R (1986) *Ayahs, Lascars and Princes – Indians in Britain 1700–1947*, Pluto Press, London

Vlaeminke & Burkimsher (1991) Approaches to citizenship, in *Citizenship in Schools,* ed K Fogelman, Fulton, London

Walford, R (1981) *Signposts for Geography Teaching,* Longman, London

Walkington, H (1999a) *Theory into Practice: Global Citizenship Education*, Geographical Association, Sheffield

Walkington, H (1999b) *Reflections of Places, Reflecting on Practice: On the Teaching of a Developing Locality in Primary School Geography*, Unpublished PhD Thesis, University of Reading

REFERENCES

Walsh, P (1993) P Lee, J Slater, P Walsh, and J White *The Aims of School History: The National Curriculum and Beyond*, Institute of Education, London

Watson, V (1996) Innocent children and unstable literature, in Voices Off: Texts, Contexts and Readers, ed M Styles, E Bearne and V Watson, Cassell, London

White, J (1993) in P Lee, J Slater, P Walsh, and J White, *The Aims of School History: The National Curriculum and Beyond*, Institute of Education, London

Whitty, G, Aggleton, P and Row, G (1996) Competing conceptions of quality in social education: learning from the experience of cross-curricular themes, in *Teaching and Learning in Changing Times*, ed M Hughes, Blackwell, London

Wilkins, C (1999) Making Good Citizens: the social and political attitudes of PGCE students, *Oxford Review of Education*, 25 (1 & 2), pp 217–30

Williamson, H (1996) *Youth Work and Citizenship*, Paper presented at the British Youth Research Conference: A New Agenda, University of Glasgow

Wilson, V and Woodhouse, J (1990) *History Through Drama*, Historical Association, London

Winston, J (1998) *Drama, Narrative and Moral Education*, Falmer Press, London

Wright, J (1992) Gymnastics in the National Curriculum, in *New Directions in Physical Education Vol 2*, ed N Armstrong, Human Kinetics, Champaign, IL

Wright, L (1987) Physical Education and Moral Development, *Journal of Philosophy of Education*, **21** (4), pp 93–102

Young, J (1999) *The Exclusive Society – Social Exclusion, Crime and Difference in Late Modernity*, Sage, London

Youth Service Development Council (1969) *Youth and Community Work in the 70s*, HMSO, London

Index